"As a believer with the simple faith of a child, the author manages to provide a well-researched and easily readable scholarly contribution on 1 Timothy. It is refreshing to read this well-balanced contribution by a female scholar on this letter that repeatedly refers to the role of woman in the church but also to other ministerial strategies. Her perspectives on the influence of this text on a contemporary faith community are enlightening."

—FRANCOIS P. VILJOEN, Professor, Faculty of Theology, North-West University

"Spencer's commentary on 1 Timothy provides an articulate defense of Pauline authorship that interacts well with critical scholarship. It is full of valuable grammatical, lexical, syntactical, historical, and theological insights. . . . Theological insights include its discussion of the heretical teaching addressed in 1 Timothy and its outstanding treatment of 1 Timothy 2:15. I enthusiastically endorse this well-documented commentary."

—PHILIP B. PAYNE, Author of *Man and Woman, One in Christ*

1 TIMOTHY

NCCS | New Covenant Commentary Series

The New Covenant Commentary Series (NCCS) is designed for ministers and students who require a commentary that interacts with the text and context of each New Testament book and pays specific attention to the impact of the text upon the faith and praxis of contemporary faith communities.

The NCCS has a number of distinguishing features. First, the contributors come from a diverse array of backgrounds in regards to their Christian denominations and countries of origin. Unlike many commentary series that tout themselves as international the NCCS can truly boast of a genuinely international cast of contributors with authors drawn from every continent of the world (except Antarctica) including countries such as the United States, Puerto Rico, Australia, the United Kingdom, Kenya, India, Singapore, and Korea. We intend the NCCS to engage in the task of biblical interpretation and theological reflection from the perspective of the global church. Second, the volumes in this series are not verse-by-verse commentaries, but they focus on larger units of text in order to explicate and interpret the story in the text as opposed to some often atomistic approaches. Third, a further aim of these volumes is to provide an occasion for authors to reflect on how the New Testament impacts the life, faith, ministry, and witness of the New Covenant Community today. This occurs periodically under the heading of "Fusing the Horizons and Forming the Community." Here authors provide windows into community formation (how the text shapes the mission and character of the believing community) and ministerial formation (how the text shapes the ministry of Christian leaders).

It is our hope that these volumes will represent serious engagements with the New Testament writings, done in the context of faith, in service of the church, and for the glorification of God.

Series Editors:
Michael F. Bird (Ridley College, Melbourne, Australia)
Craig Keener (Asbury Theological Seminary, Wilmore, KY, USA)

Titles in this series:
Romans Craig Keener
Ephesians Lynn Cohick
Colossians and Philemon Michael F. Bird
Revelation Gordon Fee
John Jey Kanagaraj

Forthcoming titles:
Titus, 2 Timothy Aída Besançon Spencer
Philippians Linda Belleville
Acts Youngmo Cho and Hyung Dae Park
1 Peter Eric Greaux
2 Peter and Jude Andrew Mbuvi
Mark Kim Huat Tan
Hebrews Cynthia Westfall

1–3 John Sam Ngewa
Luke Diane Chen
Matthew Scot McKnight
2 Corinthians Nijay Gupta
James Pablo Jimenez
Galatians Jarvis Williams
1 Corinthians B. J. Oropeza

1 TIMOTHY
A New Covenant Commentary

Aída Besançon Spencer

CASCADE *Books* • Eugene, Oregon

1 TIMOTHY
A New Covenant Commentary

New Covenant Commentary Series

Copyright © 2013 Aída Besançon Spencer. All rights reserved. Except for brief quotations in critical publications or reviews, no part of this book may be reproduced in any manner without prior written permission from the publisher. Write: Permissions, Wipf and Stock Publishers, 199 W. 8th Ave., Suite 3, Eugene, OR 97401.

Cascade Books
An Imprint of Wipf and Stock Publishers
199 W. 8th Ave., Suite 3
Eugene, OR 97401

www.wipfandstock.com

ISBN 13: 978-1-55635-991-0

Cataloging-in-Publication data:

Spencer, Aída Besançon

    1 Timothy : a new covenant commentary / Aída Besançon Spencer.

    xiv + 178 p. ; 23 cm. —Includes bibliographical references and index.

    New Covenant Commentary Series

    ISBN 13: 978-1-55635-991-0

1. Bible. Timothy, 1st—Commentaries. I. Title. II. Series.

BS2745.53 S69 2013

Manufactured in the U.S.A.

Dedicated to my coworkers in ministry at Pilgrim Church and in particular to my closest coworker, the Reverend Doctor William David Spencer.

Contents

Abbreviations | ix

Introduction to Pastoral Letters | 1
Introduction to 1 and 2 Timothy | 13
1 Timothy 1 | 21
   Excursus: Women Could Desire to Be Teachers | 28
   Fusing the Horizons: Significance of Christ's Birth | 41
1 Timothy 2–3 | 46
   Excursus: Lifting Up Hands | 53
   Fusing the Horizons: How to Use Leadership Lists | 100
1 Timothy 4:1—5:2 | 102
   Fusing the Horizons: Progress in the Christian Life | 119
1 Timothy 5:3—6:2 | 122
   Fusing the Horizons: Applying the Order of Widows to Today | 134
1 Timothy 6:3–21 | 144
   Excursus: Heresy in 1 Timothy | 147
   Fusing the Horizons: Living with Wealth | 163

Bibliography | 167
Subject Index | 173

Abbreviations

AJA	*American Journal of Archaeology*
ANTC	*Abingdon New Testament Commentaries*
BDAG	Walter Bauer, Frederick William Danker, William F. Arndt, and F. Wilbur Gingrich. *A Greek-English Lexicon of the New Testament and Other Early Christian Literature*. 3rd ed. Chicago: University of Chicago Press, 2000.
BBR	*Bulletin for Biblical Research*
CE	William D. Halsey and Bernard Johnston, editors. *Collier's Encyclopedia*. 24 vols. New York: Macmillan, 1987.
CEB	Common English Bible
CEV	Contemporary English Version
CGTSC	*Cambridge Greek Testament for Schools and Colleges*
DHH	Dios habla hoy
ECC	Eerdmans Critical Commentary
ESV	English Standard Version
GKC	E. Kautzsch, editor. *Gesenius' Hebrew Grammar*. Translated by A. E. Cowley. 2nd ed. Oxford: Clarendon, 1910.
HNTC	Harper's New Testament Commentary
HTR	*Harvard Theological Review*
ICC	International Critical Commentary
IDB	George Arthur Buttrick et al. *The Interpreter's Dictionary of the Bible*. 5 vols. Nashville: Abingdon, 1962.
JB	Jerusalem Bible
JBL	*Journal of Biblical Literature*

JETS	*Journal of the Evangelical Theological Society*
JSNT	*Journal for the Study of the New Testament*
KJV	King James Version
L&N	Johannes P. Louw and Eugene A. Nida, editors. *Greek-English Lexicon of the New Testament Based on Semantic Domains.* Vol. 1. 2nd ed. New York: United Bible Societies, 1989.
LCL	Loeb Classical Library
LEC	Library of Early Christianity
LXX	Septuagint
LSJ	Henry George Liddell and Robert Scott. *A Greek-English Lexicon.* Revised by Henry Stuart Jones. 9th ed. Oxford: Clarendon, 1968.
NASB	New American Standard Bible
NCB	New Century Bible
NCBC	New Century Bible Commentary
NEB	New English Bible
NewDocs	G. H. R. Horsley and S. R. Llewelyn, editors. *New Documents Illustrating Earliest Christianity.* 9 vols. N.S.W., Australia: Ancient History Documentary Research Centre Macquarie University, 1976–87.
NIBC	New International Biblical Commentary
NICNT	New International Commentary on the New Testament
NIV	New International Version 1983
NIVAC	New International Version Application Commentary
NLT	New Living Translation
NRSV	New Revised Standard Version
N.T.	New Testament
NTME	New Testament in Modern English
OCD	N. G. L. Hammond and H. H. Scullard, editors. *Oxford Classical Dictionary.* 2nd ed. Oxford: Clarendon, 1970.
O.T.	Old Testament
REB	Revised English Bible

RSV	Revised Standard Version
RV	Reina-Valera 1995
SBLMS	Society of Biblical Literature Monograph Series
SNTSMS	Society for New Testament Studies Monograph Series
TEV	Today's English Version
TDNT	Gerhard Kittel and G. Friedrich, editors. *Theological Dictionary of the New Testament.* Translated by G. W. Bromiley. 10 vols. Grand Rapids: Eerdmans, 1964–1976.
Thayer	Joseph Henry Thayer. *Thayer's Greek-English Lexicon of the New Testament.* Marshallton, DE: National Foundation for Christian Education, 1889.
TLG	*Thesaurus linguae graecae*
TLNT	Ceslas Spicq. *Theological Lexicon of the New Testament.* 3 vols. Translated and edited by James D. Ernest. Peabody, MA: Hendrickson, 1994.
TNIV	Today's New International Version
TNTC	Tyndale New Testament Commentaries
UBS	*The Greek New Testament,* edited by Barbara Aland, Kurt Aland, Johannes Karavidopoulos, Carlo M. Martini, and Bruce Metzger. 4th rev. ed. Stuttgart: United Bible Societies, 2001.
WBC	Word Biblical Commentary
WUNT	Wissenschaftliche Untersuchungen zum Neuen Testament

ANCIENT SOURCES

Apostolic Constitutions
   Const. Ap.
Apostolic Fathers
   Barn.   *Barnabas*
   1–2 Clem.   *1–2 Clement*
   Did.   *Didache*
   Ign. *Eph.*   Ignatius, *To the Ephesians*
   Ign. *Magn.*   Ignatius, *To the Magnesians*

    Ign. *Smyrn.*   Ignatius, *To the Smyrnaeans*
    Ign. *Trall.*   Ignatius, *To the Trallians*
    Pol. *Phil.*   Polycarp, *To the Philippians*

Appian
    Bell. civ.   Civil Wars
    Hist. rom.   Roman History

Aristotle
    Pol.   Politics

Arrian
    Epict. diss.   *Epicteti dissertationes*

Artemidorus Daldianus
    Onir.   *Onirocritica*

Athenaeus
    Deipn.   *Deipnosophistae*

Babylonian Talmud (b.)
    'Erub.   Eruvin
    Hag.   Hagigah
    Yebam.   Yevamot

Cicero
    Off.   *De officiis*

Clement of Alexandria
    Protr.   Exhortation to the Greeks

Demosthenes
    Neaer.   Against Neaera

Epictetus
    Ench.   Enchiridion

Euripides
    Iph. aul.   *Iphigeneia at Aulis*
    Iph. taur.   *Iphigeneia at Tauris*

Eusebius
    Hist. eccl.   Ecclesiastical History

Herodotus
    Hist.   Histories

Hippocrates
    Int.   Internal Affections
    Liq.   Use of Liquids
    Morb.   Diseases
    Vet. med.   Ancient Medicine

Homer
    Il.   Iliad

Irenaeus
    Haer.   *Against Heresies*
    Epid.   *Demonstration of the Apostolic Preaching*
John Chrysostom
    Hom. Col.   *Homiliae in epistulum ad Colossenses*
    Hom. Gen.   *Homiliae in Genesim*
Josephus
    Ag. Ap.   *Against Apion*
    Ant.   *Jewish Antiquities*
    J. W.   *Jewish War*
Justin
    Dial.   *Dialogue with Trypho*
    1–2 Apol.   *First-Second Apology*
Longinus
    Subl.   *On the Sublime*
Mishnah (m.)
    'Abot   *Avot*
    Hag.   *Hagigah*
    Ketub.   *Ketubbot*
    Meg.   *Megillah*
    Qidd.   *Qiddushin*
    Sabb.   *Shabbat*
    Sanh.   *Sanhedrin*
    Yebam.   *Yevamot*
Ovid
    Am.   *Amores*
Pausanias
    Descr.   *Description of Greece*
Philo
    Worse   *That the Worse Attacks the Better*
    Embassy   *On the Embassy to Gaius*
    Flaccus   *Against Flaccus*
    Spec. Laws   *On the Special Laws*
Plato
    Gorg.   *Gorgias*
    Leg.   *Laws*
    Resp.   *Republic*
    Tim.   *Timaeus*
Pliny the Elder
    Nat.   *Natural History*

Polybius
- *Hist.* — *Histories*

Pseudepigrapha
- *T. Isaac* — *Testament of Isaac*

Strabo
- *Geogr.* — *Geography*

Tacitus
- *Hist.* — *Historiae*

Tertullian
- *Exh. cast.* — *Exhortation to Chastity*
- *Mon.* — *Monogamy*

Xenophon
- *Oec.* — *Oeconomicus*

Introduction to Pastoral Letters

When Luke the evangelist wrote his Gospel, he highlighted for Theophilus, his reader, some of the features he offered, while affirming the Gospels already written (Luke 1:1–4). Following the model of this wonderful historian, I, too, would like to affirm the many wonderful commentaries written on the Pastoral Epistles, which are Pastor Paul's instructions and admonitions to two young pastors. As many of the other commentary writers of the New Covenant Commentary Series, I come from an international background, born and reared in Santo Domingo, Dominican Republic, and later in New Jersey in the United States, my mother from Puerto Rico and my father from The Netherlands. Like others in the series, I have focused on the flow of argument. My own translation is an attempt to illustrate the literal text as a basis for interpretation and stylistic analysis. I have studied the meaning of the text in light of its immediate and larger literary, biblical, historical, social, and cultural contexts. In particular, I have asked myself, how might these ancient communities have understood and received these teachings? To enrich my study, I traveled to Crete, Ephesus, Rome, and Greece, visiting many key ancient Greco-Roman sites. These were wonderful trips which were accomplished with the help and companionship of my husband, the Rev. Dr. William David Spencer, and son, Mr. Stephen William Spencer.

In addition, I have always thought that scholarship would be advanced if more women were to study and publish on these letters that relate frequently to women and to church life. Thus, as a female Presbyterian minister ordained for forty years (October 1973), I have paid consistent attention to any issues that relate to women and their role in the church. It is not, however, a commentary solely focused on "women's issues." As an active minister, who has taught New Testament theology for ministry for many years, I have also highlighted Paul's ministry strategies, his coworkers, and their community. My own initial training was in stylistics, and, thus, when appropriate, I have also highlighted Paul's rhetorical strategies.

Even though I have focused on the flow of argument, paragraphs and sentences are constructed from words and phrases. Therefore, in order to study the thoughts, I have also paid attention to semantics and grammar. I have done a close reading of the text. Like Luke, I have attempted to do a thorough investigation, but one understandable to my readers. My husband, as a theologian and a grammarian, graciously read the entire commentary. I am a "scholar," but also a believer with the simple faith of a child (Luke 18:16–17). I do believe these words, although those of the Apostle Paul, are also God-breathed, I have, therefore, not read these letters as a skeptic, but as someone who is in love with God, who inspired the words and thoughts, and in sympathy with Paul, as a friend and colleague in ministry, who was mentoring other ministers in very difficult situations.

Either Titus or 1 Timothy could have been written first. However, if Paul had just left Rome, he might have first traveled to Crete before moving on to Ephesus, Colossae, and Philippi.[1]

As I was writing the commentary, occasionally beautiful Christian melodies and lyrics based on 1 Timothy would echo in my mind, such as "Immortal, Invisible, God Only Wise" and "Now Unto the King Eternal." May my words also encourage you further to enjoy and trust God's awesome presence and words! God is our merciful, sovereign, impartial Savior and Creator, and worthy of much study, as well as praise.

Authorship of Pastoral Letters

1 Timothy, 2 Timothy, and Titus begin: "*Paul*, an apostle of Christ Jesus," or "*Paul*, a slave of God, but apostle of Jesus Christ." Because of similarity to the headings to Paul's other letters, many commentators conclude that Paul is the author of all the Pastorals.[2] Even commentators, such as C. K. Barrett, who conclude that Paul is *not* the author, agree that the external evidence supports Paul as author.[3]

Commentators ask, could the type of person who wrote these letters be the same Paul who wrote the other New Testament letters? Who is the

---

1. See Authorship and Historical Context of Pastoral Letters below.

2. See Bernard 1922; Ellicott 1865; Fee 1988; Guthrie 1990; Hillard 1919; Humphreys 1895; Johnson 1996; Kelly 1963; Lock 1924; Mounce 2000; Payne 2009; Ramos 1992; Robertson 1931; Towner 2006; Zahn 1953.

3. Barrett 1963: 4. See also Dibelius and Conzelmann 1972; Hanson 1982; Maloney 1994; Marxsen 1970; Quinn 2000.

real Paul? Is Paul the person driven with zeal to serve Jesus the Messiah, his life being on the line every day? Is he forgiving and merciful? Has he rejected his rabbinic past, relying on the Spirit, living each day open to the paradoxes of life? Or, is the author of the Pastorals a condemning man, full of fears, a hierarchically conservative man who wants everything and everyone in its order and place? Instead of rejecting his past, has he accepted fully his conservative traditions as he aims to appease his environment? As Dornier concludes: "The style of the moralist has taken the place of the style of the prophet."[4]

Although authorship has to be decided on external evidence, not subjective criteria, the Paul we meet in the Pastorals is still very much aware of the irreproachableness of his own past. In Titus and 1 Timothy, he has been released from prison and wants to make sure no believer is apprehended for the wrong reasons. He wants people to enjoy God's creation and not be ascetic—to marry, to eat. Although truth is crucial, it is so because of the health it brings. The God Paul highlights is a merciful God, Savior, hope of the world, and forgiving. God is savior before he is judge.

We have extensive external evidence supporting Paul as the author. *The Muratorian Canon* (A.D. 170–80) says that Paul addressed seven churches by name: Corinthians, Ephesians, Philippians, Colossians, Galatians, Thessalonians, and Romans, and he wrote four letters to individuals: Philemon, Titus, two to Timothy, written from "personal affection" but "held sacred in the esteem of the church catholic for the regulation of ecclesiastical discipline." *The Canon* adds that forged letters should not be received with the genuine ones, because "it is not fitting that gall be mixed with honey."[5] Papyrus 32 (A.D. 175–200), an Alexandrian text, includes Titus 1:11–15 and 2:3–8. Eusebius (260–339) states that the Epistles of Paul are universally "recognized" as true and genuine, while books "put forward by heretics under the name of the apostles" . . . "must be shunned as altogether wicked and impious" (*Hist. eccl.* 3.25).

Allusions to, and quotations of, the Pastoral Letters start early. Clement of Rome's Letter to the Corinthians (c. 95) alludes to 1 Timothy 1:17 (61:2) and Titus 3:1 (2:7; 33:1; 34:4). The *Letter of Ignatius to the Magnesians* (8:1) alludes to 1 Timothy 1:4 and Titus 3:9. Polycarp (71–155), the Bishop of Smyrna, alludes to 1 Timothy 3:8; 5:5; 6:7, 10; and 2 Timothy

---

4. In Hanson 1982: 3–4.

5. The early church did not accept pseudonymous writings as authoritative. See also Lea 1991: 535–59; Westcott 1896: 438, 441, 453, 455–56, 565; Harris 1969: 253.

4:10. Irenaeus (130–202), who "saw Polycarp in his early youth" (*Haer.* 3.4), writes that "Paul mentions Linus in his Epistle to Timothy" (*Haer.* 3.3). He titles this book, "The Refutation & Overthrow of the Knowledge Falsely So Called."[6] The *Acts of Paul* (160) includes people only found in the Pastorals (Onesiphorus, Hermogenes, and Demas). Origen (185–253/4) often refers to Paul as the author of the epistles of Timothy and Titus, and Tertullian (155–220) quotes all three Pastoral letters (1 Tim 6:20; 2 Tim 1:14; Titus 3:10–11): "I wonder since [Marcion] received a letter written to an individual, the Epistle to Philemon, that he rejected two to Timothy and one to Titus written on the subject of church order."[7]

However, the Pastoral Letters are not in p46, but, then, neither is Philemon (and no one questions Paul's authorship of Philemon). The scribe compiling p46 excluded all personal letters to individuals. (On the other hand, the Pastorals could have been included in the missing pages as the scribe was compressing his letters.)[8] Codex Vaticanus (4 c.) omits the Pastoral Epistles, Philemon, Revelation, and part of Genesis and the Psalms. The first person to deny positively the genuineness of 1 Timothy is F. Schleiermacher in 1807, on the basis of style and language. In 1835, F. C. Baur questioned all three letters. Current concerns with Paul as the author of the Pastorals result from historical, literary, ecclesiological, and theological reasons.[9]

Historical Reasons

The travel plans in the Pastorals do not seem to fit with those reported in Acts. Marxsen concludes: "the Pastorals can have been written by Paul only if he was set free again after a first Roman imprisonment."[10] As a

---

6. Irenaeus quotes 1 Tim 1: 4, 9; 2:5; 4:7; 6:20; 2 Tim 4:9–11; Titus 3:10–11, among other verses (I.16.3; III.14.1;17.1). Other early church fathers who quote the Pastorals include Justin Martyr (100–148), *Dial.* 47 (Titus 3:4), Clement of Alexandria (150–215) (1 Tim 4:1; 6:20; "the second epistle to Timothy," Titus 1:12), and Athenagoras (177–180) (quoting 1 Tim 2:2).

7. Eusebius says Paul wrote Titus 3:9 (*Hist. eccl.* 4.14.7). Theophilus, a contemporary of Jerome, cites Titus 2:15 as written by Paul as a basis for acting against those propagating the heresy of Origen (*Letter* 87).

8. Marshall 1999: 6.

9. For more on these issues as well as chronology, epistolary format, style, content, and theology see Porter 1995: 105–23. As is apparent from my stance in this commentary, I do not find these arguments convincing.

10. Marxsen 1970: 211.

matter of fact, we do have ample proof that Paul was indeed released. Paul writes in Philippians 2:24: "I trust in the Lord that shortly also I myself will come" after Timothy. He asks Philemon to "prepare for me a guest room" (22). The arrest described in Acts, Philippians, Colossians, Ephesians, and Philemon is a mild house arrest, which is usually a maximum of two years. Thus, Paul expects release. According to Acts 25:25, Governor Festus states that Paul does not deserve death and King Agrippa agrees that Paul could have been released (Acts 26:32). While, in contrast, 2 Timothy describes a more intensive period. Paul explains: "At my first defense no one took my part; all deserted me." "For I am already on the point of being sacrificed, the time of my departure has come." "Luke alone is with me." Demas is gone (Col 4:14) (2 Tim 4:6, 9, 11, 16). Nero's early years were known for his mildness and clemency (Eusebius, *Hist. eccl.* 2.22), but he changes after A.D. 64.

The early church also has proof of Paul's release. Clement, who lived in the West, wrote that Paul "reached the farthest limits of the West" (*1 Clem.* 5:7). He appears to say that Paul went beyond Italy to Spain. Eusebius quotes Origen's *Commentary on Genesis* (3:1) that Paul later was martyred in Rome under Nero: after defending himself, "the apostle is said to have set out again on the ministry of preaching and, coming a second time to the same city, found fulfillment in martyrdom. During this imprisonment he composed the second epistle to Timothy" (*Hist. eccl.* 2.22; 3.3).

Scholars have difficulty setting a later date for the Pastorals.[11] But, such late dates are not necessary since Gaius and Nero "took their divinity very seriously." In A.D. 66 Nero was described officially as "lord and saviour of the world." "The cult was already well developed during Paul's life." Especially in Titus, "the author was trying to counter the imperial cult": Christ as true Savior versus the false savior Caesar.[12] Therefore, Titus and 1 Timothy are more likely written after Paul's first Roman imprisonment before Nero began persecuting Christians (c. A.D. 62–64),

---

11. Some say the Pastorals have "no trace of" persecution such as existed in Ignatius's day (Hanson 1982: 12–13). Ignatius died in A.D. 113, whereas, Emperor Domitian, who persecuted Christians, died in A.D. 96. Some, therefore, conclude that the Pastorals have to be written before the time of Domitian, but this is too early for other critics. Another option is one or two years before Ignatius died, but for still others this is too near Ignatius's time. Another date for the letters' composition is after A.D. 112 when Trajan revived the imperial cult but before anyone was killed.

12. Hanson 1982: 186–87.

while 2 Timothy was written during Paul's second Roman imprisonment (c. A.D. 66–67).

Literary Reasons

Some scholars also see literary problems. They conclude that the Pastorals have a vocabulary distinct from the other letters, however they do not agree about the number of word differences. They notice some different words and style: *eusebeia* ("godliness"), *sōphrosynē* ("self-control"), *theosebeia* ("religion"), *semnos* ("character"), *hygiēs* ("sound"), *dynastēs* ("ruler"), *makarios* ("blessed"), and *sōtēr* ("savior"). In contrast, some words important to Paul do not occur: "evangelize," "give thanks," "boast," "spiritual," "wisdom" (*sophia*), "body," "life" (*psychē*), "in Christ." Dibelius and Conzelmann summarize: "Personal elements fade into the background, and the letter's primary purpose is to transmit regulations . . . which are not intended" for Timothy, "but for other people."[13] They conclude that the genre is household codes (*haustafel*). First Timothy is a collection of materials like the *Didache*.[14] The style is similar to Polycarp's letter to the Philippians, as is its theology and ecclesiology.[15] First Timothy 6:6–10 reproduces popular philosophical maxims on wealth.[16] However, Marxsen concludes in a circular manner that any similarities to Paul come from the "Pauline tradition."[17]

Nevertheless, Dibelius and Conzelmann accepted even many years ago that: "Recent debate has shown that the method of arguing against authenticity on the basis of statistics is inadequate."[18] According to linguists who studied the *Federalist* papers, 100,000 words of undisputed authorship are needed to compare with disputed writings, but the whole New Testament has under 140,000 words.[19] According to Sakae Kubo's *Greek-English Lexicon*, 1 Timothy has 66 words which occur only once in the New Testament. In Philippians (another letter to a positive audience), Paul uses 36 unique words in four chapters. In the first four chapters of 1

---

13. Dibelius and Conzelmann 1972: 1.
14. For example, 1 Tim 2:8 = *Did.* 7–10, 14, 15.
15. Dibelius and Conzelmann 1972: 6.
16. Hanson 1982: 4.
17. Marxsen 1970: 214.
18. Dibelius and Conzelmann 1972: 3; cf. Harrison 1964.
19. Spencer 1998b: 149; Mounce 2000: cxv.

Timothy, Paul uses 31 unique words, less than in Philippians 1–4. Most of the unique words are in 1 Timothy chapters 5–6, but, in chapter 5, Paul has a unique topic—widows.[20]

The argument about missing words is very subjective. "Savior" occurs also in Philippians 3:20 ("Savior, the Lord Jesus Christ") and Ephesians 5:23. Paul's use of *eusebeia* occurs only in the Pastoral letters. But, Peter also uses it.[21] Could that word have become important at this time in the church's life to describe the need of the church? Or could it be a key to Paul's message at this time? Or, could it be a word brought to Paul's consciousness by Peter and others? Hillard explains that differences can come from "(a) lapse of time, the author's age and new experiences; (b) different circumstances, purposes and needs; and even (c) the author's own reading, study and thought—since no active mind, and least of all men's St. Paul's, could stand still."[22]

Some of the words that do not occur also only occur in a few of Paul's letters. They are arbitrarily "important" words. For example, "spiritual" (*pneumatikos*) does not occur in 2 Corinthians, Philippians, or Philemon and "boast" (*kauchaomai, kauchēsis*) does not occur in Colossians, 2 Thessalonians, and Philemon. Hanson says the "prose is pedestrian." It has no "depth," but if any commentator sees depth of meaning, he rejects it. For example, about 1 Timothy 6:7, C. K. Barrett writes "The final nakedness of death demonstrates and underlines the initial nakedness of birth." To which Hanson replies: "But this seems over-subtle for the author's mentality."[23] Yet, the Pastorals have numerous poetical sections, such as great indeed is "the mystery of our religion: He was manifested in the flesh, vindicated in the Spirit, seen by angels, preached among the nations, believed on in the world, taken up into glory" (1 Tim 3:16 RSV).

Is 1 Timothy like the *Didache* and like Polycarp's letter?[24] The *Didache* is as much like 1 Corinthians as it is like 1 Timothy. The *Didache*

---

20. Paul also used several of these "unique" words in other forms in other letters (leaving only 53 unique words in 1 Tim).

21. 2 Pet 1:3, 6, 7; 3:11; Acts 3:12.

22. Hillard 1919: xxxii. See Mounce's (2000: civ-cx) lists of words that relate to Paul's new historical situation. Paul adapts his style as he communicates with different congregations. See Spencer 1998b: 148, app. 1.

23. Barrett 1963: 84; Hanson 1982: 107. Yet Quinn & Wacker (2000: 6) point out the Pastorals have "alliteration, assonance, rhyme, paronomasia, polysyndeton . . . asyndeton."

24. E.g., Dibelius and Conzelmann 1972: 2, 6–7.

discusses how to baptize (ch. 7), when to fast (ch. 8), how to give the eucharist and give grace (chs. 9–10, 14), and what criteria should be followed for choosing bishops and deacons (ch. 15). The *Didache* is very specific, for example, fast on Wednesdays and Fridays (8:1), whereas 1 Timothy is more general (as in 1 Tim 2:8: the men should pray "lifting holy hands without quarreling"). Polycarp's letter is much like all of the New Testament letters, because he freely quotes them. Hanson claims that 1 Timothy 6:6–10 reproduces popular philosophical maxims on wealth, but his proof comes from the third to sixth century A.D.[25]

What is the real concern? Paul now seems to want to please the world more than before and he is concerned about orthodoxy and declares clearly that Jesus is God.

Ecclesiological Reasons

Marxsen writes: "The tension of Christian existence in the new eschatological situation has been abandoned in favour of a Christian adjustment to this world." Now there is an "emphasis on the idea of tradition,"[26] a fixed tradition. Therefore, he concludes, Paul is claimed as author and Christian doctrine is a "deposit."[27] "Doctrine and offices are in harmony with apostolic authority."[28] The author appears not to argue with heretics but simply to contrast false versus true teaching. "Good citizenship" is key.[29] The bishop, deacon, elder hierarchy is close to the episcopate of the second century,[30] in contrast to Acts 14:23, where only elders are mentioned.

However, the passing on of correct tradition has always been Paul's practice, as in 1 Corinthians 11:23: "I myself *received* (*paralambanō*) from the Lord what also I *delivered* (*paradidōmi*) to you." "Received" and "delivered" are key words to describe the passing on of authoritative teaching. In 1 Corinthians 15:3, Paul repeats: "For I *delivered* to you as of first importance, what I also *received*." In Galatians 1:6, he is "astonished" they are turning to a different gospel and in 2 Corinthians 11:4, the

25. Hanson 1982: 109 cites Diogenes Laertius (third century), one century too late even for his theory!

26. Marxsen 1970: 212–13.

27. Hanson 1982: 5, 26. Dibelius and Conzelmann 1972: 1.

28. Marxsen 1970: 215.

29. Dibelius and Conzelmann 1972: 2–3, 8.

30. Hanson 1982: 4, 48.

Corinthians should not accept any different gospel. Moreover, the offices in the Pastorals are not so clear. Even Marxsen writes: it is "difficult to determine the relationship between them. We certainly cannot speak of a three-fold hierarchy, for bishop and deacons . . . are never mentioned along with the elders."[31] In Philippians 1:1, bishops and deacons are mentioned together, whereas in Ignatius' letters the bishop already has clear power over the deacon. In *Ignatius to the Magnesians*, the deacon is "subject to the bishop" and to the presbytery, and the bishop presides in the place of God (the Father) while the presbyters are in the place of the council of the apostles and the deacons in the place of Jesus Christ.[32] By the time of the *Apostolic Constitutions* (A.D. 380, also from Syria), the bishop, presbyter, deacon, deaconess, widows, virgins, women elders, and older and younger women are seated in order (2.7).

Theological Reasons

Some scholars complain that the Pastorals must be late because Jesus is clearly called God in Titus 2:13, the "Son" is never used for Christ, and the Holy Spirit is not mentioned.[33] The Pastorals have more emphasis on works. There is no mention of the cross, the law seems misunderstood (1 Tim 1:8), grace appears an exterior aid, not an interior presence, and faith has a content. Love is one virtue among many. There is an emphasis on civil "bourgeois" virtues—temperance, common sense, seriousness, integrity about money, fidelity, and respectability. In contrast, some scholars contend, Paul would have said "pride" is the root of all evil (Rom 7). "Mystery" becomes the Christian faith as a whole, not the saving action of God in Christ. Baptism appears to be a method of salvation (Titus 3:5). The heresy confronted seems similar to the Gnosticism of the second century, like Ignatius' Gnosticism, for example, where "suffering is only a semblance."[34]

But how compelling are such objections? Even in Philippians 2:6, Jesus is in the "form" of God, while the "Son" is not used in the Letter to the Philippians. Further, the Spirit is, certainly, mentioned in the Pastorals: vindication in the Spirit, the Spirit says, guarded by the Holy Spirit,

---

31. Marxsen 1970: 214.
32. Ign. *Magn.* 2; 6; also *Trall.* 2; 3.
33. E.g., Hanson 1982: 2–3, 39–40.
34. Dibelius and Conzelmann 1972: 3 citing Ign. *Trall.* 10.

and renewal by the Holy Spirit.[35] Both in Romans 7 and 1 Timothy 1 the law is good, but it is limited. Paul presents a powerful example of grace in 1 Timothy 1:12–16 and one mediator in 1 Timothy 2:5–6. Integrity about money is always a concern for Paul, for example, he disparages "*peddlers of God's word*" (2 Cor 2:17) and, similarly, godliness is not a means of gain (1 Tim 6:5). Pride is not the point of Romans 7. Rather, the point is Paul cannot do what he wants. The Pastorals have baptism allusions, as "washing of rebirth" (Titus 3:5). Even Dibelius and Conzelmann explain the author is not writing against Marcion.[36] Marxsen notes "we cannot identify [the heretics] with any of the familiar Gnostic systems."[37] Docetism is more a problem in 1 John, than in 1 Timothy.

Summary

The Pastoral Letters present us with overwhelming evidence that Paul is their author. Bernard explains that the Pastorals appear: "in Gaul and Greece in 177, in Rome in 140 (certainly)—as far back as 95, if we accept Clement's testimony—and in Asia as early as 116."[38] The letterheads themselves and the early church claim Paul as author and the Pastorals as part of the canon. The letters fit into Paul's life after his first release from prison. The Pastoral vocabulary is no less unusual than the rest of Paul's letters. Right teaching was always Paul's concern. He has the same basic faith in Jesus as always.

Nevertheless, these scholars have raised valuable questions: Can we box a person as bourgeois or prophetic? Do we really understand Paul? What is the place of the law? Where is the place of morality in the Christian life? When have we moved from concern for the salvation of others to concern for others' salvation of us? To what extent are Paul's practices examples to be copied as opposed to examples with underlying principles?

What difference does authorship make? If Paul the apostle sent from God did not write these letters, they are in reality advice from some unknown Christian. Consequently, Hanson spends much of his commentary positing "contradictions" between the Pastorals and Paul's

---

35. 1 Tim 3:16; 4:1; 2 Tim 1:14; Titus 3:5.
36. Dibelius and Conzelmann 1972: 2; Marxsen 1970: 213.
37. Marxsen 1970: 2.
38. Bernard 1922: xx.

teachings. Linda M. Maloney agrees: "Clearly, the issue of the letters' *authority* is in some sense connected with their *authorship*."[39] Their context would be second century developed Gnosticism and a church over one hundred years later. If Paul is not the author, who is? If we cannot trust when the author writes "Paul" and "Timothy," how can we trust the writer who says: "the one mediator between God and humankind, Christ Jesus, himself human, who gave himself a ransom for all" (1 Tim 2:5–6 NRSV)? And, why should we do what the letters say?

HISTORICAL CONTEXT

If, however, we trust the information given to us in the Pastoral Letters (as this author does) and assume Paul completed his plans, we may posit the following possible historical reconstruction:

1. Paul and Timothy leave Paul's house arrest in *Rome* (c. A.D. 61–62).[40]
2. Possibly, Paul may have traveled to *Spain* (Rom 15:24, 28), probably arriving at the central Roman port of Dertosa (Tortosa) (if not later after leaving Nicopolis, Achaia).
3. Paul and Titus travel to *Crete*. Paul leaves Titus behind (Titus 1:5). Possibly, Timothy had been in Crete as well or he went directly to Ephesus.
4. Paul and Timothy travel to *Ephesus*, Asia. Timothy remains (1 Tim 1:3).
5. Paul visits *Colossae* (Phlm 22).
6. Paul travels to *Philippi*, Macedonia, and probably writes Titus and 1 Timothy from Macedonia (Phil 2:24; 1 Tim 1:3).
7. Paul winters in *Nicopolis*, Achaia, where he meets Titus (Titus 3:12).
8. Paul visits *Corinth*, Achaia (2 Tim 4:20).
9. Paul meets Timothy in *Ephesus*, Asia (1 Tim 3:14; 4:13; 2 Tim 4:12).
10. Paul visits nearby *Miletus* (2 Tim 4:20).
11. Paul travels to the seaport *Troas*, Asia. He is not supported by Christians in Asia (2 Tim 1:15; 4:13–14).

---

39. Maloney 1994: 362.
40. Acts 28:14–31; Phil 1:1; 2:19, 23; Col 1:1; Phlm 1, 22.

12. Paul is arrested and incarcerated in *Rome*, where he will be joined by Timothy (c. A.D. 66) (2 Tim 1:8, 17; 4:6–8, 16, 21).[41]

---

41. Paul, of course, may have visited other places. See also Fee (1992: 4–5) for a similar reconstruction.

Introduction to 1 and 2 Timothy

SETTING—EPHESUS AND ARTEMIS

Ephesus was in the Roman province of Asia. Once Paul and Timothy were forbidden to preach in the province of Asia by the Holy Spirit (Acts 16:6, c. A.D. 50), but eventually Ephesus became the home church for the Apostle Paul's mission for about three years (Acts 20:31, c. A.D. 54–56). During these years he experienced marvels through God's work and great suffering from persecution. He wrote 1 Corinthians from Ephesus (1 Cor 16:8).[1] The hardships in Asia were so great, Paul and Timothy despaired even of life, yet God delivered them (2 Cor 1:8–9). At Paul's final imprisonment in Rome almost all of his coworkers from Asia deserted him (2 Tim 1:15).

The city and the church had people of various ethnic groups. Paul had extended discussions about Jesus in the synagogue and in Tyrannus' School.[2] Paul had many coworkers, some Jewish, including the Romans Prisca and Aquila, his fellow tentmakers, learned Alexandrian Apollos, Lycaonian Timothy, Macedonian Aristarchus, and possibly Alexander. Paul also had friends and enemies among the Gentiles: the Asiarchs,[3] the town clerk, Demetrius, and other artisans.[4] Paul's traveling companions Gaius, Timothy, Tychicus, and Trophimus were from Asia (Acts 20:4).

The disciples of John had no knowledge of the Spirit,[5] yet spiritually much happened. Although he knew only John's baptism, for example, Apollos was on fire with the Spirit. Great miracles occurred. Diseases were healed (Acts 19:11–12). Sins were confessed publicly (Acts 19:18).

---

1. Circa A.D. 56.
2. Acts 18:19, 26; 19:8–10; 20:21. See *New Docs.* 4, 1987: 231. A Jewish menorah is engraved in the steps of the second-century Celsus Library, as seen by the author, May 2010.
3. See Titus 3:1.
4. Acts 19:9, 24–25, 31, 35; 20:21.
5. Acts 18:25; 19:2. See Titus 3:13.

But where the Holy Spirit was present, so were evil spirits. These evil spirits were cast out by Paul, but they attacked the seven sons of the high priest Sceva (Acts 19:13–16). Seeking to defend the goddess Artemis, mobs attacked the Christians (Acts 19:23–41). The Holy Spirit opened a door despite many Gentile and Jewish adversaries.[6]

Many Jews were brought to Ephesus under Antiochus II and given citizenship.[7] They insisted on not worshiping the Gentile gods, being free to celebrate the Sabbath (not appearing in court), not being forced to participate in military service, and being able to send money to the temple in Jerusalem.[8]

According to Strabo, Ephesus was "the largest emporium in Asia this side the Taurus."[9] Many inscriptions called Ephesus "the first and greatest metropolis of Asia."[10] The city had around 200,000–250,000 inhabitants.[11] It was the seaway to Rome and gateway to Asia with its harbor and was connected to a major highway used by all who traveled towards the east.[12] Androclus, son of Codrus, King of Athens, who led an Ionian colonization to Ephesus, became its official founder, although ancients recognized others (Carians) were there earlier,[13] as, for example, Smyrna, an Amazon who took possession of Ephesus. Amazons are given credit for naming the city.[14] Lysimachus founded the later city of Ephesus.[15] When King Attalus Philometor died (133 B.C.), he left the Romans as his heirs, and they proclaimed the country a province, calling it Asia, the same name as the continent.[16]

---

6. 1 Cor 16:9; Acts 19:9; 20:19.

7. Antiochus II reigned 261–46 B.C. Josephus, *Ant.* 12.3 [125; 148–53]; Ramsay 1994: 103, 111; Strelan 1996: 193.

8. Josephus, *Ant.* 16.2 [27–28, 43–47, 60]; 14.10 [225–30, 262–64]; Murphy-O'Connor 2008: 78, 83.

9. Strabo, *Geogr.* 14.1.24 [C641].

10. Wood 1877: App. 3, No. 7; *New Docs* 4, 1987: 75.

11. Murphy-O'Connor 2008: 131; Trebilco 1994: 307.

12. Many years earlier, the Aegean Sea "used to wash up to the temple of Diana" but no longer (Pliny the Elder, *Nat.* 2.87 [201]; Strabo, *Geogr.* 14.1.24; 14.2.29 [C641, 663]; Ramsay 1994: 165; Murphy-O'Connor 2008: 54–57).

13. Strabo, *Geogr.* 14.1.3 [C632–33]; Pausanias, *Descr.* 7.2.7–9; 3.1.

14. Strabo, *Geogr.* 11.5.4 [C505].

15. Pausanias, *Descr.* 1. 9. 6–7; 7.3.4.

16. Strabo, *Geogr.* 13.4.2 [C624].

At least as early as A.D. 400s, Bible scholars have been elaborating on the worship of Artemis as background for the New Testament letters.[17] Pausanias summarizes the ancient sentiment: "All cities worship Artemis of Ephesus, and individuals hold her in honour above all the gods. The reason, in my view, is the renown of the Amazons, who traditionally dedicated the image, also the extreme antiquity of this sanctuary. Three other points as well have contributed to her renown, the size of the temple, surpassing all buildings among men, the eminence of the city of the Ephesians and the renown of the goddess who dwells there."[18] The temple was one of the Seven Wonders of the Ancient World. When Antipater saw the temple "that mounted to the clouds," the other wonders lost their brilliancy for, "Lo, apart from Olympus, the Sun never looked on aught so grand!"[19]

Artemis, huntress, queen of beasts, is included in the battles between the gods by Homer (*Il.* 21 [535]). Euripides calls her "Maid of the mountain-wild."[20] Ancient religions were syncretistic. Possibly the earliest temple at Ephesus was dedicated to Cybele and Demeter.[21] The queen bee was the original predominant model for the goddess. The Greek portrayal of the deities as anthropomorphic was combined with the earlier Anatolian more animalistic portrayals of deity.[22] Thus, the Artemis at Ephesus has the face of a woman but her long tapered skirt resembles the tapered abdomen of the queen bee. The Ephesian Artemis' chest is covered by her many eggs or ova.[23] The priestesses were called Melissae ("worker bees") and priests were called Essenes ("drones").[24]

17. Jerome (Heine 2002: 77).
18. Pausanias, *Descr.* 4.31.8.
19. *Greek Anthology* 9.58; Epigrams of Saint Gregory 8. 177.
20. Euripides, *Iph. taur.* 126. See also Nilsson 1971: 502, 509. She was born together with brother Apollo by the Cenchrius River in the area of Ephesus. Their parents were Zeus and Leto (Strabo, *Geogr.* 14.1.20 [C639-40]). Artemis was often pictured with bow and arrow and stag. Delos also claimed to be the birthplace of Artemis.
21. Murphy-O'Connor 2008: 99.
22. See the queen bee on coins (Ramsay 1994: 159-60; Scherrer 2000: 205).
23. Unlike breasts, the "eggs" have no nipples in statues that have been uncovered in the first century (Scherrer 2000: 213; Trebilco 2004: 22-23). Others have posited these are testicles of bulls (Murphy-O'Connor 2008: 7; LiDonnici 1992: 392-93).
24. Pausanias, *Descr.* 8. 13. 1; Ramsay 1994: 161; LSJ, 1097-98. Bees brought nourishment to the baby Zeus in some legends (Nilsson 1971: 542-44). The main function of a queen bee is to lay eggs and found new hives. This mother and queen bee "guided her swarming people" to their new abode (Ramsay 1994: 157). Xenophon

Pausanias mentions that the priestesses and priests of the Ephesian Artemis live in purity for a year "not only sexual but in all respects, and they neither wash nor spend their lives as do ordinary people, nor do they enter the home of a private man."[25] Strabo describes the priests (*Megabyzi*, literally "set free by God"[26]) as "eunuchs" who are held in great honor. Maidens (virgins) served as colleagues with them in their priestly office.[27] Thus, scholars today are unclear whether the "eunuchs" simply were not sexually active for a year or they castrated themselves.[28] But, they would model a celibate religious lifestyle in honor of the virgin goddess.[29]

The temple of Artemis was the general bank or depository of Asia. Often private citizens deposited their money there. Others donated gifts to the goddess.[30] Acts records the silversmith Demetrius reminding his fellow artisans that "we get our wealth from this business" and, when Paul persuaded "a considerable number of people" that gods made with human hands were not real, their businesses would be affected (Acts 19:25–26). The wealth of the area resulted in a reputation for luxury garments. Athenaeus repeats Democritus' boast that the Ephesians were devoted to luxury.[31] Ephesus also became a center for shipbuilding and trade. The temple was as well an asylum for the innocent.[32]

However, there was an underside to the religion of the Ephesian Artemis. Jerome notes that Paul wrote to Diana at Ephesus at: "the chief city of Asia where idolatry and the deceptions of the magicians' arts which always accompany idolatry thrived . . . They, whom the error of demons had so long held and who knew that there are spiritual beings and powers and who had perceived a certain likeness of divinity in organs and

---

(*Oec.* 7.33–35) uses the queen bee as an example for a wife.

25. Pausanias, *Descr.* 8.13.1.

26. LSJ, 1086.

27. Strabo, *Geogr.* 14.1.23 [C641]; Murphy-O'Connor 2008: 24.

28. Kroeger, "God/dess" 1995: 58. Bennett (1967: 19–20, 38–39) adds that effeminate priests and sex confusion were part of the rites of Artemis at Ephesus. See also Kroeger 1992: 193–96; Ramsay 1895, 1:93–94; Ramsay 1927: 174.

29. "Virgin" may simply refer to being unmarried. Sex is prohibited only between husband and wife (Ramsay 1895, 1:95, 136). Married women were not allowed in the temple of Artemis (Strelan 1996: 73, 120).

30. Murphy-O'Connor 2008: 23, 52, 64–66; Trebilco 2004: 25–26.

31. Athenaeus, *Deipn.* 12.525C; Murphy-O'Connor 2008: 50; Strelan 1996: 76. Artemis was called "savior" because her temple was a place of refuge (Hemer 1986: 48).

32. Murphy-O'Connor 2008: 26, 44, 123–24, 135–36, 150–51.

auguries and divinations, were in need of the apostle's commendation to God."³³ Artemis could use her arrows to protect, but also to attack. One etymology for her name was "slaughterer, butcher."³⁴ Artemis could protect mothers and kill them.³⁵ In festivals for Artemis, to keep Artemis from slaughtering the participants, "one must hold to a man's throat the sword, and spill the blood for hallowing and the Goddess' honour's sake."³⁶ Artemis's tales were not that different from legends about Amazon warriors who were required to slay a male enemy before they could marry.³⁷ Artemis was associated with ritual murder and there is evidence that human sacrifice was still practiced in the first century.³⁸ The festival of Artemis, like those of the Amazons, affirmed orgiastic religious practices.³⁹ When women went off to celebrate their festivals, they might "spend whole nights on the bare hills in dances which stimulated ecstasy, and in an intoxication perhaps partly alcoholic, but mainly mystical."⁴⁰

Ephesus was well known as a center for the study and practice of magic. Artemis at Ephesus was related to magic, the use of techniques to assure human control or power over supernatural forces.⁴¹ Magic appeals

33. Heine 2002: 77.

34. *OCD*, 126; LSJ, 248; Nilsson 1971: 509. Another etymology is "safe and sound" (Artemidorus Daldianus, *Onir.* 2.35; Strabo, *Geogr.* 14.1.6).

35. In Euripides' tales, first the angry Artemis demands the sacrifice of the maiden Iphigeneia, daughter of Agamemnon, to appease herself (*Iph. aul.*, 89–93) and then snatches her from the altar to make her priestess of her temple in Taurica, north of the Black Sea. Whenever any Greek men came to that coast, they were seized and sacrificed. Iphigeneia was forced to consecrate them to Artemis for death on the altar. "I consecrate the victim," Iphigeneia laments "in rites of that dark cult wherein Artemis joys,--fair is its name alone." While Artemis barred murderers from her altars, she "yet joys herself in human sacrifice!" (Euripides, *Iph. taur.*, 35, 40, 381–84). Clement of Alexandria refers to these sacrifices (*Protr.*, ch. 3.).

36. Euripides, *Iph. taur.*, 1458–61.

37. Herododotus, *Hist.* 4. 117; Bennett 1967: 10–11.

38. Kroeger 1995: 58, 61; *OCD*, 127. Self-castration of the eunuchs, as consecration to the goddess, could be a frenzied and bloody rite (Thomas 1995: 91).

39. Fantham 1994: 134; Nilsson 1971: 503, 509.

40. Hawkes 1968: 126, 286. The Cretan Bacchic frenzy worship continued in Ephesus (Strabo, *Geogr.* 10.3.7 [C466]; Kroeger 1992: 54). The festival of Artemis included heavy drinking (Thomas 1995: 110), though not all aspects of the festivals were unwholesome. See Murphy-O'Connor 2008: 63, 175, 177, 199; Trebilco 1994: 321–22; Arnold 1972: 17–22.

41. *Webster's Dictionary* 2001: 1155. For an example of the mysteries of Artemies, see *New Docs.* 6, 1992: 200–2. Betz 1986 includes samples of ancient spells of power. A second-century Artemis even has zodiac signs on her chest (Erdemgil 2009: 60;

to unhealthy curiosity and the desire for power over others and oneself.[42] Magic and drugs were interrelated.[43] Artemis' name, together with the names of other gods, would be repeated in incantations.[44] Some Christians at Ephesus had previously participated in magic practices. When they willingly and publicly burned their valuable incantation books, the gospel message grew and became powerful (Acts 19:18–20). Today only a column of the temple remains.[45]

ANALYTIC OUTLINE OF 1 TIMOTHY

Paul's overall purpose is to urge Timothy to promote the sound doctrine of God, Savior, who desires all to be saved and to come to knowledge of the truth by countering the false teaching threatening the life of the church at Ephesus.

I. Paul reminds Timothy to warn the false teachers at Ephesus not to teach different doctrine (1:1–20).

    A. Introduction: Paul writes Timothy, his child in faith (1:1–2).

    B. Paul urges Timothy to encourage the Ephesians not to teach different doctrine, but rather love from a clean heart and a good conscience and genuine faith (1:3–7).

    C. In contrast to what is being taught, the law is intended for the unrighteous not the righteous (1:8–11).

    D. Even the Apostle Paul was once unrighteous, but he received mercy as an example to others (1:12–17).

    E. Paul charges Timothy to keep the faith and a good conscience (1:18–20).

II. In order that all may be saved and come to knowledge of the truth, Paul promotes peaceable prayer, education, and leaders (2:1—3:16).

LiDonnici 1992: 407).

    42. Spencer 1995: 82.

    43. *Pharmakeia* could refer to drugs or witchcraft (LSJ, 1917). The Ephesian Six Letters functioned as charms to make the bearers invincible (Athenaeus, *Deipn.* 12.548c; Murphy-O'Connor 2008: 51; Meinardus 1979: 92).

    44. For an example of a syncretistic spell of attraction, see Betz 1986: 89.

    45. Yamauchi 1980: 103; Scherrer 2000: 57; Ramsay 2001: 213.

A. Paul urges godly peaceful lives so that all may be saved and come to knowledge of the truth (2:1–15).

B. Godly overseeing helps the church advance the truth (3:1–16).

III. Because God is Savior of all, Timothy should teach the words of the faith, not heterodoxy, while making sure he himself sets an example of a faithful believer (4:1—5:2).

A. Ascetic heterodoxy was predicted by the Spirit (4:1–5).

B. Since God is Savior of all people, a good minister is nourished by the words of faith, refusing godless myths (4:6–10).

C. Timothy should become an example of a faithful believer as he treats others, spiritually enriches himself, promoting his spiritual gift, so that he will save himself and those who hear him (4:11—5:2).

IV. Church leaders should be honored and justly treated so that the church is not open to attack (5:3—6:2).

A. True widows should be honored but younger widows should remarry so that the church may not be open to attack (5:3–16).

B. Elders leading well should be doubly honored and impartially treated so good deeds will be evident (5:17–25).

C. Slaves should honor masters so God is not slandered (6:1–2).

V. Timothy should fight his own fight of the faith, fleeing heterodox teaching (6:3–21).

A. Heterodox teaching robs people of the truth, while piety with contentment is its own means of gain (6:3–10).

B. Timothy instead should pursue righteousness, fighting the good fight of the faith, guarding the commandment, not open to attack until Jesus returns (6:11–16).

C. The rich should rely on God, not riches (6:17–19).

D. Timothy should guard the deposit, turning away from false knowledge (6:20–21a).

E. Final greeting (6:21b).

1 TIMOTHY 1
Warn False Teachers

INTRODUCTION (1:1–2)

Paul begins his letter in the traditional format, giving the name of the writer, then the recipient, and finally the salutation: **Paul, apostle of Christ Jesus, because of command from our Savior God and our hope Christ Jesus, to Timothy, genuine child in faith: grace, mercy, peace from Father-God and our Lord Christ Jesus** (1:1–2). Paul frequently describes himself as an **apostle** of Christ Jesus.[1] What makes this introduction distinct is that Paul highlights God as **Savior** and Jesus as **hope**. **Hope** and **savior** are also mentioned in Paul's introductory words to Titus (1:2–4), but in no other introduction by Paul.[2] Thus, although the "savior/save" word family is less frequent in 1 Timothy than in Titus, nevertheless the theme of God as Savior appears at significant points in 1 Timothy.[3] Paul is concerned that Timothy communicate God's concern to save: sinners (e.g., Paul, 1:15), everyone, including rulers, men and women (2:1–14), believers and nonbelievers (2:1; 4:10, 16), and even Timothy (4:16).

The themes of God as savior and hope reoccur in 4:10, where we learn that believers have hope because God saves. God gives hope also because God provides for the needy and the wealthy (5:5; 6:17). But, why is *Jesus* specifically **our hope** (1:1)? Jesus gives hope because he strengthens believers, appoints them to service, and, most of all, gives mercy, and overflows with grace toward sinners, which results in eternal life (1:12–16). Jesus is the victorious mediator between God and humans,

---

1. 1 Tim 1:1; 2 Tim 1:1; Titus 1:1; 1 Cor 1:1; 2 Cor 1:1; Gal 1:1; Eph 1:1; Col 1:1; and simply as "apostle" in Rom 1:1.
2. Only 2 Pet 1:1 refers to "our God and Savior Jesus Christ."
3. See Titus 1:3; 2:13; 1 Tim 1:15; 2:3–4, 15; 4:10, 16.

having given himself as a ransom (2:5–6)[4] and the Lord who will return victorious (6:14–15).

Almost every New Testament letter uses the dual salutation "grace and peace," including 1 and 2 Timothy.[5] **Grace** would be similar to the common Hellenistic greeting (*chairein*).[6] **Peace** (*eirēnē*) would be a common Hebrew greeting.[7] Thus, **grace** and **peace** is a synecdoche reminding the reader of the new (Greek) and the old (Hebrew) covenants and the mission to both Gentiles and Jews. But, only 1, 2 Timothy, 2 John, and Jude add the noun **mercy** (*eleos*) in the salutation.[8] Salvation, hope, and mercy are closely related (1 Tim 1:13–16). Because Christ came to save sinners by being merciful, he gives hope.

Timothy is the recipient of the letter, **a genuine child in faith** (1:2). **Genuine** (*gnēsios, gnēsiōs*) occurs only a few times in the New Testament (5). **Genuine child** is used also of Titus.[9] Timothy, like Titus, has a Gentile father, but, unlike Titus, a Jewish mother. Thus, **genuine** or "legitimate" probably has several allusions. (1) Timothy has a faith which is genuine, unlike the heterodox teachers at Ephesus. (2) Timothy, although of mixed ethnic parentage, should consider himself genuinely pure. His mother, Eunice, and grandmother, Lois, trained Timothy in the Old Testament from his youth (2 Tim 1:5; 3:15). As an adult, he was circumcised (Acts 16:3). (3) Timothy was a genuine **child** of Paul. Even though Timothy's father may not have been a believer,[10] Timothy had a spiritual father in Paul. Paul, who had no literal children, had a spiritual child in Timothy. In addition, they served together as father and son in the same "business"—ministry (Phil 2:22). (4) Moreover, as Paul's **child in (the) faith**, Timothy exemplified fully Paul's teachings in word and deed.[11] (5) He was also *genuinely* concerned for others (Phil 2:20).

---

4. See also 3:16.

5. 1 Tim 1:2; 2 Tim 1:2; Rom 1:8; 1 Cor 1:3; 2 Cor 1:2; Gal 1:3; Eph 1:2; Phil 1:2; Col 1:2; 1 Thess 1:1; 2 Thess 1:2; Phlm 3; Titus 1:4; 1 Pet 1:2; 2 Pet 1:2; Rev 1:4.

6. Jas 1:1; Acts 15:23; 2 Macc 11:16; Philo, *Embassy* 40 [315]; Josephus, *Life* 65 [365].

7. E.g., Matt 10:12–13; Judg 18:6; 19:20; 1 Sam 1:17; 2 Macc 1:1; Aune 1987: 176.

8. 1 Tim 1:2; 2 Tim 1:2; 2 John 1:3; Jude 2. Jude does not have "grace" (*charis*).

9. See Titus 1:4.

10. His father did not have Timothy circumcised as a child, but we do not know his beliefs about Christ.

11. See 1 Tim 4:12; 1:18; 1 Cor 4:17; 2 Tim 1:2; 2:1.

Paul probably met **Timothy** during his first missionary journey at Lystra in Pisidia, Asia Minor.[12] Timothy became a believer under Paul's teachings (Acts 14:6, c. A.D. 47-48). Lystra was a Roman colony situated along the Via Sebaste, the Imperial Roman Road that began in Antioch, Syria. A hilly country, Lystra had a lavish water supply, fertile soil, and gardens. Several coins boasted of its water supply by showing a river. Residents there would be acquainted not only with Greek and Latin but also with the ancient Lycaonian language.[13] Timothy and other new believers from Lystra probably journeyed with Paul and Barnabas to nearby Iconium and Antioch,[14] a journey of about 25-100 miles one way. At Lystra, Timothy and others witnessed a man crippled from birth spring up and walk, the worshipers of Zeus and Hermes tried to worship Paul and Barnabas, and Jews from Antioch and Iconium stoned Paul. Possibly, Timothy was one of the disciples who ran outside the city to help Paul and saw him stand up and return to the city.[15]

When Paul returned to Lystra during his second missionary journey, he wanted **Timothy** to accompany him and Silas. Timothy's reputation as a Christian had been stellar not only in his own hometown but also in Iconium, a day's journey away (Acts 16:2-3). Timothy enlisted in Paul's traveling ministry team (Acts 16:8-11), traveling to Philippi, Thessalonica, and Beroea in Macedonia.[16] Timothy eventually joined Paul, Prisca, and Aquila at Ephesus.[17] Timothy and Erastus preceded Paul to Macedonia and Corinth in Greece.[18] Timothy with many others accompanied Paul from Corinth, Greece, to Macedonia (Acts 20:4-6), being part of Paul's group of ministers who were bringing the generous donations of Christians for the starving believers in Judea.[19] Timothy was with Paul when he was under house arrest in Rome, from which Timothy left for Philippi.[20] After Paul's release, Timothy remained in Ephesus when

---

12. Timothy may have heard about Paul and Barnabas' earlier preaching ministry in nearby Iconium (Acts 13:51-14:5).

13. Acts 14:11; Ramsay 1908: 407-15. Indigenous languages, such as Lycaonian, survived among later Christians in Anatolia (Mitchell 1993, 1:173).

14. 2 Tim 3:11; Acts 14:21. Or, Paul could have been referring to Acts 16:4.

15. Acts 14:8-20; 2 Cor 11:25; Robertson 1930 (Acts): 214-15.

16. Acts 17:14-15; 18:1, 5; Phil 4:15-16.

17. Acts 19:22; 1 Cor 4:17; 2 Cor 1:1, 19.

18. Acts 19:22; 1 Cor 16:10-11.

19. Rom 15:25-27; 2 Cor 8:1-7, 10-11; 9:1-5.

20. Phil 1:1; 2:19; Col 1:1; Phlm 1.

Paul journeyed on to Macedonia (1 Tim 1:3). Paul asked him to rejoin him at his final imprisonment in Rome (2 Tim 4:9). Thus, Timothy was with Paul when he wrote eight of his thirteen letters over a period of about twenty years.

During these travels, **Timothy** witnessed many marvelous miracles but also intensive persecutions and sufferings. Eventually, he himself was imprisoned (Heb 13:23). According to tradition, Timothy was martyred for his faith during the reign of Emperors Domitian (A.D. 81–96) or Nerva (96–98) at Ephesus by being clubbed to death for protesting the orgies associated with the cult of Artemis.[21]

Not to Teach Different Doctrine, but Rather Love (1:3–7)

After the introduction (1:1–2), Paul urges Timothy to encourage the Ephesians not to teach **different doctrine**, but rather love from a clean heart and a good conscience and genuine faith (1:3–7): **As I urged you to remain longer in Ephesus, while I was going into Macedonia, that you shall transmit to some not to teach a different doctrine and not to occupy themselves with myths and endless genealogies, which give rise to speculations rather than stewardship of God's household, the one in faith. But the goal of the order is love from a clean heart and a good conscience and a genuine faith, of which, some having deviated, they twist out into talk devoid of truth, wanting to be teachers of the law, not perceiving neither what they say nor concerning what they assert.** This section has three parts: first, the negative (what not to do [1:3–4]); second, the positive (what to do [1:5]); and, third, again the negative (1:6–7).

Paul and Timothy had been in **Ephesus** in Asia together and then Paul had left Timothy behind in Ephesus while Paul crossed the Aegean Sea to **Macedonia** (1:3).[22] Paul had indicated that he planned to visit Macedonia and Asia Minor when he left his house arrest in Rome.[23] He regularly worked with his coworkers to maximize effectiveness by leaving some behind or sending some ahead, in a similar way to Jesus, who sent

---

21. Baring-Gould 1897, 1:360; Meinardus 1973: 118; Humphreys 1895: 67. Strelan (1996: 122–24) suggests his death occurred during a Dionysian festival.

22. Acts does not mention Timothy staying in Ephesus while Paul left for Macedonia. See Introduction-Authorship.

23. Phil 2:24; Phlm 22.

his disciples ahead to prepare his way, even as John the Baptist prepared the people for Jesus.[24]

Timothy's first directive is a negative one. Timothy needs to transmit a message to **some** (*tis*, 1:3). *Tis* may be masculine, feminine, or even neuter.[25] Thus, the false teachers could be men and/or women.[26] Most of the time, *tis* is used negatively to refer to people who are not orthodox in **doctrine** or practice. They are teachers of heterodoxy occupied with myths and genealogies (1:3-4); they deviate from positive attributes (1:5-6, 19); their talk is untruthful; their teaching is without knowledge (1:6-7), they renounce the faith (4:1), teach false doctrine (6:3, 20-21), follow Satan (5:15), and love money (6:10).[27] Among them are two men (Hymenaeus and Alexander, 1:20) and younger widows (5:15).

Heterodidaskaleō (1:3) was probably coined by Paul[28] to refer to teaching what is not healthy or true (6:3). Instead of turning their thoughts and time toward[29] reading Scripture, advocacy for others, and teaching (4:13), they have turned toward **myths and endless genealogies which give rise to speculations** (1:4). Some may have turned toward drinking intoxicating substances (3:8). Others have turned toward asceticism, taught by "deceitful spirits and demonic teachings" (4:1). **Myths and genealogies** also occur in Titus.[30] The Greek historian Polybius recounts that "the genealogical side (*genealogikos*) appeals to those who are fond of a story," who want to be entertained, whereas Polybius himself is interested in actual events, as a student of politics (*Hist.* 9.1.4-5; 2.4). Thus, myths are untruthful legends. Paul does not describe these myths. But, they were no doubt similar to those in Crete. Ephesus, too, had many myths about Artemis.[31] In Titus, Paul describes the myths as "Jewish" and "human commandments" (1:14), while the genealogies are "foolish"

---

24. Luke 10:1; 1:76; 3:4. See 1 Tim 1:2.

25. See also KJV, NRSV, TNIV, NLT, REB, CEV, TEV, ESV, NCB, JB, Inclusive Language Bible, NTME. In contrast see "certain men" in NIV, NASB.

26. *Tis* is used as a neuter twice (1:10; 6:7). It is used inclusively in a positive or neutral manner five times (1 Tim 1:8; 3:1, 5; 5:4, 16; Titus 1:6; 2 Tim 2:5, 21; 3:2).

27. See chart of Titus 1:10. See also Titus 1:12, 14; 2 Tim 2:18.

28. "Only in Christian wr.," BDAG, 399. Paul used *hetero* combined with other words in 1 Cor 14:21 and 2 Cor 6:14 (*heteroglōssos*) and *heterozugeō*) and he refers to "another (*heteros*) gospel" in Gal 1:6.

29. *Prosechō*, BDAG, 879; Thayer, 546; LSJ, 1512.

30. See Titus 1:14; 3:9.

31. See Introduction. Setting-Ephesus and Artemis; Strelan 1996: 53.

(3:9). As in 1 Timothy, the genealogies are **endless** (*aperantos*, 1:4). While *aperantos* can be used in a positive way to describe God as infinite (Job 36:26), here it is used in a negative way to describe activities that never come to an end; they are without conclusion.[32] These are **speculations**, arguments about topics that lead to spiritual error.[33]

How better should the Ephesians spend their time? They should turn their minds and actions toward **stewardship of God's household** (*oikonomia*, 1:4). In 1 Timothy, they are exhorted to aspire to be overseers, stewards over God's household, even the faith itself (1:4; 3:1).[34] What, then, is the goal of **stewards of God's household** (1:4)? Whereas the Sanhedrin ordered (*parangelia*) the apostles not to teach (Acts 5:28)[35] and the magistrate ordered the jailer to imprison Paul and Silas (Acts 16:22–24), Paul reminds the listeners that they were ordered by Jesus to do a positive action, to **love** (1:5; e.g., John 13:34–35). Love is an important aspect of sound doctrine and, therefore, an important theme in 1, 2 Timothy. **Faith** and **love** come from Christ Jesus.[36] Paul was redeemed by faith and love (1:14), women can be saved by them (2:15), and Timothy is to pursue them.[37] Although eventually the Ephesians learn to resist false teaching,[38] the need to love persistently is more difficult for them to attain. About thirty years later (c. A.D. 95), John warns them "you have forsaken your first love" (Rev 2:4 NIV) and shortly thereafter Ignatius exhorts them to love their bishop Onesimus, himself "a man of inexpressible love" (Ign. *Eph.* 1:3).

Such love flows out from three bases: **a clean heart and a good conscience and a genuine faith** (1:5). The **heart** represents the inward part of a person, one's thoughts.[39] Jesus describes an impure **heart** as one with evil thoughts about "murder, adultery, sexual immorality, theft, false witness, slander" (Matt 15:18–20). In contrast, Jesus taught: "Blessed are the pure in heart, for they themselves will see God" (Matt 5:8). "Love" that arises out of evil intentions cannot be genuine.

---

32. LSJ, 185, 1364.
33. 1:4 *ekzētēsis*. See Titus 3:9.
34. See Titus 1:7.
35. See also Acts 4:18; 5:40.
36. 1 Tim 1:14; 2 Tim 1:13.
37. 1 Tim 4:12; 6:11; 2 Tim 2:22.
38. Rev 2:2, 6; Ign. *Eph.* 9:1.
39. Matt 5:28; 9:3–4; 13:19; 15:8; 24:48.

Conscience (*syneidēsis*, 1:5) is an important concept for Paul and for the church at Ephesus. Paul describes himself as having a "good" or "clear" conscience before God, humans, the Sanhedrin (Acts 23:1), governor Felix (Acts 24:16), and the church.[40] If the **heart** symbolizes the inward person, the **conscience** is one aspect of the inward person, the mind's "moral personality."[41] Philo describes the conscience as an internal witness linked with God which convicts the sinner of his guilt, condemns him, holds him back, and directs his conduct. **Conscience** is "a knowing that the subject shares (*syn-eidenai*) either with himself or with someone else."[42] According to Ceslas Spicq, no other ancient writer approaches St. Paul's use of *syneidēsis* in "density and precision: Paul made *syneidēsis* into the interior faculty for the personal discernment of good and evil, the practical rule of conduct and motive for action."[43] A conscience can be defiled[44] or damaged (4:2). Lack of a good conscience and sincere faith can destroy a Christian's life (1:19). A pure conscience is necessary for Christian leadership (3:9). Love that arises out of a confused sense of right and wrong will be ineffective.

How can **love** arise out of **faith** (1:5)? Both love and faith may be found in Christ and now are reflected in Christ's followers. Love is a reflection of one's faith in Christ. People who do not love their family members have denied their faith (5:8). Those who love money wander away from the faith (6:10). Christians should have a faith that is **genuine** (1:5). *Hypokrinomai* can refer to playing a part on the stage or pretending.[45] Thus, Paul does not want a faith that is simply an act or "hypocritical."[46] The importance of a genuine love has been reiterated from a variety of synonymous terms: **heart**, **conscience**, and now **genuine**.

Some people at Ephesus have deviated from (*astocheō*) the goal: **love from a clean heart and a good conscience and a genuine faith** (1:5–6). As a result, they **twist out** (*ektrepō*) away from the truth to **talk devoid of truth** (1:6).[47] As body limbs can become "dislocated," or out of joint,[48]

---

40. 2 Cor 1:12; 4:2; 5:11.
41. *TLNT* 1994, 3:334; Titus 1:15; Rom 2:15; 9:1.
42. *TLNT* 1994, 3:334–35. See also Thayer, 602: "joint-knowledge."
43. *TLNT* 1994, 3:335.
44. 1 Cor 8:7, 12; 10:25–29.
45. LSJ, 1885–86.
46. See also Rom 12:9; 2 Cor 6:6.
47. See also 2 Tim 4:4; Heb 12:13.
48. Thayer, 200; LSJ, 523.

their Christianity has become twisted, not straight, and no longer sound.[49] What might cause people to miss the goal, a failing against which even Timothy has to guard? It is *mataiologia* (**talk devoid of truth**), because it results in wrong teaching (1 Tim 1:7). Like idols who have no real value or power, these words have no value or power. They are empty.[50] Later, Paul describes them as "profane empty talk and contradictions of the falsely called knowledge" (6:20). Such teaching was done by the younger widows who followed Satan and Hymenaeus and Philetus, who taught that the resurrection is already past (1 Tim 5:15; 2 Tim 2:16–18).

These want to be **teachers of the law** (1:7), but understand **neither what they say nor concerning what they assert** (1:7). They have no **perception** of spiritual truths based on careful faith-based thought.[51] Since such teachers do not understand spiritual matters, they do not even comprehend the spiritual implications of their own teachings, which they, nevertheless, **assert** with confidence (*diabebaioomai*).[52] Consequently, their authoritative manner of communication does not ensure the authority or accuracy of that content of the communication. Since both at Ephesus and Crete, the false teachers disputed about legal questions,[53] Paul calls them **teachers of the law**, thereby reminding us of a Jewish connection to their teachings.

Excursus: Women Could Desire to Be Teachers

If these **teachers** (1:7) included Jewish females (such as younger widows, 5:15), teaching authoritatively would be an unusual and desirable oppor-

---

49. 1 Tim 1:10; 6:3; Titus 1:9, 13; 2:2. For emphasis, Paul repeats these two verbs at the end of his letter (6:20–21).

50. See Titus 1:10.

51. *Noeō*, BDAG, 674; Thayer, 426–27. For example, Jesus realizes that his disciples have observed that when they eat something, it enters the stomach and then leaves the body. But, they have not carefully thought that this physical truth is analogous to a spiritual principle (Matt 15:16–20). The rabbinic laws of purity and impurity directing ways of eating are not what make someone pure (Matt 15:1–20). Faith helps one understand matters spiritually. See also Heb 11:3; Matt 16:9; 24:15; John 12:40; Rom 1:20; Eph 3:4; 2 Tim 2:7.

52. In Titus 3:8, *diabebaioomai* is used with positive connotations: Timothy is to "maintain strongly" the trustworthy teaching that believers should be marked by good deeds. However, in 1 Tim 1:7, the teachers have untrustworthy teaching.

53. See Titus 1:10; 3:9.

tunity for them. Of course, women could be taught and could teach the Scriptures at home, as Lois and Eunice taught Timothy authoritatively the Old Testament.[54] However, Jewish women, unlike Jewish men, were not obligated to study rabbinic and Old Testament law, nor did they receive any merit in studying the law, nor was anyone obligated to teach them. They were exempt from any requirement which necessitated their leaving the home for any period of time. They also did not participate in the synagogue "House of Study," which was a place for males only. They were regarded in the same category in rabbinic laws as Gentiles and slaves.[55] Wealthy Jewish and Greek women would be encouraged to stay within the house, active in the indoor life of household management.[56]

Among the Gentiles at Ephesus was a variety of educational expectations for women. Pre-historic Crete and Asia Minor had strong emphases on matriarchy, as reflected in legends about the Amazon women, which may be why Christian female elders taught in Crete.[57] Women would participate in the religious ceremonies of goddesses,[58] but probably not in actual physical sacrifice.[59] The Etruscan women, the initial residents of Italy who were conquered by the Romans, could take part in public events.[60] The later Greek and Roman times appear generally to have limited the public participation of women. The Athenian Greeks and the Romans were both patriarchal.

But the Macedonian conquests by Alexander the Great had changed and was still changing the role of women. Macedonian women gained more social and legal rights than other Greek women, especially Athenian.[61] As a result, women in Hellenistic Egypt had many social and legal rights because Hellenistic queens were successors of the Macedonians. Thus, in Hellenistic Greece, some women scholars and prose writers can be found in Alexandria, as the Neopythagorean philosophers Perictione or Hypatia, leader of the Neoplatonic School (fourth through fifth century A.D.).[62] But,

---

54. 2 Tim 1:5; 3:14-15.

55. *M. Qidd.* 1:7; *Hag.* 1:1; *Sukkah* 2:8; Spencer 1985: 47-57.

56. Philo, *Spec. Laws* 3.31 [169-71]; *Flaccus* 11 [89]; Spencer 1985: 50. See also Xenophon, *Oec.* 7.23, 35.

57. See Titus 2:3-5; Bennett 1967: 75; Winter 2003: 141.

58. Hood 1971: 117.

59. Euripides, *Iph. taur.* 41. See also Introduction. Setting. Ephesus and Artemis.

60. Goodwater 1975: 10-11; Swidler 1976: 22-23.

61. Lightfoot 1913: 56; Acts 16:13-15, 40; 17:4, 12.

62. Nevertheless, education was not promoted for women, even by the wealthy

even though the situation may have been become better for Gentile women since many women were no longer forbidden to pursue higher education, still very few women were teaching in a professional sense in salaried positions in great houses or running a school as a sophist.[63] Many Athenian and Eastern women were still sequestered in the home, married women in Ephesus (at least in the second century A.D.) even being forbidden to enter the temple of Artemis.[64] Early marriage limited opportunities for women. The learned professions were still usually reserved for men. Women were also excluded from law schools, since arguing publicly in court was forbidden, being considered "immodest."[65]

Thus, when confronted with heterodox teaching and learning, neither the Jewish nor Gentile women may have been well prepared to withstand it. Further, what little teaching the Gentile women in Ephesus did receive might have been syncretistic.

Paul himself was an accurate **teacher of the law** (*nomodidaskalos*, 1:7) after his years of study as a Pharisee following his own teacher, Rabbi Gamaliel.[66] A **teacher of the law** is synonymous with, or even superior to, a scribe, since Gamaliel was head of a school.[67] A devout Jewish youth would begin study of the Scriptures at five, study of the interpretation and application of the Scriptures (the Mishnah) at ten, and study of the Talmud (the scholars' interpretation of the Mishnah) at fifteen (*m. 'Abot* 5:21). A scholar might be ordained as a teacher at forty to become an academic professional involved in a career in justice, government, and/or education. For the Jews, knowledge of scriptural exegesis was the determining factor in judicial decisions. These doctors of the law were highly

---

(Pomeroy 1975: 131, 136–39; Pomeroy 1984: 66–71; Goodwater 1975: 15).

63. Winter 2003: 116.

64. Pomeroy 1975: 189. Artemidorus Daldianus (of Ephesus) (*Onir.* 4.4) wrote that death is the penalty for a married woman who entered the temple of Artemis of Ephesus; Bennett 1967: 33.

65. Winter 2003: 178. Nevertheless, a few Roman women gave public speeches (Pomeroy 1975: 175–76).

66. Acts 5:34; 22:3; 26:5; Phil 3:5–6. See also Luke 5:17.

67. E.g., Zenas, Titus 3:13; Plummer 1922: 152; Robertson 2005: 87; Bruce 1990: 175.

regarded and were given places of honor at banquets and synagogues.[68] The law and study of it were highly esteemed. Rabbi Meir explains: "He that occupies himself in the study of the Law for its own sake . . . is deserving of the whole world. He is called friend, beloved of God, lover of God, lover of mankind . . . And it gives him kingship and dominion and discernment in judgement; to him are revealed the secrets of the Law."[69] No wonder Josephus concludes his history by explaining that the Jewish people "give credit for wisdom to those alone who have an exact knowledge of the law and who are capable of interpreting the meaning of the Holy Scriptures." He adds, "though many have laboriously undertaken this training, scarcely two or three have succeeded" (*Ant.* 20.12 [264–65]).

No wonder the Ephesians wanted to become **teachers of the law**. However, in contrast to a genuine **teacher of the law**, the Ephesians, even though they spoke with authority, had no spiritual understanding (1:7). Paul, who did, rarely defended himself by referring to the Jewish oral laws.[70] In his own writings, **law** normally refers to the Scriptures, usually the Pentateuch and sometimes the Prophets,[71] as in 1 Timothy 1:8–9, where "law" appears to refer to Moses' laws.[72]

THE LAW FOR THE UNRIGHTEOUS NOT THE RIGHTEOUS (1:8–11)

Both Paul and the church recognized the value of the law: **But we know that the law is good** (1:8).[73] However, Paul adds a conditional clause: **if someone makes use of it lawfully**, explaining: **knowing this, that to the righteous law is not given, but to the lawless and disobedient, godless and sinners, unholy and profane, patricides and matricides,**

68. Matt 23:6–7. See also *m. 'Abot* 3:19; 4:6; 6:3; Jeremias 1969: 237–40.

69. *M. 'Abot* 6:1. See also *m. 'Abot* 1:2; 3:6, 8; 6:6, 7.

70. See Acts 22:3; 25:8; Phil 3:5.

71. Ten commandments: Rom 2:17–22; 4:14; 5:13; 7:1–7; 13:8–9; Moses' laws: Acts 23:3; 1 Cor 9:8–9; Gal 4:21–23; Eph 2:15; Prophets: Rom 3:10–19; 1 Cor 14:21. Paul also uses *nomos* to describe a principle (Rom 3:27; 7:21–25; 8:2); as a contrast to grace (Rom 4:16; 6:14; 10:4; 1 Cor 9:20; Gal 2:21).

72. Paul refers to serious crimes mentioned in the O.T. in 1:9–11, such as murder (because humans are created in God's image) (Gen 9:6; Exod 20:13; Lev 24:17) honoring parents (Exod 20:12; Lev 19:3; Exod 21:15, 17), adultery (Deut 22:20–27), homosexual behavior, lying (Lev 18:22; 19:11–12; Exod 20:16), and selling slaves (Exod 21:16; Deut 24:7). In contrast, in Roman society trafficking in slaves was a regular, daily event (Bradley 1994: 2, 7–8).

73. See also Rom 7:12.

murderers, immoral persons, male homosexual offenders, slave-dealers, liars, false swearers, and whatever is opposed to healthy teaching (1:9–10). A **lawful** use applies the law to those who are not righteous (1:8–9). Paul uses fifteen illustrations of what is not righteous.[74] **Lawless** (*anomos*) can refer in general to Gentiles (1 Cor 9:21), but in this context clearly applies to those who do evil deeds.[75] The focus of the law is negative, not positive. It tells people what *not* to do.[76] *Bebēlos* (**godless**) is an important word Paul uses to describe the activity occurring at Ephesus and the myths being told.[77] *Bebēlos* refers to unholy acts that lead to lack of piety.[78] Paul himself was accused of profaning the temple at Jerusalem because he was thought to have entered with a Gentile (Acts 24:6). *Bebēlos* summarizes what the Old Testament laws of purity intended to avoid.[79]

Pornos is a general term for a sexually **immoral person** (1:10). "Sexual immorality" (*porneia*) is a broad term referring to any sexual activities done in a way not pleasing to God. It includes sexual immorality done outside of monogamous heterosexual marriage ("adultery" or "incest") or when not married ("fornication") or even mental sexual sin as use of pornography, or even looking at someone with lust.[80] *Pornos*, like other unholy actions, begins with internal desire, such as lust, that eventually exhibits itself externally.[81] It is often part of idolatrous celebrations (1 Cor 10:7–8). Along with murder, homosexual actions, lying, and slander, continued unrepentant behavior will keep believers from

---

74. See Titus 1:13. He begins with the more general terms in pairs: **to the lawless and disobedient, godless and sinners, unholy and profane,** and then, specifically, **to patricides and matricides,** as well as **to murderers, immoral persons, male homosexual offenders, slave-dealers, liars, false swearers,** and ends with a general summary: **whatever is opposed to healthy teaching.**

75. Luke 22:37; 23:32–33; 2 Thess 2:8; 2 Pet 2:8. Paul uses four Greek words that begin with the *a* privative: no law, no obedience, no piety, and no holiness. *Anupotaktos* is used in Titus 1:6 and *anosios* in 2 Tim 3:2 for the heterodox.

76. See also Rom 3:20.

77. Four of its 5 occurrences in the N.T. are in 1, 2 Tim (1 Tim 1:9; 4:7; 6:20; 2 Tim 2:16).

78. 1 Tim 1:9; 2 Tim 2:16. Hebrews describes Esau as *bebēlos* because he sold his birthright for one meal (12:16).

79. Aaron and his descendants as priests were to "distinguish between sacred and *profane* (*bebēlos*), and between clean and unclean" (Lev 10:10).

80. Matt 5:27–28; John 8:41; 1 Cor 5:1; 6:15–20; 7:1–2.

81. Matt 15:18–19.

The Law for the Unrighteous Not the Righteous (1:8–11)   33

inheriting God's kingdom.⁸² *Pornos* refers to people guided by their own physical pleasure.⁸³ The Jerusalem council highlighted *porneia* as one of three things Gentile Christians should guard against (Acts 15:20). The remedy is self-control and the opposite is the fruit of the Spirit.⁸⁴

Arsenokoitēs (1:10) refers to a male who engages in anal intercourse primarily with a person of his own sex (rarely a male with a female).⁸⁵ It is a more specific term than *pornos*. The term probably alludes to Leviticus 18:22 and 20:13. Here Paul may be referring to the sexual confusion in the worship of Artemis in Ephesus, including among the eunuch priests.⁸⁶

Paul had spent two years in Rome and most likely had become knowledgeable about Emperor Nero. This one man had committed nearly every sin listed in these verses. He murdered his mother Agrippina and his wife Octavia (Josephus, *Ant.* 20.8 [153]). He would kill men as a game, dropping their bodies down the sewers. He had gluttonous feasts that lasted from noon until midnight, set up temporary brothels along the shore whenever he floated down the Tiber to Ostia, and seduced boys and married women. He even raped the Vestal Virgin Rubria. Having tried to turn the boy Sporus into a girl by castration, he went through a wedding ceremony with him. He practiced every kind of obscenity. He ended up killing every member of his family and countless innocent others (Suetonius, *Nero* 26–29, 33-37). His degradation became so legendary that graffiti about him appeared on the city walls: "Nero, his own mother, murdered" (*Nero* 39). Nero definitely deserved the law to convict him of sin and punish him for his crimes.⁸⁷

Such destructive actions contrast with healthy maturing growth. **Healthy teaching**⁸⁸ **is in conformity with the glorious gospel of the blessed God with which I myself was entrusted** (1:11).⁸⁹ Paul's specific

---

82. 1 Cor 5:9–11; 6:9; Gal 5:19–21; Eph 5:5; Rev 21:8; 22:15.

83. See also 1 Cor 6:13.

84. 1 Thess 4:3–6; Gal 5:19–23.

85. It is formed from *arsēn* ("male") and *koitē* ("bed") BDAG, 135; Kroeger n.d.; Polycarp, *Phil* 5.3; Belleville 2009: 33–34.

86. Bennett 1967: 37–39; Kroeger 1992: 193–96. See also Rom 1:26–27.

87. See Rom 7:7; 1 Cor 15:56.

88. See Titus 1:13.

89. The glorious gospel is opposed to being in conformity with the unlawful use of the law (1:8). "Sound" has become a dead metaphor for many today, connoting "dead" orthodoxy (*hygiainō* and *hygiēs* are used literally in Luke 7:10; John 5:6). However, Paul uses a metaphor in the present participle (1:10; 6:3) to highlight teaching which

personal **gospel**, "good tidings"[90] is that Christ Jesus "appointed into ministry" Paul himself, a former "blasphemer and a persecutor and a violent person" who received mercy because Christ Jesus' grace "overflowed with faith and love" (1:12–14). Or, in a general sense, the good news is that "Christ Jesus came into the world to save sinners" (1:15). Indeed, God is a Savior "who wants all humans to be saved and to come into a knowledge of truth" (2:4; 4:10). Christ Jesus himself is "a ransom in behalf of all" (2:6). Jesus' own call was to bring "good news" to the needy.[91]

This news is **glorious** (1:11) for the needy who need forgiveness, empowerment, and affirmation (such as Paul). God deserves glory and honor for the salvation that God brings.[92] As early as Moses' song, after God saved the Israelites from the pursuing Egyptians, God's glory became recognized: "Let us sing to the Lord, for he is gloriously glorified ... I will glorify him" (Exod 15:1, 2 LXX).[93] From God emanates a glory that surrounds God's good news. This good news has been **entrusted** to Paul[94] to then entrust to others, such as Timothy and Titus (Titus 1:3), who are to guard it (1 Tim 6:20), and, as well, entrust it to other believers (2 Tim 2:2).

The Apostle Paul, Once Unrighteous, Received Mercy (1:12–17)

To understand the good news, Timothy is reminded of Paul's former life of "bad news." As Paul explains, the law should be applied to the unrighteous (1:8–11), exemplified at one time by Paul himself, but he received mercy as an example to others. As Adam is a prototype of those who sin in knowledge, while Eve is a prototype of those who sin because of deceit (2:14), Paul is a prototype of those who sin out of ignorance but are then forgiven (1:12–17):[95] **I have gratitude to the one strengthening**

---

results in continuous healthy maturing growth instead of unorthodox destructive "disease" and continued infancy.

90. See also 2 Tim 1:8.
91. Luke 4:18; Isa 61:1.
92. E.g., 1 Tim 1:17; 2 Tim 4:18; Ps 96:2–7.
93. After the completion of the tabernacle, a cloud covered it as it was "filled with the glory of the Lord" with the result that Moses could not enter the tabernacle (Exod 40:34–35).
94. See also 1 Cor 9:17; Gal 2:7; 1 Thess 2:4.
95. See also Heb 5:2.

me, Christ Jesus our Lord, that he considered me faithful, having appointed me into ministry, formerly being a blasphemer and a persecutor and a violent person, but I received mercy since being ignorant I acted in unbelief** (1:12–13).

The Lord's grace toward Paul (1:14) resulted in Paul's grace (**gratitude**) toward the Lord (1:12). Grace is like a circular flowing airstream. Paul is similar to the thankful healed Samaritan leper who remembered to thank Jesus (Luke 17:15–19). The leper was healed and saved, and Paul was saved and **strengthened** (*endynamoō*, 1:12) and continues to be strengthened. In the Old Testament *endynamoō* is used to describe the indwelling of the Holy Spirit.[96] Paul too is being indwelt by the Holy Spirit[97] by means of **Christ Jesus**, in order to become effective in **ministry**.[98] The Lord **appointed** Paul soon after Paul's first encounter with Jesus while going to Damascus: "to bear my name before Gentiles and also rulers and people of Israel."[99] When Paul was first converted from persecuting Jesus and Jesus' disciples to preaching that Jesus is the Son of God, he became more and more "effective" in proving that Jesus was the prophesied Messiah, as the Lord "empowered" Paul to preach (2 Tim 4:17).[100]

Paul describes his former self with three negative attributes: **a blasphemer and a persecutor and a violent person** (1:13). These three words are related because blasphemers and persecutors can be violent. **Blasphemy** has two basic types: against God and against humans.[101] Blasphemy against God can include claiming to be God[102] or saying or doing things only God can do (like forgive sins, Matt 9:2–3) and dishonoring and speaking against God.[103] Blasphemy against humans includes insulting them[104] and speaking untruths about them.[105] Paul probably

---

96. Judg 6:34; 1 Chr 12:18.

97. See also Acts 9:17.

98. In contrast, in Phil 4:11–13, Paul is empowered to be content in all situations, which can include ministry but is not limited to it.

99. Acts 9:15; Rom 1:5, 16; Gal 2:7–8.

100. Acts 9:1–5, 20–22.

101. E.g., Stephen's accusation, Acts 6:11. See also Titus 2:5.

102. John 10:33; Matt 26:64–65.

103. Rom 2:24; 14:16; 1 Tim 6:1; Titus 2:5; Jas 2:7; Rev 13:1, 5–6.

104. Matt 27:39; Acts 13:45; 1 Pet 4:4.

105. Rom 3:8; 1 Cor 10:30; Titus 3:2; 2 Pet 2:2, 12.

considered that he did both since he did not recognize Jesus as God and he dishonored Christians.

A **violent** person (*hybristēs*) inflicts both verbal (Luke 11:45) and physical acts of abuse, but primarily physical abuse. Verbal abuse seems a precursor to physical abuse.[106] The same word is used for violent battering from a storm.[107] Acts describes Paul as attacking, dishonoring, and physically abusing Christians, condemning them to prison and to death (Acts 8:3). He "punished" them in synagogues to cause them "to blaspheme." He was "enraged at them" (Acts 26:11). He treated the Christians the way he later was treated, for example, by the Jews from Antioch and Iconium who stoned Paul and dragged him outside Lystra.[108] In contrast, Paul worked within the law. Of course, he thought he was acting in accordance with God's will. Paul may have heard the Christian message, but he was not able to understand it (**being ignorant**, *agnoeō*, 1:13) because it did not fit his presuppositions. In a similar way, Jesus' disciples could not comprehend why the Messiah had to suffer and that he would resurrect (Mark 9:32).[109] Saul (Paul) may have **persecuted** Christians for about a year (Acts 8:1—9:4, c. A.D. 34–35). Possibly, Paul had some Christians inflicted with forty minus one stripes (*m. Mak.* 3:10–13) or he had them stoned (*m. Sanh.* 7:4–5). He certainly had them killed (Acts 26:10).

But the same Lord who saved and strengthened Paul had also been merciful with him: **But our Lord's grace overflowed with faith and love, the one in Christ Jesus** (1:14). Normally when **faith** and **love** occur together, they refer to human faith and love of a church, a household, or an individual.[110] However, in 1 Timothy 1:14 and 2 Timothy 1:13, faith and love reside in Jesus.[111] Understandably, love is an attribute of Jesus because God is love (1 John 4:16), but how can faith reside in Jesus? Do

---

106. E.g., Matt 22:6; Luke 18:32; Acts 14:5.

107. Acts 27:10, 18, 21.

108. Acts 14:19; 2 Cor 11:23–26; 12:10.

109. See also 2 Pet 2:12.

110. E.g., 1 Tim 4:12; 6:11; 2 Tim 2:22; 3:10; 1 Thess 1:3; 3:6; 5:8; Col 1:4; Phlm 5; Rev 2:19.

111. The article after "love" creates an appositive. Whose faith and love?—the one in Christ Jesus. For a similar interpretation, see Quinn & Wacker 2000: 132; Mounce 2000: 53, 55; Fee 1988: 52; Bernard 1922: 31; Ellicott 1865: 34. Eph 6:23 mentions that love and faith can come from "God the Father and the Lord Jesus Christ." Other interpreters conclude that the faith and love are human actions toward Jesus, e.g., Lock 1924: 15; Robertson 1931: 564.

not humans rather have faith or trust *in* Jesus? *Pistis* can refer either to the One "in whom confidence can be placed" who is the epitome of faithfulness—God—or to the one who trusts the One who is trustworthy. **Faith** or "faithfulness" is a virtue that Christians can have, having received it from God.[112] When **grace** overflows from the Lord, streaming out with the grace flow faith and love, the type of faithfulness and love that are distinctive to Christ Jesus (1:14).[113] This is what Paul received instead of the punishment he deserved.

Paul's point is summarized in the saying and doxology that follow: **The word is trustworthy and worthy of all acceptance, that Christ Jesus came into the world to save sinners, of which I myself am first** (1:15). The phrase **the word is trustworthy** (*pistos ho logos*) occurs five times in the Pastoral Letters, but each time fits well in the context. *Pistos ho logos* is an authoritative, accurate teaching from God expressed in a pithy saying or summary statement that can be passed on to others as fully reliable.[114]

---

112. BDAG, 818, 820.

113. Faithfulness (*emeth*) and love (*hesed*) are two central characteristics of God, e.g., Ps 117:2; Gen 24:27, 49: 32:10; Exod 34:6.

114. See Titus 3:8.

"The Word Is Trustworthy... "

Passage	Teaching	Alternate
1 Tim 1:15	"that Christ Jesus came into the world to save sinners"	
1 Tim 3:1	"if anyone aspires to overseeing, (s)he desires a good work"	2:15[115]
1 Tim 4:9–10	"for this we work and strive, since we hope on the living God, who is Savior of all humans, especially believing ones"	4:8[116]
2 Tim 2:11–13	"for if we died together, also we will live together, if we persevere, also we will reign, if we will deny, he also will deny us, if we become unfaithful, that one remains faithful, for he is not able to renounce himself."	2:8–10[117]
Titus 3:8	"that those who have trusted in God may be careful to devote themselves to doing what is good"	3:4–7[118]

However, on account of this I received mercy, that in me first Christ Jesus might reveal all compassion for an example for the ones about to believe in him for eternal life (1:16). Because Christ Jesus came into the world to save sinners, Paul received mercy. **Example** (*hypotypōsis*) might better be translated a "prototype." *Hypotypōsis*[119] occurs twice in the Pastoral Letters. In 2 Timothy, *hypotypōsis* refers to the "healthy words" which Timothy heard from Paul (1:13). In 1 Timothy, an aspect of that teaching is exemplified by Jesus' actions toward Paul. Paul

---

115. Most scholars think 3:1 is the saying; cf. Dibelius and Conzelmann 1972: 28–29.

116. Mounce 2000: 48; Humphreys 1895: 249 agree 4:9–10 is the saying; others think 4:8 is the saying (Fee 1988: 105; Lock 1924: 51; Robertson 1931: 618 Ellicott 1865: 75–76).

117. Mounce 2000: 49; Fee 1988: 249; Bernard 1922: 120 agree 2:11–13 is the saying; others think 2:8–10 is the saying (Lock 1924: 96; Humphreys 1895: 249; Ellicott 1865: 139).

118. Humphreys 1895: 249 agrees Titus 3:8 is the saying; others think 3:4–7 or 3:5–8a is the saying (Towner 2006: 789; Mounce 2000: 49; Fee 1988: 207; Robertson 1931: 607; Bernard 1922: 120; Ellicott 1865: 215).

119. The preposition *hypo* appears to intensify the noun *typos* (Robertson 1934: 634).

is an individual who was a sinner (a synecdoche).[120] He was saved from punishment by Christ Jesus, who showed **compassion** (*makrothymia*) toward Paul by being merciful toward him, forgiving him (1:16). The word family *makrothymia/makrothymeō*[121] literally signifies the holding of strong feelings over a long time, but it can refer to endurance (Jas 5:1–11) and **compassion**. One of God's central self-revelations was made to Moses at Mount Sinai: "The Lord, the Lord, a God merciful and gracious, *slow to anger*, and abounding in steadfast love and faithfulness" (Exod 34:6 NRSV). *Makrothymeō* is a synonym for merciful, gracious, and abounding in steadfast love. God holds on to strong feeling over a long time, being compassionate, which results in **mercy**. *Makrothymeō/ia* is used in this sense of compassion as a synonym for mercy several times in Hebrew literature. According to Proverbs 19:11, "a merciful man is *compassionate*" (LXX). Jesus the son of Sirach says, in comparison to eternity, a human life is like "one drop from the ocean or a single grain of sand. That is why the Lord is *patient* with people; that is why he lavishes his mercy upon them" (Ecclus 18:10–11 REB). Jesus the son of Sirach's analogy is similar to Peter's which says that "one day for the Lord is as a thousand years, and a thousand years as one day. The Lord is not slow about his promise, as some count slowness, but is *compassionate* toward you, not wanting any to die, but all to reach repentance" (2 Pet 3:8–9). Paul calls *makrothymeō/ia* a characteristic of love (1 Cor 13:4), and a fruit of the Spirit (Gal 5:22–23).[122]

The root *typos* ("type, archetype, pattern, **model** to be initiated") is used elsewhere by Paul to describe Paul and his coworkers.[123] For the Philippians, Paul and Timothy are models of believers who persevere despite suffering,[124] and, for the Thessalonians, Paul, Silas, and Timothy are models of believers who work and are not idle.[125] The rhetorician Quin-

---

120. A part representing a whole. See Spencer 1998b: 209.

121. *Makros*, "lasting long" and *thymos*, "feeling and thought, esp. of strong feeling and passion (LSJ, 810).

122. If *makrothymeō* is translated as **compassionate**, it clarifies several of Jesus' parables. The laborer who had never paid the fifteen years worth of salary he owed to the king asked him to be *compassionate* and he would pay him everything. By granting more time, the king would be merciful (Matt 18:26, 29), but the king forgave the whole debt. In Luke 18:1–8, God will show compassion to the elect by procuring the justice for which they ask. See Spencer 1990b: 60–61.

123. E.g., Moses is given a pattern to imitate, Heb 8:5. See also BDAG, 1020.

124. Phil 3:13–19. See also 1 Thess 1:6–7.

125. 2 Thess 3:7–12. See also Titus 2:7; 1 Tim 4:12.

tilian explains that a *hypotypōsis* is "any representation of facts which is made in such vivid language that it appeals to the eye rather than the ear." It is a compelling illustration explaining in full detail how something was done (*Inst.* 9.2.40). Education by model is such an effective and vivid teaching tool.

Christ's mercy and compassion toward Paul, a sinner, serve as a **model** for those people considering belief in Jesus (**the ones about to believe**, 1:16) in order to obtain eternal life.[126] Some of those potential believers are already at Ephesus—even including the heterodox teachers (1:3–7)—while others are still to come, such as the rulers for whom they are to pray (2:1–2).

Reflecting on these marvelous truths about God, Paul, like many rabbis or devout Jews,[127] breaks out into a blessing or prayer to God: **Now to the Ruler of the ages, imperishable, invisible, only God, be honor and glory into the ages of the ages (forever and ever), amen** (1:17).[128] Who is the **Ruler** or King of the ages? Paul appears to refer to Jesus since Christ Jesus is the most recent referent (1:14–16). Jesus told Pilate that he was born to be king (John 18:37) and the angel tells John that the Lamb "is Lord of lords and King of kings" (Rev 17:14). The name of the rider of the white horse, who is called "Faithful and True," is "Ruler of rulers and Lord of lords" (Rev 19:11, 16).[129] Yet, since God is one, Paul could be referring to the Trinity.[130] God the Father is also possible since only God the Father is **invisible**.[131] Later in the letter, Paul appears to refer to Jesus as "the blessed and only Sovereign, the Ruler of rulers and Lord of lords," but to God the Father "whom no human has ever seen or can see" (6:15–16).[132] God's desire was always to rule directly over the people with a prophet or judge to whom God would reveal his will, but the Israelites preferred instead a king such as the Gentile nations had. The ruler could

---

126. See Titus 1:2.

127. "Blessed is he" is a common interjection when speaking of God, "the Holy One," e.g., *m.'Abot* 3:2; 4:22.

128. See also other doxologies by Paul: 1 Tim 6:15–16; 2 Tim 4:18; Rom 11:36; 16:27; Gal 1:5; Eph 3:20–21; Phil 4:20. Ps 9:16 LXX also has "into the ages of the ages."

129. See Titus 2:13. Mounce agrees that the immediate context suggests Jesus is the "King" (2000: 60).

130. E.g., Ellicott 1865: 38.

131. Paul refers to the "Lord" in v. 14 and "God" in vv. 4, 11 and "Father" in v. 1.

132. Towner 2006: 151–52; Harris 1992: 256.

become a type of idol.¹³³ Nevertheless, even in the Old Testament, God continued to be called **the King**. This is what the prophet Isaiah called God when he saw the Lord, "the King, the Lord of hosts" "sitting on a throne" (Isa 6:1, 5).¹³⁴ Other Jews would also describe God as King, as did the Sanhedrin court when it admonished witnesses: "The King of kings, the Holy One, blessed is he, has stamped every man with the seal of the first man, yet not one of them is like his fellow" (*m. Sanh.* 4:5). Rabbi Akabya ben Mahalaleel, a contemporary of Paul, advised, know "'before whom thou art about to give account and reckoning'—before the King of kings, the Holy One, blessed is he" (*m. 'Abot* 3:1).¹³⁵

In 1 Timothy, Paul reminded his listeners that God is the unique Ruler-one who lasts forever (**Ruler of the ages**), is not mortal, not being seen, the only God, who deserves eternal honor (1:17). *Aphthartos* (**imperishable**) signifies not liable to decay, unlike an athlete's crown (1 Cor 9:25). Opposite would be the idols created by humans (Rom 1:23), such as Artemis of Ephesus, or the emperors who were declared to be divine, such as Octavius Augustus (Luke 2:1), whom the Roman Senate decreed at his death in A.D. 14 a god of the State.¹³⁶

God's everlasting power and deity are **invisible** (*aoratos*), yet they are reflected in the world God created (Rom 1:20). The marvel has been that the invisible God, who is Spirit and cannot be seen, has become visible in Jesus Christ.¹³⁷ In particular, in 1 Timothy, God's attribute of compassion became visible through God's compassionate treatment of Paul (1:15–16).

Fusing the Horizons: Significance of Christ's Birth

Christmas is for many people a time of great physical, emotional, and financial stress.¹³⁸ Paul explains a major reason why Jesus came to earth. He

---

133. 1 Sam 8:5–8; 12:11–12.

134. See also Jer 10:10.

135. See also *m. 'Abot* 4:22; Tob 13:10–11, 15.

136. *OCD*, 151. Emperor Nero claimed to have descended from the divine Augustus (*OCD*, 729). Ephesus, as a leading city, was given authority in 29 B.C. by Emperor Octavius to set up a sanctuary dedicated to the cult of Roma and to his deified father, Julius Caesar (Mitchell 1993: 100).

137. 1 Tim 6:16; John 1:18; 4:24; Col 1:15–16. On Rom 1 see Spencer 1991.

138. For example, next to January and March, most funerals occur in December.

did not come to give humans a heavy burden (cf. Matt 11:28–30), rather to alleviate a great burden: to save sinners (1:15). He saved the great sinner Paul who, in pursuit of what he thought was a just cause, violently persecuted countless Christians and blasphemed the Lord Jesus. Another example is the soldier Basilides. Potamiaena was a student of Origen in Alexandria, Egypt in the 200s. She was beautiful but determined to remain a virgin until she married, despite pressure from lovers. Because of her faith, she was sentenced to death. A soldier, Basilides, led her away to her death. People were making sexual jokes at Potamiaena's expense but Basilides felt compassion for her and treated her kindly. She thanked him and offered to pray for him, even though he was bringing her to her death. Boiling pitch was poured over her body, while Basilides watched. Afterwards, Basilides had to take an oath based on the divinity of Emperor Septimus Severus and to the shock of all his fellow-soldiers, he refused. Under no circumstances would he take this oath because he was now a Christian. Basilides was a persecutor of Christians but he received mercy from God, after having received mercy from Potamiaena (Eusebius, *Hist. eccl.* 6.5).

Thus, Christmas should be a time of mercy. No one today is too violent or evil or hopeless to receive God's mercy and become transformed. God is invisible (1:17). Nevertheless, Jesus can become visible again through people today, like Paul and Basilides, who are transformed to serve. Christmas should be a time in which to remember because Christ is merciful to us, therefore we can be merciful to others, and even to ourselves, showing our compassion in service to the extent that we are being strengthened by Christ (1:12).

KEEP FAITH AND A GOOD CONSCIENCE (1:18–20)

First Timothy 1:18–19 refers back to 1:5 as an internal summary of the first chapter:[139] **This order I am entrusting to you, child Timothy, according to the prophecies preceding you, that you may fight with them the good fight, having faith and a good conscience, which some, having rejected for themselves with respect to the faith, suffered shipwreck, of which is Hymenaeus and Alexander, whom I delivered to**

---

139. "Order" (*parangelia*), "faith" (*pistis*), "conscience" (*syneidēsis*) all occur in 1:5 and "child Timothy" in 1:2.

Satan, that they might learn not to slander (1:18–20). Paul is entrusting to Timothy an order of "love from a clean heart and a good conscience and a genuine faith" (1:5). This love has been demonstrated and made possible by Christ Jesus who "came into the world to save sinners" (1:15). Therefore, Timothy has been charged to exhort certain people at Ephesus "not to teach a different doctrine and not to occupy themselves with myths and endless genealogies" (1:3–4) nor to misuse the law (1:8).

Timothy had been well spoken of by the believers in Lystra and Iconium (Acts 16:2). Possibly, some believers had prophesied then about Timothy. Timothy's spiritual gift had been given to him when the elders laid hands on him (1 Tim 4:14). That is why Paul entrusted this commission to Timothy. As an evangelist (2 Tim 4:5), Timothy is particularly gifted to respond to heterodox teachers. But, as well, the Holy Spirit had prophesied about future false teachings at Ephesus (1 Tim 4:1; Acts 20:29–30). Because Timothy knew, from **prophecy** (1:18), that the teachings at Ephesus were indeed heterodox, he does not have to be unsure about their truth or falsehood. Therefore, he can fight this campaign with confidence. Prophecy reproves and calls all to account (1 Cor 14:22–25). The words of prophets should not be despised, because prophets are moved by the Holy Spirit (1 Thess 5:19–20; 2 Pet 1:21). Some prophets, for example, had been moved by the Holy Spirit to forewarn Christians about the future heterodox teaching at Ephesus.

This **order** of ministry is now explained in the imagery for a soldier waging war: fight . . . **the good** fight (*strateuō, strateia*, 1:18).[140] The professional soldier[141] was a normal aspect of ancient life (e.g., Luke 3:14). The Roman Emperor Augustus established a permanent standing army, composed of Roman citizens and *auxilia* (soldiers raised from the provinces). The military had *praefecti* (commanders) or tribunes, under which were centurions and decurions and then soldiers.[142] The New Testament shows soldiers working with centurions and with Governor Pilate.[143] They arrested Jesus, attended to the crucifixion, guarded Peter, guarded and protected Paul when he was under arrest.[144] Timothy is not

---

140. Paul develops these same two words as an extended metaphor to appeal to the Corinthians (2 Cor 10:3–4), a city overrun with military personnel, situated under the Acrocorinth (Spencer 2001: 168). See 1 Tim 6:12.

141. *Stratiōtēs* (2 Tim 2:3) (LSJ, 1653).

142. *OCD*, 155, 120–21, 872.

143. E. g., Matt 8:5, 9; 27:27; Mark 15:16; Acts 10:7; 23:22–23, 31; 27:1, 31–32, 42.

144. Matt 27:27; Luke 23:36; John 19:23, 32, 34; Acts 12:4, 6, 18; 23:23, 31; 28:16.

to comport himself as a soldier under leave, but as an active soldier. His "enlisting officer" is Paul (1 Tim 1:18). Like a good soldier he should be attentive to his orders. But, in contrast to a soldier who might have to serve in a war with which he differs, Timothy serves in a **good** campaign. His tools are not javelins or swords or arrows, but, first, the prophecies he received, and, second, the twin virtues of **faith and a good conscience** (1:19).

Faith is an important theme in Paul's letters, including the Pastoral Letters (56 refs. in 13 chs.), but it is especially important in 1 Timothy (33 refs. in 6 chs.).[145] Faith is a virtue that Christians can have, having received it from God, the One who is the epitome of faithfulness (1:14). The object of faith for Christians is Jesus Christ (1:16; 3:16).[146] **The faith** may also describe all of Christianity, its message of trust in Jesus, and its impact on a Christian's life.[147] Faith and a good conscience are mentioned together three times in 1 Timothy. They are (along with a "pure heart") a basis for love (1:5) and they accompany perseverance in the Christian walk (1:18–19). If they do not accompany (as virtues) the Christian walk (1:19a), they affect the ability to persevere in the Christian walk (1:19b). In 3:9, a **clean conscience** is the receptacle or environment in which faith (as a synecdoche for all of Christianity) must reside.

Consciences should be both **good** and "clean." Initially, only Christ can cleanse the conscience perfectly and permanently from sin and evil so that humans can draw near to God in confidence.[148] The faith and the cleansed conscience that Christ gives then become weapons to arm Christians in their daily walks. But, especially at Ephesus, the interior faculty for the personal discernment of good and evil, that interior conversation that might be shared with another, needs to be maintained, along with trust (or faith) in Jesus and in his promises and precepts for living.[149] The danger at Ephesus is the *searing* of the conscience (1 Tim 4:2), while the danger at Corinth is a *weak* conscience becoming soiled or wounded (1 Cor 8:7, 12).

By rejecting conscience, **Hymenaeus and Alexander** (1:19b–20) have replaced "the internalizing of the norm of godliness, for an external

---

145. Paul uses this word family (*pistis*; *pisteuō*; *pistos*) more frequently only in Rom (61 refs. in 16 chs.) and Gal (27 refs. in 6 chs.) (Kohlenberger 1995: 802–5).

146. For "faith" as a virtue, see 1 Tim 1:5, 19; 2:7, 15; 4:12; 5:12; 6:11.

147. 1 Tim 1:2, 4; 4:1, 6; 5:8; 6:10, 12, 21.

148. Heb 9:9–10, 14; 10:2, 19, 22.

149. See 1 Tim 1:5.

law structure."¹⁵⁰ They have abandoned the conscience with its organic, interior ability to discuss and discern what is good and evil, with an external misuse of the law (1:8–10; 4:3–4). The conscience is guided in its everyday life by faith, trust in the living God, to guide and to teach one. As a result of rejecting the conscience as a "steering wheel" or a harbor guide, their ship of faith has **suffered shipwreck** (1:19). And, when a ship is shipwrecked, not only are passengers wounded and made infirm, but lives and cargo are lost as well.¹⁵¹

Having been shipwrecked already, Hymenaeus and Alexander are already in Satan's domain because **Satan** is the one who causes illness, infirmity, and death.¹⁵² Paul then leaves them there. He **hands** them **over** (*paradidōmi*) to Satan (1:20). In the same way, God **hands over** people to the results of their own evil choices.¹⁵³ Although *paradidōmi* can be used in a positive way (as in being **handed over** to God's grace, its negative use refers to the act of being arrested, tortured, and killed.¹⁵⁴ Satan here is "the soldier" who imprisons. Paul, though, intends that his decision to hand them over will have a positive result: Hymenaeus and Alexander will learn not to **slander** (*blasphēmeō*, 1:20). Apparently Hymenaeus and Alexander had been acting in a diabolical way: lying, deceiving, bearing false witness instead of furthering the truth, peace, righteousness, and love.¹⁵⁵ Paul has allowed them to remain in this severe type of discipline because, unlike Paul, they did not sin out of ignorance, and, unlike the women in 2:11–14, they were not deceived out of lack of education. Apparently Hymenaeus did *not* learn not to slander because he continued to swerve from the truth by claiming that the resurrection had already taken place. Paul concluded then that Hymenaeus was not "God's" (2 Tim 2:17–19).

---

150. Towner 2006: 158.
151. E.g., Acts 27:18–19, 21–22, 33–34, 41, 44.
152. E.g., Luke 13:16; 2 Cor 12:7; Job 1:9–19; 2:4–7.
153. E.g., Rom 1:22–26; Acts 7:41–43; 2 Cor 5:5.
154. E.g., Acts 14:26; 15:40; Matt 4:12; 10:19, 21; 18:34; 24:9; Luke 21:12; Acts 8:3; 12:4; 22:4; 27:1; 28:17.
155. See Titus 2:5.

1 TIMOTHY 2–3
Peaceable Prayer, Education, and Leadership

Paul's appeal[1] in 2:1 (**therefore**) alludes to an "order" to Timothy in chapter 1 (1:18).[2] Paul's appeal in chapter 2 has to do with the nature and consequent purpose of God. God is a savior God "who wants all humans to be saved and to come into knowledge of truth" (2:3-4). If chapter 1 (as regards the church) mainly deals with what they are *not* to do (teach different doctrine), chapters 2-3 mainly deal with what they are to do. In order that all may be saved and come to knowledge of the truth, Paul promotes prayer that results in peace, peaceable prayer lifestyles, peaceable learning, and godly leaders who promote peace with outsiders (2:1—3:16).

GODLY PEACEFUL LIVES (2:1-15)

Paul has Timothy begin this process of leading people to salvation by appealing to Timothy and the believers at Ephesus to pray: **Therefore, I am encouraging you, first of all, to make prayers for needs, reverent prayers, intercessions, thanksgivings on behalf of all humans, on behalf of rulers and all of the ones in a place of prominence, in order that we may live a tranquil and quiet life in all Godliness and holiness** (2:1-2).

Prayer is **first** in terms of importance and priority in time (2:1). The Savior God must be active and present for salvation to occur. **Prayer** is described in four of its aspects in a pleonasm.[3] The noun *deēsis* and verb *deomai* principally refer to petitionary prayer or a forceful urging in regard to some **need**.[4] They can be used for humans communicating to

---
1. See Titus 2:15 on "appeal" (*parakaleō*).
2. See 1:18 internal summary.
3. "Pleonasm" is the repetition of synonyms for "prayer" for emphasis (Spencer 1998b: 203).
4. See Spencer 1990b: 112-15.

humans and humans communicating to God.[5] *Proseuchē* is a prayer addressed to God.[6] Being limited to God (or the gods), it emphasizes the sacred nature of the act (**reverent**), as in Jesus' lesson to *pray*: "Our Father, the One in the heavens, hallowed be your name" (Matt 6:9). These two prayers (*dēesis, proseuchē*) summarize the types of prayers of the widow, whose hope is only in God (1 Tim 5:5). Her prayers include her need and her reverence toward God. In summary, *dēesis* "gives prominence to the expression of personal need, *proseuchē* to the element of devotion."[7]

The third aspect of **prayer** is *enteuxis* (**intercession**). Outside the New Testament, *enteuxis* and *entugchanō* refer to "*lighting upon, meeting with*" someone and, thereby, obtaining an audience and conversing with them.[8] In the New Testament, it includes the idea of an audience with someone, but even more purposeful, as in petitioning against someone (as in a complaint)[9] or petitioning for someone, as in an intercession. The Holy Spirit and Jesus **intercede** or advocate for believers.[10] Believers can follow their example and intercede to God for other people or other needs (1 Tim 2:1; 4:5).

Thanksgiving (*eucharistia, eucharisteō*) is an important word family for Paul. Out of a total 53 New Testament references, 35 are used in Paul's letters (66%).

The word family (*eucharistia*) is a reminder that Jesus, when on earth, gave thanks for food before distributing and eating it, including at the "Eucharist."[11] Jesus appreciated the Samaritan who thanked him after being healed (Luke 17:12–19).[12] This attitude of appreciation was one Paul wanted to encourage in other Christians, which he himself modeled (1 Tim 1:12–14). The Lord's Prayer follows the sequence of adoration followed by petition for need (Matt 6:9–13). In 1 Timothy 2:1, the suppliant begins with need, then moves to a more reverent attitude, then continues with a focus on others, and concludes with a positive attitude.[13] For when

---

5. E.g., a man covered with leprosy, "falling upon his face, *begged*" Jesus to make him clean (Luke 5:12). See also 8: 28, 38; 9:38.

6. *Pros* ("to") limits *euchē* ("vow" or "prayer") (Spencer 1990b: 131–39).

7. Thayer, 126.

8. LSJ, 576–78.

9. E.g., Acts 25:24; Rom 11:2.

10. Rom 8:27, 34; Heb 7:25.

11. E.g., Matt 15:36; 26:27; Mark 8:6; 14:23; Luke 22:17, 19; John 6:11, 23.

12. See also Spencer 1990b: 126–31.

13. Cf. Phil 4:6.

we thank God, our thanks are an acknowledgement or confession of belief in God's work in the world and in our lives.

Timothy and the other believers should pray for everyone (2:1). Paul begins with a more specific term (**rulers**, *basileus*) and then continues with a more general or abstract phrase: **everyone currently ("being") in a position of prominence** (*hyperochē*). Paul wants them to pray for such rulers as Emperor Nero and King Agrippa II (Acts 25:13; 26:2), the proconsul in Ephesus, and any kings or queens in Asia Minor. A **ruler** would be someone wealthy and powerful with a staff and an army over a country or city-state.[14] Paul also wants them to pray for anyone having authority or **prominence**, such as, the provincial Roman consul or governor, the local political and religious leaders, and the local Jewish and Christian leaders.

In Titus 3:1–2 and Romans 13:1, Paul exhorts the Christians to be subject to those in positions of authority.[15] In 1 Timothy, he explains that the advantage of praying for those in leadership is that they can help Christians to live in tranquility.[16] Both *ēremos* and *hēsychios* include the idea of **quiet**, stillness, and rest.[17] *Hēsychios* (adj.) in 2:2 is the same word family as *hēsychia* (noun) in 2:11–12[18] showing that what Paul wants for women, he also wants for all Christians: a state of calm and rest. This life was to be lived out in **godliness** (*eusebeia*) **and holiness** (*semnotēs*). Godly living is an important trait for Christians, especially as they live in a secular world.[19]

People living in tranquility furthers God's purposes: **This is good and acceptable before our Savior God, who wants all humans to be saved and to come into knowledge of truth** (2:3–4). Living a "quiet life" "in all godliness and holiness" is **good** because it helps God to reach God's desire of salvation for all humans. Jesus explained that not many will remain faithful,[20] nevertheless, God wants all people to believe in

---

14. E.g., Matt 11:8; 18:23; 22:2–7; Luke 14:31.
15. See Titus 3:1.
16. Keener (1992: 102, 121–22) reminds us that Jews also prayed for the emperor.
17. LSJ, 777–79.
18. See 1 Tim 2:11.
19. Titus 1:1; 2:12. *Eusebeia* was also a secular concept referring to a "right relationship" to the god/dess that blessed the city (Strelan 1996: 28–29). For Paul, a right relationship to God would also bless the secular people. On *semnos*, see Titus 2:2.
20. Matt 7:14; Luke 18:8. Sider (2005) similarly notes that few Americans take seriously the Christian worldview (e.g., 126–130).

God and to persevere in their faith and thus to be saved.[21] To be **saved** is to be forgiven one's sins (1:13–15) and, thus, be purified, made acceptable to a holy **God**.[22] A believer is purified by God, but must work on being pure in practice. In the process of being saved, a believer should come to a thorough **knowledge**[23] **of the truth**. Otherwise, false knowledge can mislead a believer away from truth[24] and, eventually, away from salvation, as in the case of Hymenaeus and Alexander (1:20). The importance of truth is a continual theme for Paul.[25] Paul is adamant that as an apostle he is telling the truth (2:7). The church also should be founded on the truth (3:15). Truth is durable, dependable, real, and an essential aspect of God's nature.[26]

One aspect of truth is to know **God** (e.g., Eph 1:17) and God's nature which is apparent in the next sentence: **For God is one, one is also a mediator between God and humans, human Christ Jesus, the One having given himself as a ransom on behalf of all, the witness to his own times, for which I myself was appointed a preacher and apostle (I speak truth, I do not lie), a teacher of Gentiles in faith and truth** (2:5–7). A Jew would heartily affirm the first clause (2:5), as Moses summarizes: "Hear Israel, the Lord our God (*elohim*), the Lord is one" (Deut 6:4). In Deuteronomy, as a result, believers are to love the Lord with their whole being (vv. 5–6). Jews were renowned in ancient times for their belief in one God, symbolized, for example, by Judith's proclamation to the Gentile magistrates: We "acknowledge no god but the Lord" (Jdt 8:20 REB). The Roman historian Tacitus describes the Jews as despising the gods, having "a purely spiritual monotheism . . . for them, the Most High and Eternal cannot be portrayed by human hands and will never pass away" (*Hist.* 5.5). Why did Paul include the clause **God is one** in this chapter? He appears to imply that God is unique in that God genuinely wants people to be saved (2:4). God also is the only being capable of saving people and the only deity before whom a human needs approval. The Godhead is also able to accomplish salvation completely. The One

---

21. See Titus 1:3; 2:13; 1 Tim 1:1; 4:10.

22. See Titus 3:5.

23. *Epignōskō*, see Titus 1:1.

24. E.g., 1 Tim 4:1–3; 6:5; Titus 1:14.

25. *Alētheia, alētheuō, alēthēs, alēthōs, alēthinos* occur 55 times in letters attributed to Paul (Rom - 9; 1, 2 Cor - 11; Gal - 4; Eph - 7; Phil - 2; Col - 2; 1, 2 Thess - 5), 15 times in the Pastoral Letters.

26. *TLNT* 1: 67–68; BDAG, 42–44.

who requires purity from humans and the One who can accomplish that purity are the same. Later in 1 Timothy, monogamous marriage or a *one-flesh* union will reflect humans being created in the image of *one* God.[27]

The pagan Gentiles might find several offensive aspects in Paul's statement. First, many would believe in a variety of gods for a variety of purposes and people. As Artemidorus explained, "What the gods signify for men, goddesses signify for women. Gods are more auspicious for men than goddesses; goddesses are more auspicious for women than gods" (*Onir.* 4.75). At Ephesus, many would place gods in a hierarchy with Artemis at the top. The temple of Artemis at Ephesus (Artemision) was also renowned as an asylum for the innocent yet simultaneously Artemis could be a slaughterer.[28] Some would think she should be the **mediator** (2:5). Others would conclude she would not save **all** (v. 4). In addition, Ephesus had shrines sacred to Zeus, Cybele and Demeter (mother of the gods), Apollo (Artemis' brother), Asclepius (god of healing), Aphrodite, Dionysus, Hygeia, Pan, Isis, Hecate, Marnas (river god), Leto (Artemis' mother), Athena, Serapis, Eros, and deified emperors, such as Augustus.[29] Paul, in contrast, asserts that there is only one God who can serve all needs, including salvation, for all people.[30]

The pivotal teaching in Deuteronomy 6:4 also contains within itself the allusion to plurality within the one God. **One** can refer, for example, to two people united in marriage (Gen 2:24) or to all humans when they have one language (Gen 11:1, 6). *Elohim* is an abstract plural word for **God**, but it has a singular verb when referring to the unique living God (e.g., Gen 1:26–28). The Lord has *one* "name" but three persons ("the Father and the Son and the Holy Spirit").[31] Thus, after God's revelation to Paul[32] and his own reflection, he can assert that God is one but yet that one God has three persons.[33]

Christ Jesus is the only **mediator** between God and humans. Paul places in juxtaposition the term **human** (*anthrōpos*): **humans, human**

---

27. E.g., 1 Tim 3:2, 12; 5:9. See also Spencer 2009: 28–30.
28. See Acts 19:27 and Introduction. Setting. Ephesus and Artemis.
29. Scherrer 2000: 58–61, 70, 80, 86–87, 92–94, 134–35, 151, 170–71, 188, 198–201, 209–13. Mitchell (1993: 2:19, 28) groups indigenous cults in ancient Anatolia as four: for Zeus, mother goddesses, *Mēn*, and champions of divine justice and vengeance.
30. See also Spencer 1995.
31. Matt 28:19. See Spencer 2009: 28–29.
32. Acts 9:4–5; Gal 1:11–12, 16–17; 1 Thess 2:13.
33. See also, e.g., 2 Cor 13:13.

(2:5). Even though Jesus was born a male, Jesus only uses the generic self-description **human**[34] because if Jesus is to represent humans (male and female) he himself must be "human" first of all. He is the counterpart to "the *Adam*," "humanity" (made of male and female) (Gen 1:26–28). A **mediator** (*mesitēs*) is in a middle (*mesos*)[35] position between several parties (Gal 3:20), in this case two: God and humans. Job cried out to God the dilemma: "If I wash myself with soap and cleanse my hands with lye, yet you will plunge me into filth, and my own clothes will abhor me. For [God] is not a mortal, as I am, that I might answer him, that we should come to trial together. There is no *umpire (mesitēs)* between us, who might lay his hand on us both" (Job 9:30–33 NRSV). But, Jesus is this unique "umpire" or **mediator** (God *and* human). As Paul also explains to the Corinthians, God is "the one reconciling [humans] to himself through Christ" (2 Cor 5:18). Humans did not obey God's first covenant. Jesus set them free from the sins committed under the first covenant so that they could become heirs under a new covenant.[36]

What kind of **mediator** is **Jesus**? He is **the One having given himself as a ransom on behalf of all, the witness to his own times** (2:6). *Antilytron*[37] hearkens back to Jesus' words to his disciples: "the Son of Humanity did not come to be served but to serve and to give his life a **ransom** for many."[38] In that context, Jesus uses his own example as a model for servant as opposed to tyrant leadership (Matt 20:25–27). In 1 Timothy 2, Paul uses the concept as an explanation of the means by which God saves all people. It has already been done willingly by Jesus. Jesus has given his life in exchange for[39] his function as a **ransom** was displayed in Jesus' lifetime, the "lamb" who was sacrificed.[40]

As a witness to Jesus (the One who mediates between God and humans by having been a ransom), Paul was appointed: **for which I myself was appointed a herald and an apostle** (2:7). A *kēryx* in ancient

---

34. Not the usual term for "male," *anēr*, though even it sometimes is used for groups including women. "Son of Man" may be rendered "the Human One" (CEB) or the Son of Humanity (e.g., Luke 9:58). Spencer 1995: 99–101. See also Strauss 1998: 246–47.
35. Thayer, 401.
36. Heb 8:6–9:15; 12:24.
37. See Titus 2:14.
38. Matt 20:28 [*lytron anti*]. See also Mark 10:45.
39. Thayer, 50.
40. E.g., 1 Cor 5:7. See also Titus 1:3.

times was a **herald**. As Philo explains: the herald's staff is "an emblem of covenants of reconciliation, for wars come to be suspended or ended through heralds establishing peace; wars where no heralds are admitted create endless calamities both for the assailants and the defenders."[41] An **apostle**, as an eyewitness of the resurrected Jesus, is a messenger sent off by Jesus to represent Jesus, proclaiming God's reign.[42]

Paul reiterates the truth of his calling and message: (**I speak truth, I do not lie**)[43] and adds a third role to **herald** and **apostle**: **a teacher of Gentiles in faith and truth** (2:7). **Teacher** and "apostle" are two primary spiritual gifts Paul uses for self-description.[44] Although he baptizes a few people, he does not define himself as an evangelist (in contrast to Timothy).[45] As a teacher (*didaskalos*), Paul instructs persons or causes them to learn. The primary effect of the *didaskalos* is on "the intellect, and someone qualified exercises the influence."[46] A *didaskalos* "teaches definite skills."[47] Jesus, when on earth, taught, preached, and healed (e.g., Matt 4:23). The twelve apostles also taught because teaching was one of the ways in which the reign of God is furthered (Mark 6:30). According to Jesus, the greatest person in God's kingdom both obeys and teaches others Jesus' commands (Matt 5:19). Teaching is one aspect of making disciples (Matt 28:19–20). Of course, true and false teaching is a major problem at Ephesus[48] that Paul can address by being a teacher of truth (2:7).

Paul's primary focus is teaching **Gentiles**, as Ananias was told by the Lord: Paul was his "chosen vessel . . . to bring his name before Gentiles and also rulers and people of Israel."[49] The church at Ephesus most likely had Gentiles and Jews. Even though Paul had to leave the synagogue at Ephesus, he was heard by Jews and Gentiles throughout the area.[50]

---

41. *Embassy* 13 [100]. See also 2 Tim 1:11; Rom 10:14–15; 2 Cor 5:18–20.
42. Acts 26:16–18; Gal 1:11–12; 1 Cor 9:1; 15:5–8. Spencer 2004: 137–38.
43. See 1 Tim 1:4; Titus 1:2.
44. 2 Tim 1:11; 1 Cor 12:28–29. **Herald** (*kēryx*) is never listed as a spiritual gift. See also Acts 11:26; 15:35; 18:11; 20:20; 28:31.
45. 1 Cor 1:14. See 2 Tim 4:5. Paul also speaks in tongues (1 Cor 14:18; 12:28–30).
46. Behm, *TDNT* 4:1019.
47. Rengstorf, *TDNT* 2:149.
48. See 1 Tim 1:6–7.
49. Acts 9:15; 13:47; Rom 1:5, 13; 11:13; Gal 2:9; Eph 3:8–9.
50. Acts 19:8–10, 17, 26; 20:21.

Nevertheless, Paul's strategy was first to speak at the synagogue of each city where Jews and Gentile God-fearers could hear him.[51]

After encouraging Timothy to begin with prayer at the larger societal level, Paul wants Timothy to instruct the men and women in peaceable prayer lifestyles (2:8–10). In Greek, Paul begins verse 8 **Therefore, I want to pray the men** placing the infinitive (**to pray**) before the direct object (**the men**) (**Therefore, I want the men to pray in every place, lifting holy hands, without anger and disputing** [2:8]). Here, Paul uses *anēr* to refer to males. Verse 9 begins **likewise women** leaving out (ellipsis) the main verb, the infinitive, and the article (**I want to pray the**). In this way, verses 8 and 9 are connected. Both sections deal with prayer in a congregational setting and appropriate lifestyles in the midst of prayer. Apparently, the men and women had differing problems at Ephesus.

Excursus: Lifting Up Hands

Lifting up one's hands while standing in prayer was the common ancient way for men and women to pray. Jesus assumes his disciples will stand praying (Mark 11:25). Both the Pharisee and the tax-collector stand praying.[52] Once people stood, normally they would lift their hands toward heaven. The hands represent the human. The lifting of them reach toward and bless God. For example, when the temple was dedicated, Solomon stood before the altar and "spread forth his hands toward heaven."[53] Sometimes the Jews even lifted up their hands while prostrated on their knees (Ezra 9:5). A regular part of the Jewish synagogue service was "The Lifting of the Hands" as a euphemism for prayer. First, benedictions were given including recitation of the *Shema'* ("Hear"),[54] and prayer was initiated by the *archisynagogus* ("ruler of the synagogue") while the congregation stood and affirmed "Amen," then the Scripture was read in Hebrew and translated, followed by an exposition (with the preacher seated), concluding with a blessing (also called "Lifting of the Hands").[55] Justin Martyr's explanation of the second century Christian service in Rome has many similarities to the Jewish ser-

---

51. Acts 13:5, 14; 14:1; 17:1–2, 10, 17; 18:4, 19.
52. Luke 18:11, 13. See also 1 Sam 1:26; *m. Taan.* 2:2.
53. 1 Kgs 8:22 KJV. See also Exod 9:29; Job 11:13; Pss 63:4; 88:9; 143:6.
54. Deut 6:4–9; 11:13–21; Num 15:37–41.
55. *M. Meg.* 4:3; Schürer 1979, 2:448–55.

vice. It begins with reading of the Scriptures, then the president gives an exposition, then all stand up and the president offers prayers followed by a congregational "Amen." The Eucharist is then taken (*1 Apol.* 65–67). The prayers in 1 Timothy 2:8 appear not to be limited to the ruler of the synagogue[56] or the president. Rather, there is a communal aspect to worship, as in 1 Corinthians 14:26 ("whenever you gather, *each* has . . . ").[57]

The men at Ephesus were using this time allotted to prayer to dispute with one another. *Dialogismos* (**disputing**) refers to the internal conversation (e.g., Matt 15:19; Luke 5:21–22) that then can become external.[58] It can be motivated by desires to attack, challenge (Luke 5:21–22), promote oneself (Luke 9:46; 20:14), and produce feelings of fear or confusion (Luke 24:38; Matt 16:7–8).

Orgē (**anger**) also refers to an internal impulse.[59] God's internal impulse of "wrath" is always just, punishing evil, as Paul explains, "Beloved, never avenge yourselves, but leave room for the *wrath* ("punishment") of God" (Rom 12:19 NRSV).[60] Rulers' "wrath" should also serve just punishment (Rom 13:4–5). But *orgē* among humans is more an internal impulse harmful to others (Eph 4:31), as James warns: "Let everyone be quick to hear, slow to speak, slow to *anger* for a man's *anger* does not produce God's righteousness" (1:19–20). Thus, the men at Ephesus were using the time of prayer to dispute with one another, impulsively allowing their internal destructive thoughts to harm each other and not promote the very activity they sought—attentive communication to God.

Josephus records a pertinent example where some men began quarrelling during the prayer section of a synagogue service. The ruler of the synagogue challenged Josephus for misusing funds. At the end of their altercation, some men tried to kill Josephus, but, with the assembly in his favor, Josephus escaped (*Life* 57–58 [294–303]). This illustration shows how even if people appear to be involved in a pious activity like prayer it can be misused to create fighting and not peace.

---

56. Male and female rulers of the synagogue have been found, e.g., Brooten 1982: 5–33.

57. Men and women prayed (and prophesied) in Corinth (1 Cor 11:4–5).

58. E.g., Luke 9:46–47; 20:14; Matt 16:7–8.

59. Thayer, 452.

60. See also Rom 1:18; 2:5, 8; 3:5; 4:15; 5:9; 9:22; 12:19; Eph 5:6; 1 Thess 1:10; 2:16.

The women **likewise** had problems during prayer: **Likewise (I want the) women (to pray) in well behaved deportment with respect for others and wisely to adorn themselves, not in gold-braided hair or pearls or expensive apparel, but (to adorn themselves) with what is proper for women professing religion, through good actions** (2:9–10). Since the false teaching at Ephesus emphasized the external literal keeping of laws[61] as opposed to fulfilling genuine virtues in action, this difficulty manifested itself among the women in attention to their external apparel, rather than to the Christian virtues. In a city concerned for wealth,[62] the Christian women too were concerned to flaunt their wealth, possibly in a sexually suggestive manner. Thus, Paul is not against gold and pearls *per se*, but the obsession with and flaunting of wealth. Rather, the wealthy are to use their resources "to do good, to be rich in good works, to be generous, ready to share" (6:18).

Paul uses two synonyms for clothing (2:9). Neither is the common word for "a piece of clothing."[63] *Katastolē* (**deportment**) can refer to "outward attire, either the character one exhibits in personal deportment or someth. to cover the body."[64] A *stolē* was "a loose outer garment for men which extended to the feet" worn by kings, priests, and persons of rank.[65]

Himatismos (**apparel**, 2:9) is used by Paul to describe clothing that could be coveted (Acts 20:33) and in the Gospels to describe the nicely dressed former demoniac.[66] In 1 Timothy, **apparel** is modified by the adjective "very expensive" (*polytelēs*) (2:9).[67] Thus, *katastolē* and *himatismos* combined with *polytelēs* identifies "very expensive clothing" that implies the women's perspective needs reorientation.

Paul, instead, describes the right type of external appearance as exemplary character, which is demonstrated by good actions, not attire.[68] *Katastolē* is modified by three words: *kosmios* (**well behaved**), *aidōs* (**respect for others**), and *sōphrosynē* (**wisely**) (2:9). This same word family

---

61. See 1 Tim 1:5–11.
62. See Introduction. Setting. Ephesus and Artemis.
63. BDAG, 475: *himation*.
64. BDAG, 527.
65. Thayer, 589. *Katastolē* is *stolē* intensified by the preposition *kata* (Robertson 1934: 606).
66. Mark 5:15; Luke 8:35.
67. BDAG, 850.
68. See also 1 Sam 16:7.

is used to describe positive character traits of overseers (1 Tim 3:2) and slaves,[69] thus, it is not a sex-specific term. The verb *kosmeō* can refer to organizing, decorating, making attractive, or preparing for use a house, grave site, temple, or lamp.[70] Thus, he uses a phrase with a wordplay: *katastolē kosmiōs* can be understood as "attractive clothing" or **well behaved deportment**. The women's intention is to have attractive clothing, instead Paul wants them to have well behaved deportment. How, then, can people be genuinely "attractive"? If they have the dual traits of **respect for others** (*aidōs*) and **wisdom** (*sōphrosynē*) (2:9).

Aidōs (2:9) is a frequent virtue for Greek philosophers,[71] but rare in the Bible. It refers to "*reverence, awe,* **respect** *for the feeling or opinion of others or for one's own conscience, and so shame, self-respect.*"[72] Ceslas Spicq summarizes: "It is then a restraint, a dignity, a modesty, or a discretion that keeps one from excess; thus a self-respect and a sense of honor that is often identified with modesty" or "the religious fear that one experiences in the presence of the sacred."[73] It can refer to women or men (3 Macc 1:19; 4:5). In the context of 1 Timothy 2, its opposite is **gold-braided hair or pearls or expensive apparel** (2:9). Thus, Paul wants the women in worship to dress themselves in a way that does not shame others. Their honor or attractiveness is in their character and actions.

Sōphrosynē (**wisely**) and *aidōs* (**respect**, 2:9) both relate to restraint of oneself (as does *hēsychia* in 2:11).[74] *Sōphrosynē* (**wisely**) comes from the root *sōphrōn* ("wisdom").[75] Paul repeats this same virtue in 2:15 and uses it in self-description (Acts 26:25). Although the ancients might have used it as a virtue for women,[76] in the New Testament *sōphrosynē* and its word-family are used as a positive trait for women and men. **Respect**

---

69. See Titus 2:10.
70. Matt 12:44; 23:29; 25:7; Luke 21:5.
71. *TLNT* 1:41–42.
72. LSJ, 36; Thayer, 14.
73. *TLNT* 1:42, 44.
74. Other Bible interpreters have used **to adorn** (*kosmeō*) as the main infinitive of the sentence, moving it to the beginning of 2:9, while still assuming **I want the** is an ellipsis, but then they miss the full parallelism of 2:9 with 2:8, e.g., Towner 2006: 204–5; Mounce 2000: 108–9; Robertson 1931, 4:569; Ellicott 1861: 50; Bernard 1922: 44 vs. Marshall 1999: 446–47; Witherington, 2006: 224; Barrett 1963: 55; Liefeld 1999: 92–95; Payne 2009: 311; Belleville 2009: 53.
75. See Titus 2:2.
76. Mitchell 1993, 1:189. Pomeroy 1984 writes *sōphrosynē* is mentioned "more frequently than any other quality on women's tombstones" (70).

and wisdom would contrast with some of the pagan religious festivals for women.[77]

The women were *not* to adorn themselves with **gold-braided hair or pearls or expensive apparel** (2:9b). **Not in braided hair and gold** is more clearly translated as a hendiadys:[78] **gold-braided hair**. Hair could be braided with hundreds of golden ornaments and pearls[79] that glittered and tinkled with every movement of the head. Neil concludes: "It would be difficult to find in the way of jewellery a vainer or more artificial form of female adornment,"[80] a problem at Ephesus and throughout the province of Asia (1 Pet 1:1; 3:3). Zinserling adds that "Jewelry reached the zenith of extravagance in Hellenistic times . . . The hair was knotted on top of the head, bound up with ribbons, parted and smoothed down, twisted in plaits around the head."[81] Xenophon of Ephesus declared that braided hair and purple chiton made women erotically attractive (*Anthia & Habrocomas* I.11.5-6). Braiding of hair was important in some pagan cults, such as the cult of Artemis of Ephesus or the cult of Isis.[82] Paul had already warned the elders at Ephesus (Acts 20:33) that he did not covet their **gold** and **expensive apparel**, the same words used in this passage (*chrysion, himatismos*). He concludes this sentence repeating the earlier positive action (2:9a) in different words: **(to adorn themselves) with what is proper for women professing religion, through good actions** (v. 10). Jerome summarizes: "Let her pearls be of another kind and such that she may sell them hereafter and buy in their place the pearl that is 'of great price'" (*Epist.* 107.5).

Even though Paul directs these commands (2:8-10) to men and women in particular, they are not necessarily true of all men and women everywhere, nor are they necessarily sex-specific in all places. Women can fight during prayer. Men can flaunt their wealth in worship too.

Paul then continues with a clear command: **let a woman**[83] **in silence learn in all submission** (2:11), a bold and radical command for

---

77. Hawkes 1968: 286; see Introduction. Setting. Ephesus and Artemis.

78. In a hendiadys ("one by means of two") one noun connected by "and" to another noun (here in the same case) functions as an adjective modifying the first noun. See also Neil 1920: 200-202; Lanham 1991: 82; Keener 1992: 105.

79. BDAG, 616.

80. Neil 1920: 200.

81. Zinserling 1972: 44.

82. Balch 1981: 101-2.

83. **Woman** is a more likely translation than "wife" because neither the sentence nor the context includes a personal pronoun (or even an article) to differentiate

Paul's time. Paul switches from the plural for "women" (2:9, 10) to the generic singular (**woman**, 2:11), most likely, to introduce or set up the illustration of Eve which follows (2:13-14). Afterwards, Paul repeats the singular (2:15a) but returns back to the plural ("they," 2:15b). Paul uses the imperative **let learn** (*manthanō*). This is the first imperative in the letter.[84] The women were to learn, especially by study.[85] *Manthanō* could refer to the acquisition of knowledge or skill gained by instruction,[86] such as when the centurion Claudius Lysias "learned" Paul was a Roman citizen (Acts 23:26-27). *Manthanō* can also refer to the thoughtful pondering for further understanding of the significance of Scripture, a message, nature, a person, or experience,[87] as when Jesus challenged the Pharisees to "learn" the meaning of "I desire mercy and not sacrifice" (Matt 9:13) or when Paul challenged the Corinthians to "learn" the meaning of "Nothing beyond what is written" (1 Cor 4:6). Paul, who himself was considered a learned man even by Governor Porcius Festus and a student of Rabbi Gamaliel (Acts 22:3; 26:24), wanted the women to acquire knowledge and reflect on the significance of Christian truth. As a man rabbinically trained, Paul would know that women were not obligated to study nor did they receive any merit in studying nor was anyone obligated to teach them.[88]

Paul emphasized that women were to learn **in silence**[89] because the ancients considered this the best way to learn, as Simon, the son of Paul's teacher, Rabbi Gamaliel, summarized: "All my days have I grown up among the Sages and I have found naught better for a man than silence; and not the expounding [of the Law] is the chief thing but the doing [of it]; and he that multiplies words occasions sin."[90] **Silence** had positive connotations among the ancient Jews because the Old Testament has

---

"woman" from "wife." For example, Eph 5:22 begins "the women to their *own* men," as does 1 Cor 7:2; 14:35; and 1 Pet 3:1. Col 3:18-19, which is a brief summary of Eph 5:22-33, has the definite article. In contrast, 1 Tim 3:11 has no article or pronoun with "women."

84. It is one of only five present imperatives third person singular verbs in 1 Tim. Most imperatives (second person singular) in the letter are addressed to Timothy.

85. LSJ, 1079.

86. BDAG, 615.

87. Matt 9:13; 24:32-33; 1 Cor 4:6; Eph 4:20; Phil 4:11; Col 1:7; Titus 3:14.

88. See 1 Tim 1:7.

89. Or "quietness." "Silence" is emphasized by being placed before the verb in 2:11 and by being repeated at the end of 2:12.

90. *M. 'Abot* 1:17. For more references, see Spencer 1985: 77-80.

Godly Peaceful Lives (2:1–15)   59

positive connotations for **silence**, for example, "Those who have knowledge use words with restraint... Even fools are thought wise if they keep silent, and discerning if they hold their tongues" (Prov 17:27–28 TNIV). *Hēsychios* (adjective), *hēsychia* (noun), and *hēsychazō* (verb) in the New Testament always have positive connotations. *Hēsychios* has positive connotations in 1 Timothy 2:2 when all Christians are encouraged to lead a "quiet" life,[91] a life free from persecution by rulers. In an educational setting, it refers to the state of calm, restraint at the proper time, respect, and affirmation of a speaker. It does not necessarily refer to not speaking. When the circumcision party heard from Peter how the Lord had saved Cornelius and his household, "*they were silenced* and praised God saying: 'Then also to the Gentiles God gave repentance that leads to life'" (Acts 11:17–18). Thus, the first act they did after they "were silent" was speak!

This *hesychia* word family may be found especially in the Old and New Testaments to refer, literally, to rest, not work, and especially not fight.[92] "Not fighting" also affects the way people interact when verbally communicating. Thus, the word family can refer to the **silence** when someone is not able to answer a challenging question or someone acquiesces to another's arguments or someone is won over by another's arguments.[93] "Stillness" is a proactive inner quality that can withstand the temptation of sin (Gen 4:7) and pursue good, rather than evil.[94] The Lord honors the person who is "lowly and *still* and (who) trembles at (his) words" (Isa 66:2). Many of these elements of "quiet" could be important to the female students: learning, especially by study, of God's new covenant, not by means of fighting nor by openness to evil, but with humility and cooperation (*hypotagē*).[95]

What enabled Paul to make such a radical command? Because he followed the example of rabbi Jesus who had insisted that his disciple Mary learn even though a woman's primary ancient responsibility was homemaking (Luke 10:40–42).[96]

Learning (*manthanō*) and **teaching** (*didaskō*) are interrelated actions (2:11–12). After all, *teaching* is *learned* (Rom 16:17). And, those

---

91. See similar examples: 1 Thess 4:11; 2 Thess 3:12; Job 14:6.

92. Exod 24:14; Josh 5:8; Judg 3:11, 30; 5:32; 8:28; 18:7; Ruth 3:18; 2 Kgs 11:20; 2 Chr 14:1; 23:21; Job 11:19; 37:17; Prov 26:20; Jer 26:27; 29:6–7; Ezek 38:11; Luke 23:56.

93. Neh 5:8; Job 32:1; Luke 14:3–6; Acts 11:18; 21:14.

94. Prov 11:12; 15:15; 1 Pet 3:4.

95. See Titus 2:5 on *hypotassō/hypotagē*. See also Spencer 1985: 74–77.

96. See Spencer 1985: 57–63.

who learn will teach, as Hebrews explains: "For though by this time you ought to be teachers, again you need someone to teach you the first principles of God's words" (Heb 5:12). The rabbis also taught that a good learner "learns in order to teach and . . . learns in order to practice" (*m. 'Abot* 6:6). Not all Christians will have the spiritual gift of teaching systematically, yet they should pass on to others what they have learned.[97] Therefore, *de* (**but**), introducing 2:12, is most likely adversative **but, to teach, a woman, I am not permitting, certainly not**[98] **to domineer over a man, but to be in silence** (2:12). Women at Ephesus are to learn, but not to teach. Paul highlights **to teach** by placing the infinitive first in the sentence instead of the usual Greek word order: **I am not permitting** (subject and its verb) for **a woman** (object) **to teach** (object of verb).

References to Teaching *Word Family*

references	Didaskō (verb) "to teach"	Didaskalos (noun) "teacher"	Didachē (noun) "teaching"	Didaskalia (noun) "teaching"	Didaktos (adj.) "taught"	Didaktikos (adj.) "apt in teaching"
No. in N.T.[99]	97	59	30	21	3	2
No. in Paul's letters	16	7	6	19	2	2
No. in Pastorals	5	3	2	15	0	2
% N.T.	5%	5%	6%	71%	0	100%
% Paul's letters[100]	31%	43%	33%	79%	0	100%

Teaching is an important theme in the Pastoral Letters. In almost every case, its usage in the Pastorals is greater than expected from their length relative to the whole New Testament. The references to *didaskalia*

---

97. Col 3:16; John 6:45; Isa 54:13.

98. When *oude* joins two prohibited actions, the second action can intensify the first one, as in 1 Tim 6:16; Rom 8:7; 11:21. *Oude* may then be translated "certainly not," "moreover," "especially not." In summary, Paul does not allow women to continue this teaching destructive to men, even as Eve's teaching was destructive to Adam.

99. Based on Kohlenberger et. al. 1995: 207–9.

100. Pastorals are 2.66% of the N.T., 11.3% of Paul's writings, and Paul's letters are 23.45% of the N.T. "Paul's letters" are all letters ascribed to Paul. Length is determined by number of Greek pages.

and *didaktikos* are especially frequent (71%, 100%). The frequency of this word family is understandable in light of the difficulties with heterodoxy at Ephesus at this time. Paul's goal is "healthy" teaching,[101] as opposed to heterodox,[102] demonic teaching (1 Tim 4:1) or teaching for shameful gain (Titus 1:11).[103] Teaching should be an important emphasis for Timothy,[104] Titus (Titus 2:1, 7), Paul,[105] the elders (male and female),[106] and other faithful people (2 Tim 2:2). For Paul, teaching is one of the spiritual gifts given to individuals for the edification of others, especially to equip other Christians for ministry and to help them mature.[107]

In light of the heterodox teaching and learning at Ephesus,[108] Paul highlights the women in particular as needing to learn but not yet **teach**, most likely because of their unpreparedness in withstanding heterodoxy, a heterodoxy that may have been especially appealing to the women at Ephesus.[109] Paul focuses on teaching because the teacher especially is one who must be qualified to teach the truth and Paul wanted to make sure they understood *God*'s teachings.[110] However, all women everywhere were not dissuaded from teaching. Prisca, along with her husband Aquila (admired coworkers of Paul), certainly taught Apollos with great accuracy (Acts 18:25–26) and the female elders at Crete were to teach (Titus 2:3). In addition, women had a long history as religious leaders: prophets, wise women, apostles, church overseers, and ministers.[111]

Paul in 2:12 does not use the imperative (as he does in 2:11 [**let learn**]). Rather, he uses the first person singular present indicative (**I am not permitting**). The present tense basically denotes linear action. Its most frequent use is descriptive.[112] When Paul uses the present active

101. See Titus 1:13. 1 Tim 1:10; 2 Tim 4:3; Titus 1:9; 2:1 refer to "healthy teaching."
102. 1 Tim 1:3; 6:3. See Titus 1:11.
103. See Titus 1:7.
104. 1 Tim 4:11, 13, 16; 6:2; 2 Tim 4:2.
105. 1 Tim 2:7; 2 Tim 1:11; 3:10.
106. 1 Tim 3:1–2; 5:17; Titus 1:6–9; 2:3.
107. Rom 12:7; 1 Cor 12:28–29; 14:6; Eph 4:11; Col 1:28.
108. See similar situation in Titus 1:11.
109. E.g., 2 Tim 3:6–7. See 1 Tim 1:7.
110. See 1 Tim 2:7.
111. See Spencer 1985: 96–120.
112. Robertson 1934: 879. In other words, Greek has aspect *and* time. The grammarian Caragounis (2004: 318–20) demonstrates knowledge of both time and aspect in numerous ancient and modern grammarians. Payne (2009: 320–25) also explains why the first person singular present active indicative indicates Paul's own personal

indicative first person singular in 1 Timothy, he appears to describe an action that he is encouraging Timothy to do now. Sometimes the present active indicative first person singular simply describes what Paul himself is doing at that moment: "I am entrusting, I am encouraging, I am wanting, I am writing, I am coming."[113] Along with his self-description comes an implied action that Paul wants from Timothy at the present time. For example, he is giving this "order" to Timothy to do at this time (1:18), he is encouraging prayer at this time to help the Christians have a quiet life (2:1–2), he wants the men not to quarrel while praying, a problem they had at this time (2:8), he is writing now with the expectation of coming later (3:14). Thus, in the same manner, this restriction related to women teaching will not always apply.

The verb **permit** (*epitrepō*) is not that frequent in the New Testament.[114] In the New Testament, it refers not to commands, but to allowable acts, analogous to God's permissive will as opposed to God's perfect (and proactive) will. For example, Jesus said that Moses "*permitted* you to divorce your wives because your hearts were hard. But it was not this way from the beginning" (Matt 19:8 TNIV).[115] At times, it is a term of polite conversation: "First *allow* me to say farewell" (Luke 9:61). It is also used for obtaining a governmental *allowance* to do a certain act, as when Pilate *permitted* Joseph to take Jesus' body (John 19:38).[116] Thus, it is not so much that Paul *commands*[117] women not to teach, but that they do not have his permission at this time.

Paul also does not permit a woman **to domineer over** (*authenteō*) **a man, but to be in silence** (2:12b). Volumes have been written on *authenteō*.[118] Verbs of ruling such as *authenteō* take the genitive, therefore,

---

advice or position for a situation that is not universal. "The ongoing sense of the present tense verb is to be noted" (Belleville 2009: 57). Porter (1992: 21, 29) agrees that the present indicative indicates action in progress. While Campbell (2008: 13, 63) writes that to state that 2:12 refers to "an action in progress" is "erroneous," yet he states that the present tense-forms "often" depict "a process or action *in progress.*"

113. See 1 Tim 1:18; 2:1, 8; 4:13; 5:1, 13, 14, 21; 6:13. Mounce (2000: 122) reduces this argument to the present tense. However, my comment refers to the *first person singular* present indicative. Nevertheless, even statements in the first person singular present indicative may apply today, but only to analogous situations.

114. 18 refs., 3 times by Paul.

115. Also Mark 5:13; Luke 8:32; 1 Cor 16:7; Heb 6:3. 1 Cor 14:34 appears to fit in this category although the "law" is unclear.

116. Acts 21:39–40; 26:1; 27:3; 28:16; Esth 9:14; 1 Macc 15:6.

117. E.g., *parangellō*: 1 Tim 4:11; 5:7; 6:17.

118. Sanford Hull lists the many exegetical difficulties in 1 Tim 2:8–15 (Hull 1987: 259–65). *TLG* lists no verb forms of *authentein* before the third century A.D. L&N,

Godly Peaceful Lives (2:1–15)   63

a man (*anēr*) is clearly its object. The difficulty arises with interpretation because this verb occurs nowhere else in the Bible. Although some scholars have argued that *authenteō* has positive connotations ("to exercise authority"), these positive connotations come from later ecclesiastical use (A.D. 370 and later).[119] The noun cognate used by Jewish writers contemporary to Paul clearly has negative connotations. Josephus uses *authentēs* to render "assassins" (murderers of Galilean Jew[s] on their way to a festival in Jerusalem). He describes Antipater, Herod's son, as an *authentēs* because he was accused of killing his family members.[120] Philo describes the person who has tried to destroy the virtues as his "own murderer" (*Worse* 21 [78]). The Wisdom of Solomon describes bad parents as *authentai* who "*kill* defenseless souls by their own hands" (12:6). Contemporary Roman writers also used *authentēs* with negative connotations. The historian Appian (A.D. 95–165) used *authentēs* for "murderer."[121] Diodorus of Sicily also used *authentēs* in negative contexts: "the *perpetrators* of the sacrilege" and "the *author* of these crimes."[122] *Authenteō* is similar to the negative type of leadership Jesus portrays for the Gentile rulers (*archōn*). Their leadership is described with two words *katakurieuō* and *katexousiazō* (Matt 20:25), formed from the root preposition "under" (*kata*), which vividly describes the position of the person being ruled. *Katakyrieuō* signifies to "*exercise complete dominion.*"[123] *Katexousiazō* signifies to wield "*authority over*" or "*tyrannize*" *"over someone."*[124] Liddell and Scott's *Lexicon* agrees: *authenteō* signifies "*to have full power* or *authority over,*" "*commit a murder*" and *authentēs* refers to a "*murderer.*"[125] Thus, Paul would be prohibiting women from having absolute power over men in such a way as to destroy them.

---

474 defines *authenteō* as "to control in a domineering manner." See also Payne 2009: 361–73.

119. See the extensive discussion in Payne 2009: 361–92; Belleville 2005: 209–17; Belleville 2009: 58–59; Kroeger 1992: 87–103, 185–88.

120. *J.W.* 2.12 [232–40]; 1.30 [582].

121. *Hist. rom.; Bell. civ.* I.7.61; III.13.115; IV.17.134.

122. XVI.61.1; XVI.5.4. Some scholars have posited that the noun and verb have different root meanings, e.g., Köstenberger & Schreiner 2005: 45, 102. However, the grammarian A. T. Robertson indicates that the verb *authenteō* comes from the noun *authentēs* (1934: 147–48).

123. LSJ, 896.

124. LSJ, 924; BDAG, 531. *Katakyrieuō* is used of the demons who "overpower" the Jewish exorcists so that they are left naked and wounded (Acts 19:16).

125. LSJ, 275.

If Paul had intended to use a word with positive connotations signifying a woman should not have authority over a man, he could have used any of the following, some of which were even used elsewhere in the Pastorals and some by Aristotle to describe the marriage relationship itself.

Words for "Authority" Not Used in 1 Timothy 2:12[126]

Greek words for "authority"-	N.T. References	References in Paul's letters	References in Pastorals
Archō[127] ("to rule"), archōn	123	6	0
Basileuō ("to rule"), basileus, basilissa	140	14	4 (1 Tim 1:17; 2:2; 6:15)
Despotēs,[128] oikodespoteō ("to be master of a house"), oikodespotēs	23	5	5 (1 Tim 5:14; 6:1, 2; 2 Tim 2:21; Titus 2:9)
Episkopeō ("to oversee"), episkopē, episkopos	11	4	3 (1 Tim 3:1, 2; Titus 1:7)
Epitassō ("to command"), epitagē	17	8	3 (1 Tim 1:1; Titus 1:3; 2:15)
Exousiazō ("to have authority"), exousia	106	30	1 (Titus 3:1)
Hēgeomai ("to lead"), hēgemōn	48	11	2 (1 Tim 1:12; 6:1)
Hyperechō ("to have power over"), hyperochē	7	6	1 (1 Tim 2:2)
Kyrieuō ("to rule over"), katakyrieuō	11	6	1 (1 Tim 6:15)
Oikonomeō ("to manage a household"), oikonomia,[129] oikonomos	20	11	2 (1 Tim 1:4; Titus 1:7)
Poimainō ("to shepherd"), poimēn	29	2	0
Proïstēmi ("to lead"), prostatis	9	9	2 (Titus 3:8, 14)

126. See also Spencer 2009: 81–84. Numbers are based on Kohlenberger 1995.
127. Term used by Aristotle, *Pol.* I.II.8 [1254a]; 12 [1254b].
128. Term used by Aristotle, *Pol.* I.II.2 [1253b].
129. Term used by Aristotle, *Pol.* I.II.1 [1253b].

Authenteō (2:12) as a verb of ruling takes the genitive case of the person over whom the destructive domination is executed.¹³⁰ In contrast, *didaskō* (**to teach**) takes the accusative case for the person and topic taught.¹³¹ Consequently, grammatically **man** is most likely the object only of *authenteō*.¹³² Thus, Paul is limiting women from teaching and from having a destructive power (**domineer**) over men. Rather, they are to be **in** "**silence**" (2:11–12). As a consequence, women at Ephesus will become part of the health-producing educational process: learning peacefully, co-operatively, not teaching yet, while not harming their teachers.

Why might Paul have chosen to use *authenteō* (**domineer,** 2:12) when writing Ephesus? Artemis of Ephesus was modeled on the queen bee.¹³³ After the young queen has stung to death any other competing queen bees, she leaves the hive on a mating flight. The seven or eight drones who mate with her die because their reproductive organs are torn out after mating.¹³⁴ Similarly, the cult of Artemis at Ephesus was associated with ritual or actual murder. Catherine Kroeger explains: "In Ephesus women also assumed the role of the man-slaying Amazons who had founded the cult of Artemis of Ephesus . . . Evidence of actual human sacrifice has been discovered at the lowest level of the great Artemisium."¹³⁵ Consequently, *authenteō* might very well allude to the traditional destructive pagan feminine principle at Ephesus. If the women were actually killing men, Paul would have used a stronger verb than **I am not permitting**. Rather, he was using *authenteō* metaphorically to describe destructive attitudes of the women toward the men, modeling themselves on Artemis, the "slaughterer,"¹³⁶ or, even on Eve, for, when she ate the fruit forbidden by God, it resulted in death (Gen 3:3–4).

I. H. Marshall summarizes: "In the context it seems most likely that through their being 'deceived' there was a false content to their teaching

---

130. BDAG, 150. The genitive case often expresses possession, but it may serve as the object.

131. BDAG, 241. The accusative case usually is the object of a transitive verb.

132. In contrast, when the object modifies both verbs, Paul may place it in the first clause, e.g., 1 Tim 4:11; 6:2.

133. See Introduction. Setting-Ephesus and Artemis. Statues uncovered of Artemis and coins of Ephesus often include the figure of a queen bee, e.g., Scherrer 2000: 205, 213; Kroeger 1992: 71. See Ephesus Museum, Selçuk, Turkey.

134. Michener & Michener , "Bee," *CE* 3:763.

135. Spencer 1995: 61. See also Kroeger & Kroeger 1992: 185.

136. See Introduction. Setting. Ephesus and Artemis.

and that this element included some kind of emancipatory tendency."[137] While some agree women were probably "promulgating the heresy" and *authentein* is a "difficult word to define," they conclude: "Paul does not want women to be in positions of authority in the church; teaching is one way in which authority is exercised in the church." Women may not "authoritatively teach the gospel to men (possibly overseers) in the public assembly of the church."[138] A. T. Robertson has raised a question many

137. Marshall 1999: 441, 442. Others have similar conclusions. *Didaskein* "forbids women to teach a wrong doctrine." Paul does not allow a woman "to proclaim herself author of man," going back to the sense of *authentēs* as the responsibility of the subject in the accomplishment of an act or function (Kroeger 1992: 81, 99, 103, 185, 192). *Authentein* has the connotation "to domineer." Some kind of "disruptive behavior, which perhaps included boisterous affirmation of the heresies, seems to lie behind these instructions" (Fee 1988: 73). See also REB: "I do not permit women to teach or dictate to the men" and CEV: "They should be silent and not be allowed to teach or to tell men what to do" (2:12). The second verb (*authenteō*) modifies the first verb (*didaskō*), similar in function to a pleonasm or hendiadys: I am not permitting a woman to teach with self-assumed authority over a man. In other words, the connecting *oude* combines two conceptually different elements to express a single idea (Payne 2009: 337–59). See also TNIV: "I do not permit a woman to teach or to assume authority over a man" (2:12). The footnote has "Or teach a man in a domineering way." "Paul is addressing women who have been involved in teaching the heresy" or have assumed the teaching role inappropriately "out of a desire to dominate in the public meeting" (Towner 2006: 223–24). "Paul may here be warning against a domineering use of authority, rather than merely any use of authority" (Keener 1992: 109). *Authenteō* is not "gender-specific," as John Chrysostom advises husbands not to "be despotic or *domineer* the woman" (*Hom.* 10 *Col.*). The verb "characterizes the nature of the teaching rather than the role of women in church leadership in general" (Witherington 2006: 227–28). "It is inconsistent to regard the dress code in 1 Timothy 2:9 as culturally relative and, therefore, temporary, but the restriction on women's ministry in 2:12 as universal and permanent. All these instructions are part of the same paragraph, the same flow of thought" (Groothuis 1997: 214). "There is no first-century warrant for translating *authentein* as 'to exercise authority'... Rather the sense is the Koine 'to dominate, to get one's way.'" "To define a purpose or goal actually provides a good fit: 'I do not permit a woman to teach so as to gain mastery over a man,' or 'I do not permit a woman to teach with a view to dominating a man'" (Belleville 2005: 216, 219).

138. Mounce 2000: 120, 126, 130. Others have similar conclusions: Paul "prohibited wives from teaching their husbands in public worship" and "to have authority over their husbands in that same context" (Gritz 1991: 135). Women are "debarred from occupying whatever position in a given local church would be equivalent to the pastoral epistles' governing elder" (Moo 1991: 186–87). A woman by nature is "formed to obey," for the government of women has always been regarded by all wise persons as a "monstrous thing; and, therefore, so to speak, it will be a mingling of heaven and earth, if women usurp the right to teach. Accordingly, he bids them be 'quiet,' that is, keep within their own rank" (Calvin n.d.: 2178). "Virtually every word in verses 11–12 is disputed." "The debate over the meaning of *authentein* has been vigorous.

years ago about women not teaching: "One feels somehow that something is not expressed here to make it all clear." "One wonders if there was not something known to Paul about special conditions in Corinth and Ephesus that he has not told" because Paul's affirmation of female prophets in 1 Corinthians 11:5 "is not easy to reconcile" with "his demand for silence by the women" in 1 Corinthians 14:34-40 and 1 Timothy 2:8-15.[139] Grenz summarizes: "Paul temporarily bars women from teaching in keeping with the close connection he makes between possessing wisdom or knowledge and being actively involved in the teaching and admonishing role in the church. That the ban will one day be lifted, however, is indicated by Paul's instruction to Timothy to entrust sound doctrine to persons who in turn could teach others."[140]

Many commentators (egalitarians and hierarchalists) over the years are agreed that 2:12 is difficult to understand. Many have come to appreciate that for Christian women to learn in silence (2:11) is an exemplary virtue for all Christians. Many have also recognized that women were in some way promulgating or at least participating in the heresy at Ephesus. However, when commentators come to interpret verse 12, some (hierarchalists) emphasize the latter part of the verse (*authentein*), seeing teaching as one aspect of "authority" (interpreting *authentein* positively) and taking **silence** as somewhat literal. In contrast, others (egalitarians) tend to emphasize the earlier part of verse 12 (*didaskein*) and verse 11, seeing *authentein* as a misuse of power. Authority, then, becomes an aspect of teaching. Was the key problem at Ephesus gender roles and female relationship to leadership or right knowledge and female relationship to orthodoxy? Is 1 Timothy mainly about order or salvation? Is the key problem at Ephesus (and today) role reversal or lack of submission to truth? My own conclusion is that 1 Timothy is primarily about Paul's great themes: right knowledge, salvation, and submission to truth.

Paul explains his earlier sentence with an illustration[141] (2:11-12): **For Adam first was formed, then Eve, and Adam was not deceived,**

The meaning 'exercise authority' is most likely. See ESV: "I do not permit a woman to teach or to exercise authority over a man" (2:12a). In particular, Henry Scott Baldwin has pointed out that the verb must be separated from the noun in constructing the definition of the term" (Schreiner 2005: 97, 102).

139. Robertson 1931: 570; Robertson: (Acts) 1930: 363.
140. Grenz 1995: 130.
141. It is a mistake "to approach the study of *gar* with the theory that it is always or properly an illative, not to say causal, particle. It is best, in fact, to note the explanatory

but the woman, having been deceived, came to a state of transgression (2:13–14). Paul's illustration is an "analogy" ("a form of reasoning in which one thing is inferred to be similar to another thing in a certain respect, on the basis of the known similarity between the things in other respects").[142] **Adam** and **Eve** both were humans formed by God, but they sinned. Eve, being deceived, affected herself and others. Paul's technique is not unlike the rabbis who used analogies to make the Old Testament relevant to present and on-going circumstances.[143]

Paul begins with the basics: **Adam first was formed, then Eve** (2:13). *Plassō* signifies "*form, mould,* prop. of the artist who works in soft substances, such as earth, clay, wax" and, metaphorically, "*mould, form* by education, training, etc."[144] This same verb is used in Genesis 2:7: "God *formed* the human, dust (soil "heaped up"[145]) from the ground."[146] But, *plassō* can also have a metaphorical sense in the Bible, for example, the Lord **forms** the Messiah "with understanding" (Isa 53:11). Moses employs a similar wordplay[147]: God, the "father" purchased and made and *formed* Israel (Deut 32:6). God had not **formed** Israel literally, but "formed" Israel conceptually as a nation liberated from Egypt and, then, taught Israel what it meant to be a holy, separated nation.[148] Habak-

---

use first" (the instruction in v. 12 is illustrated by Adam and Eve) (Robertson 1934: 1190). Cf. Mounce 2000: 131. In reality, explanatory, causal, and illative are very close. That is why the context is crucial to determine "the precise relation between clauses or sentences" joined by *gar* (Robertson 1934: 1191). *Gar* in 4:10 seems to be also explanatory or an "appendix to the train of thought" (Robertson 1934: 1190) citing the saying introduced in v. 9. *Gar* in 5:15 gives an example of how the adversary has been victorious. In 5:11 *gar* could introduce an explanation of what happens when younger widows are on the list—their sensual desires alienate them from Christ or a cause (why not place the younger widows on the list? Answer: Because their sensual desires alienate them). Verse 6:7 could be explanatory (an example that elaborates on v. 6) or causal (why contentment is enough). See Payne 2009: 399–402.

142. Webster's 2001: 74. Lanham (1991: 10) defines "analogy" as "reasoning or arguing from parallel cases." In Greek, it is "proportion" (LSJ, 111). Keener and others have independently noticed this analogy (1992: 117 n. 118).

143. See Spencer 1985: 89–90 for examples how rabbis even used "prefall" illustrations in this way.

144. LSJ, 1412. See also Belleville 2009: 55.

145. LSJ, 2000.

146. Paul also used the verb in Rom 9:20–21 alluding to Isa 29:16; 45:9.

147. In Greek "paronomasia," a play (pun) on sense (or sounds) of words. A word may be used first in its proper sense, then its derived sense (Lanham 1991: 3, 110; LSJ, 1342). See also 1 Tim 2:9.

148. Deut 31:24–29; 32:4. See also Isa 43:1, 7; 44:21; 49:8.

kuk, too, declares God "formed" him in order to "discipline his training" (*paideia*, 1:12 LXX). The psalmist reminds God that God "made me and *formed* me," which then leads to the request he be instructed so that he can learn (*manthanō*) God's commandments (118:73). The Athenian in Plato's dialogue on *Laws* describes the "good legislator" who trains (*paideuō*) and also molds (*plassō*) with laws the banqueter who is "unwilling to submit to the proper limits of silence and speech" (*Leg.* II. 671C). Plato also describes stories that nurses and mothers tell children in order to "*form* their souls" (*Resp.* II. 377C).

Thus, in this wordplay, Paul describes Adam as **formed** literally and also metaphorically (2:13). God exhorted Adam: "You are free to eat from any tree in the garden; but you must not eat from the tree of the knowledge of good and evil, for when you eat of it you will certainly die" (Gen 2:16–17 TNIV). Eve had not yet been created. Afterwards, God educates Adam why he needs "help equal to himself,"[149] which no other created being can satisfy, before he creates Eve (2:18–22). Adam was created before Eve and also educated before Eve. In the same way as Paul is the **first** or prototype of all sinners (1:13–16), a prototype of someone sinful (but ignorant) who receives God's mercy, Adam is a prototype of someone born and educated first.

Verse 13 then follows from **to be in silence** (2:12). Others interpret verse 13 in light of *authentein* in verse 12, thereby claiming that verse 13 shows God's prescriptive intention of male authority and male church leadership.[150] However, *authentein* is a weak basis on which to establish male authority because of its negative connotation in pre-ecclesiastical usage and the rarity of its usage in the New Testament. In contrast, in my opinion, these commentators do not clearly show how verse 13 relates to verse 14.[151] Since vv. 13 and 14 are connected by "and," they should relate in some way. Some commentators[152] indicate that 1 Timothy 2:13 is a similar argument to 1 Corinthians 11:8–9 (and, I might add, 11:3). However, the application in 1 Corinthians 11 does not affect church leadership at all. Women can still pray and prophesy—only their attire

---

149. Spencer 1985: 23–29.
150. E.g., Mounce 2000: 130.
151. Mounce (2000: 135) notes that v. 14 "may be difficult to interpret." He does agree that "in some way, Adam and Eve are parallel to the Ephesian men and women."
152. E.g., Mounce 1991: 130; Schreiner 2005: 106.

is affected.¹⁵³ 1 Timothy 2:13 is descriptive, not prescriptive, even as the "curses" in Genesis 3:16–19 are descriptive, not prescriptive.¹⁵⁴

Eve, in contrast, is a prototype¹⁵⁵ of someone who sins because (s)he is deceived: **And so Adam was not deceived, but the woman, having been deceived, came to a state of transgression** (2:14). Why was Adam not **deceived** but Eve was? Verses 13 and 14 are connected by the simple connective *kai* ("and"), which may be translated **and so**,¹⁵⁶ as in Matthew 5:15 when a lamp is placed on a lampstand "and so" it gives light to all in the household. Adam having been **formed** first is the key idea in the first clause that affects the second clause: why Adam was not deceived. I have suggested that **form** (2:13) has to do with education. Others have suggested that **first formed** has to do with precedence in authority as a firstborn.¹⁵⁷ But does the Bible ever claim that every male who is firstborn has precedence in authority that affects knowledge of the truth? In addition, firstborn children are not always chosen to rule, as in the example of David, the youngest son, in Jesse's family, chosen by the Lord to rule Israel.¹⁵⁸ And, when is resistance to deception a characteristic of only firstborn sons? If God established that the firstborn always rules, it is a law that God does not follow!¹⁵⁹ **First** also is not necessarily superior, as Philo explains as he looks at creation: the principle of order is this, creatures "begin at what is lowest in its nature, and end in the best of all" (*Creation* 22.67). In other words, humans are superior to animals because they were created in God's image.

What does education have to do with deception? **Deception** is basically based on telling a lie or lies and misleading by half-truths. Paul, most likely refers back to the earliest use of *apataō* in the Bible when used by Eve herself as she made her excuse to God: "The serpent *deceived* me

---

153. Probably, 1 Cor 11:3–16 is closer to 1 Tim 2:9–10 since both discuss the proper attire for prayer. See Spencer 1990a: 41–50. Payne (2009: 403) notes that the similarity between 1 Cor 11 and 1 Tim 2 is that since woman was "formed" out of man, she should respect man as her source.

154. See Spencer 1985: 34–42.

155. See 1 Tim 1:16.

156. Robertson 1934: 1183.

157. E.g., Hurley (1981: 207–8) explains that the firstborn inherited responsibility of leadership in the home and in worship.

158. 1 Sam 16:11–12; 1 Chr 2:13–15.

159. See Webb (2001: 136–39) for an extensive list. The younger Ephraim is chosen over the firstborn Manasseh (Gen 48:14–19); elder Esau serves younger Jacob (Gen 25:23).

and I ate" (Gen 3:14). Adam, in contrast, does not claim he is deceived. Rather, he blames God for having given him Eve and blames Eve for having given him the forbidden fruit (Gen 3:13). The dialogue between the "crafty" serpent and Eve shows elements of the process of deception and its lies. First, the serpent raised a challenge in the form of a question, why did God make a certain command? He also rephrased the command to make it impossible to obey: "Why has God said, Do not eat from any tree in the garden?" (Gen 3:2). Eve and Adam would starve if they could not eat of any tree! Then, the serpent made several promises that were completely false: (1) "You shall not surely die" and (2) they would be as gods knowing good and evil (3:5–6). They did die (5:5). They learned only evil, not good, and became less like God. Eve, too, in her dialogue with the serpent made God's commandment more difficult than it was (they were not to "touch" the tree, 3:4). Then, she catalogued the positive values of the forbidden fruit (nutritious, aesthetic, and educational [3:7]), values she could have gotten elsewhere. Deception here was an interactive process of informational distortions between the serpent and Eve enticing Eve away from what was good and true.[160]

Lies as these are not told in order to protect someone or to do something good. Rather, they may be done for reasons of self-aggrandizement (power) or sexual oppression.[161] Possibly false teachers might also want power over others. The Bible highlights false teaching as a major way to deceive.[162] Unsuspecting people can be deceived (Rom 16:18). In 1 Timothy 2:13–14 and 2 Corinthians 11:3, Eve is used as a prototype for persons who are deceived by Satan by teachings that lead them away from the truth. In 2 Corinthians, Eve illustrates the danger to the whole church of Corinth, while in 1 Timothy she illustrates the danger for the women at the church in Ephesus. However, **deception** is not limited to women. Paul himself says he was deceived by sin (Rom 7:11). Nevertheless, Eve has become for Paul a prototype of someone who sins because of deception. Adam certainly sinned. In contrast to Eve, he is a prototype of someone who sins, but not by means of deception.[163] He knew what

---

160. See Spencer 1985: 30–34. Eve was *not* deceived in taking the initiative over the man, but in questioning God's word (Payne 2009: 409; Belleville 2005: 222).

161. Exod 8:29; 22:16; Judg 14:15; 16:5; 2 Sam 3:25.

162. E.g., Gen 3:2–14; Rom 16:18; 2 Cor 11:3–6; Eph 5:5–6; Col 2:8; 2 Thess 2:3, 10; Jas 1:26.

163. Chrysostom (*Hom. Gen.* 17. 18–19) also notes that Adam was not ignorant or deceived.

he was doing. In Romans 5:12–21 and 1 Corinthians 15:22, Adam is significant for what he brought into the world—death. All humans die and live in a world of death and suffering because Adam sinned and brought death into the world.[164] Adam contrasts with Christ whose death brings life to all (Rom 5:17–21; 1 Cor 15:22).

Paul uses two synonyms for **deceive** (*apataō* and *exapataō* [2:14]). He adds the intensifying (perfective) preposition *ek* to *apataō* to indicate Eve was deceived "*thoroughly.*"[165] As a result of being thoroughly misled by falsehoods, she **came to a state of transgression** (2:14). Paul uses the perfect tense of *ginomai* ("become"). Usually, the perfect has an extensive force, presenting a completed state or condition. It "begins with the punctiliar and goes on with the durative."[166] God did not create Eve in a state of transgression. Her act of eating the forbidden fruit affected her state or condition. Genesis, later, narrates the progressive effects of her and Adam's sin.

Paul describes Eve's sin as **transgression** (2:14, *parabasis*). In the New Testament, *parabasis* and *parabatēs* refer to the breaking of God's laws.[167] The law indicates what one should do. "Transgression" (literally "going aside" or "going over")[168] is not going along with the law, but, rather, *going aside* it, disobeying the law. Paul does not say Eve became a "transgressor" (*parabatēs*), which would have more easily fit in this sentence. The focus is not so much who she became (a "transgressor") but rather the state or condition in which she entered, a state of deviation or violation of the law. She "went aside" from the true path to a false path.

How then does the illustration of Eve relate to the women at Ephesus? The women at Ephesus were reminiscent of the woman in Eden: Eve. The Ephesian women who were learning a body of heretical beliefs and teaching it to others, submitted to heterodox teachers that brought spiritual death to their listeners. Eve, too, had in her time been deceived into believing certain heterodox teachings: if she touched the fruit of the tree of the knowledge of good and evil, she would become like God, yet she would not die. She authoritatively passed on her teachings to Adam. Her eating the fruit symbolized her "belief." Sadly, he learned. He too ate the

---

164. Paul's view contrasts with Sir 25:24: through "the woman . . . we all die."
165. LSJ, 586.
166. Robertson 1934: 893.
167. E.g., Rom 2:23, 25, 27; 4:15; 5:14; Gal 2:18; 3:19; Heb 2:2; 9:15; Jas 2:9, 11.
168. LSJ, 1305; Thayer, 478.

forbidden fruit. The entire state of humanity and nature was affected by their actions: enslavement to sin and death. Eve's deception affected the state into which she entered. So, too, if the women at Ephesus continued in being deceived by false teaching, they too would enter a **state of transgression**. And, as the earth became fallen, so too the church at Ephesus would fall. (Already some women were "turning after Satan" [5:15].)

Instead, Paul had begun a process to address the educational limitations on women, especially in such a syncretistic area as Ephesus, by commanding that the women learn the truth so they could understand fully the Christian message, not be deceived, and, then, when they taught, they would bring spiritual life and salvation to their listeners.

Paul states clearly that Eve need not stay in her state: **But she will be saved through the Childbirth, if they might remain in faith and love and holiness with wisdom** (2:15). Salvation is an important theme in the Pastoral letters.[169] The verb *sōzō* is always used in a spiritual sense by Paul and in the Pastorals it refers to the forgiveness of sins and purification by means of God's mercy so that believers persevere in order to know the truth, lead a holy life, and inherit God's kingdom. God, the Trinity, is involved in the process of salvation.[170] Paul then uses the preposition *dia* with the genitive case of **childbirth** (*teknogonia*) to signify **through** an intermediate personal agent. The agent comes "in between the non-attainment and the attainment of the object in view,"[171] as in Matthew 1:22: "The Lord spoke through the prophet." The prophet is the intermediate agent between the Lord (the source) and speaking (the ultimate end). In the same way, in "the man *through* the woman" (1 Cor 11:12), God is the ultimate agent, but the woman is the intermediate agent between God and a man's birth.[172] One historic interpretation was to understand the

---

169. See 1 Tim 2:3–4; Titus 1:3; 2:14; 3:4–7.

170. 1 Tim 1:15; 2:4; 4:16; 2 Tim 1:9; 4:18; Titus 3:5–7. For a succinct summary of key elements in Paul's understanding of salvation, see Rom 10:9–10; 1 Cor 15:2–11; Eph 2:4–10. Most of the N.T. references use *sōzō* metaphorically for a spiritual sense, salvation from eternal death. However, the N.T. also uses *sōzō* literally to refer to preservation from death (Matt 8:25; 14:30; 27:40, 42, 49; Mark 3:4; 13:20; 15:30–31; Luke 6:9; 23:35, 37, 39; John 12:27; Acts 27:20, 31) including from illness (Matt 9:21–22; Mark 5:23, 28, 34; 6:56; 10:52; Luke 8:48, 50; 18:42; John 11:12; Acts 14:9) and demon-possession (Luke 8:36). LSJ (1748).

171. Robertson 1934: 581–82.

172. Paul does *not* use *dia* and the accusative case which would then mean "a woman will be saved 'because of, for the sake of, on account of' the childbearing" (Robertson 1934: 583). Childbirth (or childbearing) would then somehow cause women to be saved.

use of the singular article to refer to **The Childbirth**,¹⁷³ the great Childbirth by Mary which produced the Savior Jesus. Ignatius, who lived in the first century, used a similar synonym for childbirth (*ho toketos*) to refer to Jesus: "the virginity of Mary and her childbirth were hidden from the ruler of this age, as was also the death of the Lord" (*Eph.* 19:1).¹⁷⁴ Thus, the source or ultimate agent, by the use of the passive voice, would be implied to be Christ Jesus (2:5), the intermediate agent would be the childbirth by Mary, and the ultimate end would be salvation. Even though Eve came into a state of transgression (2:14), through another woman, Mary, salvation came. Even Eve was **saved** as a type of the women at Ephesus. Paul probably alludes to Genesis 3:15, the *protevangelium*, the woman's seed who bruises the serpent's head.¹⁷⁵ Jesus as the Messiah is the child who fulfilled that final victory over Satan. Paul uses a similar hermeneutic, an allusion, in Galatians 3:16 declaring the singular of "offspring" (*sperma*) in Genesis 12:7; 13:15; 24:7 is a reference to Christ. *Teknogonia* ("childbirth") may also be an allusion to Genesis 3:16: Eve "shall bring forth children."

In Genesis, the Lord suggests that through the means of **childbirth** redemption will occur (Gen 3:15). Thus, one reason the Old and New Testaments trace genealogies is to trace the potential or prospective birth of the Redeemer. For instance, Lamech named his son "Noah" with the hope he would bring relief from Adam's curse (Gen 5:29; 3:17–19). Simeon and Anna perceived the child Jesus was the predicted Messiah (Luke 2:25–38). In the immediate context of 1 Timothy 2, Christ is mentioned as the mediator between God and humans (2:5–6), and Christ being revealed in the flesh is a central Christian proclamation (3:16). The heresy at Ephesus included teachings that forbade marriage and promoted abstinence from foods and a desire to be ascetic that, instead of promoting holiness, resulted in sensuality and self-indulgence.¹⁷⁶ As in Neo-Platonism, matter was viewed as evil and childbirth too might be perceived as evil.

---

173. The Greek article retains some of the demonstrative force, serving as a pointer (Robertson 1934: 754–58). See also Payne 2009: 429–31. **Childbirth** brings out the punctiliar sense, the event of a childbirth with a resulting child (Payne 2009: 432–33).

174. See also Gal 4:4 for the use of "woman" to refer to one unnamed woman-Mary. *Apocr. Gen.* uses "this childbearing" to refer to Noah (2:15). The angel describes the baby Jesus as "the one to be born" (*to gennōmenon* [Luke 1:35]). See Payne 2009: 439 for more early church examples.

175. See Irenaeus, *Haer.* 3. 22.4; 23.7; 4. 40.3; 5. 19.1; 21.1; *Epid.* 33.

176. 1 Tim 4:3; 5:11–15; 6:9.

Artemis herself was the virgin goddess. In contrast, Paul's teachings here by implication (but stated directly later), presuppose that matter is good because all God created is good, food and clothing are good (4:4; 6:8). God wants believers to enjoy God's material gifts but not place hope on them (6:17). Even the use of wine may be necessary (5:23). Marriage too is good, as well as household management, and childbearing.[177] The noun form (*teknogonia*, 5:14) in 2:15 has the same root as the verbal form (*teknogoneō*).[178] In a church with a low view of marriage and childbearing (4:3), Paul describes the Christian message from the perspective of **The Childbirth** to set the stage for the younger widows to understand a later command in the letter (5:14).

Interpretations of 1 Timothy 2:15a may be categorized broadly based on their understanding of the literal (physical) or metaphorical (spiritual) sense of **save** and **childbirth/childbearing**:

(1) **save** is literal and **childbirth** is literal: for example, "God ... will deliver her through childbearing" (The Voice); "a wife will be brought safely through by giving birth to their children" (CEB);

(2) **save** is metaphorical and childbirth is literal, where **childbearing** is a synecdoche for the role of mother: for example, "she shall be saved in childbearing" (KJV); "salvation for the woman will be in the bearing of children" (REB);

(3) **save** is metaphorical and childbirth is literal, where **childbirth** is a synecdoche for Childbirth by Mary: for example, "she will be saved by the Child-bearing" (NTME); "women are saved through the birth of the Child" (New Translation).

I do not accept the first interpretation because *sōzō* elsewhere in Paul's letters, including the Pastoral Letters, has a metaphorical sense.[179] I do not accept the second interpretation because **childbirth** is not the same as rearing children or undertaking a domestic role, as in *teknotropheō* or *oikodespoteō* (1 Tim 5:10, 14). This interpretation would contradict Paul's understanding elsewhere that salvation comes by grace through faith (Eph 2:4–10; Rom 4:2–5:1), as Paul explains God "saved us" "not

---

177. 1 Tim 3:4–5, 12; 5:10, 14.

178. Neither word occurs any where else in the N.T. or LXX. In contrast, the more frequent *tiktō* (verb) has no comparable noun.

179. Nevertheless, the death of the mother in childbirth was a major concern in biblical times (e.g., *m. Sabb.* 2:6; Cohick 2009: 135–37, 140; Cox & Ackerman 2009: 140). See also Keener 1992: 118–19.

out of works, the ones in righteousness, which we ourselves prepared, but according to his mercy" (Titus 3:5). Since Paul encouraged men and women to devote themselves to the ministry as single, if they are not tempted sexually (1 Cor 7:8–9; 1 Tim 5:3), why would he identify childbearing as a requirement for salavation for all women (married, single, and barren)? A woman can be involved in childbearing and in all the domestic motherly roles and still not be saved if she does not believe in Jesus. (1 Tim 2:15 does *not* say a woman shall be saved through faith, love, and holiness.) Schreiner concludes that women "will experience eschatological salvation by adhering to their proper role, which is exemplified in giving birth to children."[180] But, do men experience salvation by adhering to their proper role? Roles do not save; in contrast, Galatians 3:26—4:7 teaches that male and female are one when it comes to faith and being saved as heirs of Abraham. I prefer the third interpretation because it fits best in the context, the established meanings of the words, and harmonizes with Paul's other teachings, including those in the Pastorals.[181]

Paul returns now to the plural number (**they might remain**, 2:15b) because the analogy or illustration of Eve has concluded. If Eve was the singular, who are the plural **they**? Certainly it includes the plural women in the church (2:9–10), but it also applies to the orthodox teachers, including Timothy, who will teach the women. Paul uses a conditional ("third class") clause indicating the condition has not happened, thus some doubt is involved, but it has some expectation of realization. The women already have **faith, love, holiness**, and **wisdom**, but they need to persevere (**remain**)[182] in these virtues because they were saved in order to develop these qualities of God's character.[183] Why did Paul pick these particular four qualities? **Faith** and **love** are important themes in the Pastorals (1 Tim 1:5).[184] From an educational perspective, **faith** describes both the content of the message that Paul wants to impart and a means

---

180. Schreiner 2005: 118, 120.

181. For further examples, see Payne 2009: 421–22 n. 14. CEV has all renderings: "brought safely through childbirth," "saved by having children," "saved by being good mothers," and "saved by the birth of a child" (that is, by the birth of Jesus)." See also NLT.

182. Paul uses *menō* with the sense of "continue" or "persist" (e.g., Rom 9:11; 1 Cor 3:14; 7:8, 11, 20, 24, 40; 15:6).

183. See Titus 3:8. Christ is faithful; loving (1 Tim 1:14; 2 Tim 1:13); holy; and wise (1 Cor 1:24, 30 *sophia*).

184. See 1 Tim 1:19.

by which to persevere in the Christian walk.[185] Some at Ephesus have renounced or may renounce the faith.[186] In 3:1 Paul will encourage all to desire to be an overseer or minister. Faith is one key aspect of being an overseer or minister (3:9, 11, 13). Thus, **faith** is a foundation of the three qualities to follow. **Love** is an important aspect of sound doctrine.[187] A negative aspect of the women's attire while in prayer may have been flaunting wealth or sexual suggestiveness. Therefore, Paul adds the quality of **holiness**. *Hagiasmos* or sanctification is God's will for all believers.[188] When people are set free from sin, then they (out of gratitude and with God's help) set on the road of becoming holy in effect so that they can obtain eternal life (Rom 6:22). Procksch summarizes: in *hagiasmos* action is emphasized. It is "the moral form which develops out of [atonement] and without which there can be no vision of Christ."[189] In the Pastorals, a synonym is *eusebeia*, which is a quality for all believers and a quality of Christ's teachings (1 Tim 2:2; 6:3). *Hagiasmos* (**holiness**) is modified by *sōphrosynē* (**wisdom**). *Sōphrosynē* is built on the root *sōphrōn*, soundness or wholeness of mind, having control over the sensual desires ("self-control").[190] **Wisdom** helps one become holy. Paul uses this adjective for self-description before the Roman governor Festus (Acts 26:25). The opposite is madness (Acts 26:4). Although *sōphrosynē* was a popular virtue for Greek women in biblical times,[191] in the New Testament it is not limited to women. These four qualities are good for the women to persist in, but they are not simply for women, but for all Christians. Even Timothy is exhorted by Paul elsewhere to persist in faith, love, holiness, and wisdom or self-control.[192]

---

185. 1 Tim 1:4, 16, 18–19; 2:7; 3:13, 16; 4:1, 3, 6; 5:8.

186. 1 Tim 4:1; 5:15; 6:10, 21.

187. See 1 Tim 1:5.

188. 2 Tim 2:21; Rom 6:19, 22; 1 Thess 4:3–4, 7. The verb form (*hagiazō*) is an important O.T. concept that goes back as early as Gen 2:3 (God "sanctified" the seventh day) and as Exod 13:2 (in Passover: "Sanctify to me every firstborn").

189. Procksch & Kuhn, *TDNT* 1:113.

190. See Titus 1:8; 2:2.

191. Pomeroy 1984: 70. The Neopythagoreans also used *sōphrosynē* for married people (Mitchell 1993, 1:189). See 1 Tim 2:9.

192. 1 Tim 4:7–8, 12; 6:11–12; 2 Tim 1:7; 2:22.

Godly Overseeing (3:1-16)

Paul has been urging godly peaceful lives so that all people may be saved and come to knowledge of the truth. This is accomplished by prayer for all (2:1-7), living a peaceable life of prayer (2:8-10), learning peaceably (2:11-15), and having godly overseeing (3:1-16). Before discussing any virtues, Paul presents the importance of desire: **The word is trustworthy: If anyone aspires to overseeing, (s)he desires a good work** (3:1). This is Paul's second authoritative, accurate teaching from God expressed in a pithy saying or summary statement that can be passed on to others as fully reliable.[193]

Paul addresses women and men since **anyone** (3:1, *tis*) is generic,[194] using two synonyms: *oregō* (**aspires to**) and *epithymeō* (**desires**). *Oregō* has the literal sense of "stretch out" and, metaphorically, "reach after, grasp at, yearn for" or "aspire to."[195] Thus, Christian men and women are to "stretch" themselves in order "to grasp" the office of overseeing. *Oregō* can be a negative **desire** (as to love money which results in drawing one away from the faith and giving one pain, as in 1 Tim 6:10) or a positive desire (to live as a "pilgrim" on earth, living to prepare for a heavenly citizenship as in Heb 11:16). *Epithymeō*, a strong passion turned toward something, although largely negative, can also have positive connotations.[196] Thus, desires need to be evaluated. But, in 1 Timothy 3:1, the aspiration is good because the goal is good.

The object is **overseeing** (*episkopē*, 3:1). *Episkopē* is a feminine abstract noun,[197] in contrast to *episkopos* (**overseer**), which specifies a concrete person, in verse 2. **Overseeing** or the "office of *episkopos*"[198] can refer to the functions of an apostle (Acts 1:20) or to leadership in general (Ps 108:8 LXX). Often it refers to an act of judgment, an "inspection,

---

193. See 1 Tim 1:15; Titus 3:8.
194. See NRSV, NIV, ESV, NEB, JB, NLT vs. KJV, NASB, *Did.* 15:1.
195. LSJ, 1246-47; BDAG, 721. Its related noun *orguia* literally refers to stretching out one's arms (Thayer, 452; Acts 27:28).
196. See Titus 2:12.
197. The Greek feminine *episkopē* appears to function like the Hebrew abstract feminine (GKC: 393).
198. LSJ, 657.

investigation, visitation,"[199] frequently done by God,[200] but also by humans.[201]

Episkopos (**overseer**, 3:2) is a synonym for *presbyteros* ("elder"),[202] God's stewards or managers of a household, in this case God's household, and for God's shepherds (*poimēn*), as in Acts 20:28. Paul has already addressed the elders at Ephesus as shepherds over a flock. The root idea of *episkopos*, an **overseer**, may be seen in its etymology, one who "looks upon" or "observes" another, so as to "watch over" or care for the other.[203] Jesus is the perfect "Shepherd and Overseer" of the lives of the sheep (1 Pet 2:25), after whom elders or overseers should model themselves.[204] Xenophon, for example, describes the "overseers" in "well ordered cities" who enforce the laws passed by the citizens "commending the law-abiding and punishing law-breakers." The wife should do the same for household laws (*Oec.* 9:14–15). Thus, the task of an "overseer" in the Bible includes aspects of care, organization, and judgment. Most of the attributes in the list are *not* roles but rather virtues, except for "hospitable, apt in teaching, managing his/her own house well." Thus, an overseer is a teaching minister with gifts of organization and hospitality.

A believer aspires to leadership not by grasping power over others (1 Pet 5:3 *katakyrieuō*), but by aspiring to become the type of person described in the following verses (3:2ff.). Women, too, who learn the content and virtues of a sound Christian faith could aspire to and prepare to be overseers. *Episkopē* (**overseeing**, 3:1) may refer to only 3:2–7, but it probably refers to both offices (*episkopos* and *diakonos*, 3:2–12), since **therefore** (3:2) immediately follows 3:1 and precedes the interconnected offices, concluding with the explanatory statement as to the value of leadership: "For the ones having served well acquire a good foothold

---

199. Thayer, 242.

200. E.g., Gen 50:24–25; Exod 3:16; 13:19; 30:12.

201. E.g., Num 7:2; 14:29; 16:29. Thayer explains that *episkopē* is an "act by which God looks into and searches out the ways, deeds, character, of men, in order to adjudge them their lot accordingly, whether joyous or sad" (Thayer, 242); e.g., Luke 19:44; 1 Pet 2:12; Exod 30:12.

202. See Titus 1:5, 7. Cf. Belleville 2009: 66.

203. LSJ, 657; Thayer, 242–43; 579.

204. Eleazar, a priest and son of Aaron, oversaw the whole tabernacle and all inside it including the oil, incense, and daily offering (Num 4:16). The tabernacle, households, the army, and building efforts had overseers (Judg 9:28; 2 Kgs 11:15, 18; 2 Chr 34:12, 17). Kelly explains that *episkopos* denotes "a wide variety of functionaries, e.g. inspectors, civic and religious administrators, finance officers" (1963: 73).

for themselves and much confidence in the faith, the one in Christ Jesus" (3:13).

What are the virtues necessary for this **good work**? **It is necessary the overseer to be not open to attack, a one-woman man, sober, wise, well behaved, hospitable, apt in teaching, not given to getting drunk, not pugnacious, but gentle, not contentious, not loving money** (3:2–3).[205]

Such a godly overseer should not be **open to attack** (*anepilēptos*) from outsiders (3:2). *Epilambanō* can simply refer to holding or grabbing onto someone in a neutral or helpful way,[206] but it can also refer to laying hold of someone in order to arrest or beat someone. In the latter sense, for example, a crowd in Jerusalem "seized" Paul in order to kill him (Acts 21:30). Also, some Philippians "seized" Paul and Silas to bring them before the magistrates (Acts 16:19–20). The Ephesians would well remember the crowd that "seized" Gaius and Aristarchus, bringing them to the theater (Acts 19:29).[207] Thus, in the often disturbing political Roman context,[208] Paul's goal was not so much that overseers be "perfect," but that the nonbelievers have no legal basis by which to arrest them. The same will be required of widows (5:7). *Anepilē(m)ptos* phrased in a positive way is having "a good testimony from the outsiders" (3:7). Paul himself, having recently been imprisoned in Rome, would know well that Christians could not avoid all arrest or beatings, but his goal is to make sure arrests are not done for criminal behavior by Christian leaders.[209]

Can women and single men ever be **overseers**? First, Paul indicates that "anyone" should aspire to "overseeing" (3:1), thereby, opening up the positions to all. Second, how shall we understand language that appears in the Greek or in translation to be exclusive: "husband of one wife," "his own house," "his children," "a man," "he take care," "he fall," "he must have"?[210] Does the gender language limit the position of overseer to married men only?

A one-woman man (3:2) is also used in Titus (1:6) and for the *diakonos* ("minister," "one-woman *men*," 3:12). A widow in the praying

---

205. See Titus 1:6–9.
206. E.g., Matt 14:31; Mark 8:23; Luke 9:47; Acts 17:19; 23:19; Heb 8:9.
207. See also Luke 20:20; Acts 18:17; 21:33.
208. See Titus 1:6.
209. Also Peter's later concern in 1 Pet 2:12–15.
210. 3:2, 4–7 KJV.

order was also to be a "one-man woman" (5:9). Normally, the modifiers in Greek follow the noun modified, but, in all these cases, they precede the noun, thereby emphasizing the modifiers "one woman" (or "one man"). The adjective also restricts the noun. Paul refers not just to a **man**, but to a **one-woman man**. The total concept expressed would be that a male overseer, if married, must be a man who is faithful and devoted and focused on only one woman. This phrase is another way to express that the men are to love "their own wives as their own bodies" (Eph 5:28). Here are different ways Bible versions have translated the phrase:

Different Translations of* mias gunaikos andra *(one-woman man, 3:2)

Translation	Bible version
"a man of one woman"	ESV footnote
"(the) husband of (but/only) one wife"	KJV, ESV, NIV, NASB, REB, NTME, NRSV footnote, NLT footnote, CEV footnote
"married only once/not have been married more than once"	NRSV, JB, NLT footnote, TEV footnote, NEB footnote
"have only one wife/married to one wife"	TEV, NEB footnote, NLT footnote, CEV footnote, RV
"have never been divorced"	CEV footnote
"faithful to his one wife"	NEB
"faithful to his wife"	TNIV, NLT
"faithful to their spouse"	CEB
"faithful in marriage"	CEV

Paul's directive would contrast with the Roman and Greek practice of not considering it "adultery" if a married man had sexual relations with a slave, concubine, or a prostitute. Roman slaves legally never married, they cohabitated (*contubernium*), although, to the slaves, their marriages were valid. The slave women could not be accused of adultery.[211] Xenophon assumes a married man could have a sexual relationship with

---

211. Pomeroy 1975: 193; Fantham 1994: 300, 306, 323; Winter 2003: 41.

a household slave: "When a wife's looks outshine a maid's, and she is fresher and more becomingly dressed, they're a ravishing sight, especially when the wife is also willing to oblige, whereas the girl's services are compulsory" (*Oec.* 10.12). Demosthenes explains: "Mistresses (*hetaira*) we keep for the sake of pleasure, concubines for the daily care of our persons, but wives to bear us legitimate[212] children and to be faithful guardians of our households" (*Neaer.* 122). *Hetairai* were "women, slave or free, who traded their sexual favours for long or short periods outside wedlock."[213] They could be streetwalkers or accomplished courtesans. Adolf Berger and Barry Nicholas explain: Roman law "took cognizance only of adultery by the wife . . . Adultery by the husband was never as such a crime, but his illicit intercourse with a respectable woman constituted the crime of *stuprum* under the *Lex Julia*, and in the fifth century (*Cod. Just.*5.17.8) his adultery in the matrimonial home or his adultery with a married woman anywhere entitled his wife to divorce him."[214] If a man were faithful and devoted and focused only on his wife, he would have no room in his heart or in his time for other intimate female (or male) relationships.

Having a wife and a mistress would be similar in reality to polygamy.[215] Although Greeks and Romans espoused monogamy, in practice a man might have more than one regular sexual relationship. Paul's directive would also contrast with legal polygamy (as expressed in the translation "have only one wife"). Polygamy was possible with Jews, even though monogamy was preferred and more common. For example, King Herod had nine wives.[216] *The Mishnah* readily discusses the rights of "co-wives," and a man being married to two or three or four wives.[217] A man could

---

212. "Legitimate" (*gnēsiōs*) is the same term used for Timothy and Titus by Paul (1 Tim 1:2; Titus 1:4).

213. *OCD*, 512.

214. *OCD*, 10–11.

215. Tertullian concludes that "none but monogamists are to be chosen for the order of the priesthood." He adds that men have been "deposed from office for digamy," *Exh.cast.* 7. In contrast, Ngewa (2009: 62) uses "a one-woman man" to allow polygamy among African officers whose behavior is "chaste and mature." But, are not they then "two-women men"?

216. Ilan 1995: 85–88. See also Josephus, *Ant.* 17.1 [14]. Justin Martyr describes Jewish men as taking as many wives as they desired (*Dial.* 134, 141).

217. E.g., *m. Yebam.* 1:1–4; 16:1; *m. Ketub.* 10:1–2, 4–6.

remain married to two women, but not a woman to two men (*m. Yebam.* 10:1, 4). Jewish law also contains, according to Tal Ilan: "no definition of or provision against adultery by the husband against his wife, since he may marry more than one woman; the wife, on the other hand, must remain strictly faithful to her husband. The only way a man can commit adultery is with another's man's wife."[218]

Paul's directive would also eliminate some cases of divorce.[219] In effect, **a one-woman man** (3:2) would be a man who is "joined fast to his wife" and "one flesh" with her.[220] Thus, the emphasis in the text is not on overseers being men, with one wife, but on the type of man who should be in leadership. A single chaste man (or woman) would not contradict Paul's prescription. Such a man yet has no wife to whom to be faithful. If single men could not be overseers, then Paul, maybe even Timothy, could not be overseers. Even Jesus, the greatest "Overseer" of our lives (1 Pet 2:25), could not be an overseer! However, the advantage of a single person is that he or she could focus on the Lord's affairs, as opposed to the married person, who is concerned to please the spouse (1 Cor 7:32–34).

An additional question to consider is the nature of language that may appear sex specific but is in reality generic. If 1 Timothy 3:2 and Titus 1:6 are sex specific, how, then, will we interpret Malachi 2:15, "let none be faithless to the wife of his youth" (RSV)? Does that mean that Malachi allows wives to be faithless to their husbands? I think not.

Some of the masculine pronouns in English translations are necessary because of the nature of the English language requiring a pronoun for the third person singular or a shorter sentence, but they do not necessarily render any sex specific pronouns in the literal Greek, as we see in the following chart:

---

218. Ilan 1995: 135. Belleville agrees "that marital faithfulness was a greater challenge for the husband in that society" (2009: 68).

219. Matt 19:12. Paul is not against remarriage of a widow(er): 1 Tim 5:14; Rom 7:1–3; 1 Cor 7:8–9, 39; Towner 2006: 251.

220. Matt 19:5–6; Gen 2:24. For a discussion of the meaning of "one flesh," see Spencer 2009: 25–31.

Comparison of Greek and an English Translation in Regard to Gender

Literal Greek Translation	ESV Translation[221]
"the own house well managing" 3:4	"he must manage his own household"
"having children" 3:4	"his children"
"the own household . . . take care" 3:5	"his own household . . . he care"
"not newly planted" 3:6	"he must not be a recent convert"
"having been deluded . . . might fall" 3:6	"he may become puffed up with conceit and fall"
"to have a good testimony . . . might fall" 3:7	"he must be well thought of . . . he may not fall"

Nowhere does the Greek text have a masculine pronoun in 3:4–7 except for the modifier **own** (*idios, idia, idion*) of **household** (*oikos*, 3:4, 5). Since **own** modifies the noun **household** (*oikos*), it must be grammatically "masculine," in this case an *o* declension. *Episkopos* (**overseer**) as an antecedent also has a "masculine" or *o* declension. In the same way, "conscience" (*syneidēsis*) has a "feminine" or *a* declension in 4:2 (the same pronoun as in 3:4, 5 **own**), although no one would argue that only females were affected by seared consciences. We here are concerned with grammatical gender that has to do with class or kind, a way to categorize words, not sex or real gender.[222]

Thus, in summary, probably the translations "faithful in marriage" (CEV) or "faithful to their spouse" (3:2 CEB) render best the intention of the more literal **a one-woman man**. Further, the overseer's relationship with his (or her) spouse is an important, but not the only, quality for leadership. How can people be faithful and persistent in following God if they can not be faithful and persistent in their earthly one-flesh relationship?[223]

Both the lists of elders' qualifications in 1 Timothy 3 and Titus 1 include references to not being open to attack from outsiders, to cultivating

---

221. The ESV renders the generic *tis* as "someone" (3:5).

222. See Spencer 1995: 121–25. In addition, in Hebrew (and in English) and sometimes in Greek "the masculine as *prior gender* includes the feminine" (GKC, 391).

223. See also 1 John 4:20.

sobriety, wisdom, hospitality, good doctrine, not being pugnacious, not greedy, and having cooperative children.[224] Both lists place a priority on not giving the society a reason to attack and on maintaining faithfulness in marriage. In 1 Timothy, more emphasis in the list is placed on wisdom, good behavior, and the ability to teach. Some qualities are mentioned only for the church at Ephesus: good behavior, gentleness, peaceableness, and safeguarding a new convert. While the celebrants of Artemis might be more encouraged to participate in intoxicated orgiastic practices and the magical control of gods and humans (e.g., Acts 19:19), in contrast, Paul was encouraging self-control, order, and gentleness. Although Ephesus was a place of great wealth[225] and the heterodox teachers also were promoting their own financial gain,[226] the Christian overseers were not to be greedy. Good teaching and models are important during times of wrong teaching and controversy and speculation.

Kosmios (**well behaved**, 3:2) is a synonym for "wise" (*sōphrōn*). *Kosmios* is the same quality that the women who were flaunting their attire and the slaves who were not acting in a trustworthy manner needed to develop.[227]

Philoxenos (3:2, literally, one who "loves" a "stranger" or "guest friend") is the care of strangers. "Loving strangers" or being **hospitable**[228] is a trait all Christians are to offer.[229] Having a positive attitude toward strangers is a trait that goes back through Jewish history. Moses summarizes God's self-revelation as the "God of the gods and Lord of the lords, the Mighty, the Great, the Strong, and the Wonderful, who is not partial and does not take bribes, executing justice for orphan and widow and loving every stranger, giving each one food and clothing" (Deut 10:17–18). The Hebrews, therefore, were to love the stranger because they modeled after God and they were once strangers themselves (Deut 10:19). They were to feed and leave food for strangers.[230] Jesus, as God incarnate, also taught the importance of hospitality: "I was a stranger and you gathered me in" (Matt 25:35) and he invited the disciples to "Come,

---

224. See Titus 1:6ff.
225. See Introduction. Setting-Ephesus and Artemis.
226. See Titus 1:10–11.
227. See 1 Tim 2:9; Titus 2:9–10.
228. Thayer, 654, 432; LSJ, 1938; BDAG, 1058.
229. Rom 12:13; 1 Pet 4:9; Heb 13:2; 3 John 5–8.
230. Lev 19:9–10; Deut 14:28–29; 24:19–22; 26:12–13.

eat breakfast" with him (John 21:12). Believers are to be hospitable even to enemies (Rom 12:20-21).[231]

Apt or skillful at teaching (3:2) is a key characteristic for an overseer at a time when the church is confused about which teaching is sound and unsound.[232] The women at Ephesus need to learn.[233] The women at Crete need to teach.[234] Believers need to be taught so they can teach others (2 Tim 2:2). Teaching is so important that elders who teach should be paid more than others (1 Tim 5:17-18). Effective teaching is often combined with wisdom.[235]

These first seven qualities in the list are all positive (3:2). The next two are negative (3:3). **Not given to getting drunk** is an antithesis of **sober**. Not **pugnacious** is an antithesis of **gentle** and **not contentious**.[236] The men at Ephesus already were quarreling in the midst of prayer (2:8). The heterodox were also disputing about words (6:4). The overseer, who has been forgiven and ransomed by the Messiah, must have a different style. To be **pugnacious** is to be "ready with a blow," whether physical or verbal.[237] Sometimes pugnaciousness is considered an asset for a man, but a deficit for a woman. Here it is not an asset for either. Instead, the overseer, like every other Christian, should aim to be gentle and reasonable.[238] **Gentleness** is one of the qualities of a wise teacher (Jas 3:17). Jesus, too, is gentle and reasonable (2 Cor 10:1). Some Corinthians saw this trait as a sign of weakness, not strength (2 Cor 10:1). The synonym, **not contentious** (*amachos*) or "peaceable," can refer to those who are "unconquerable" because they take no part in battles.[239] Instead they should "love from a clean heart and a good conscience and a genuine faith" (1 Tim 1:5).

In 3:4-7, Paul moves from adjectives to more elaborate descriptions: **managing his/her own house well, having children in submission, with**

---

231. Some believers renowned for their hospitality include Abraham and Sarah, the poor widow of Zarephath, the wealthy Shunammite, Elisha, Job, Zacchaeus, and Lydia (Gen 18:1-8; 1 Kgs 17:10-16; 2 Kgs 4:8-16; 6:22-23; Job 31:32; Luke 19:1-10; Acts 16:14-15, 40). See Spencer & Spencer 1990b: 48-50; idem 1998a: 95-99.

232. 1 Tim 1:10; 2 Tim 4:3-4; Titus 1:9.

233. See 1 Tim 2:11.

234. See Titus 2:3.

235. E.g., Jas 3:1, 13, 15, 17 *sophia*; Acts 26:25 *sōphrosynē*.

236. See Titus 1:6.

237. Thayer, 516, 519.

238. See Titus 2:3.

239. LSJ, 78.

all respectfulness. **But, if anyone does not know how to manage his/ her own household, how will (s)he take care of God's church?** (3:4–5). In Titus, the emphasis is on "having faithful children, not in accusation of wildness or disobedience,"[240] whereas in 1 Timothy the emphasis is on management of a household. In a similar way, as an overseer's faithful relationship to a spouse mirrors the overseer's faithful relationship to God, an overseer's ability to oversee a household should help in overseeing God's household (3:2, 4–5). Both overseers (*episkopos*) and ministers (*diakonos*) are exhorted to **manage** (*proistēmi*) their households (3:4, 12). *Proistēmi*[241] (3:4, 5) normally has to do with leadership. The overseers and ministers lead by "standing before" the church and their households. This is also a spiritual gift that must be done with "earnestness" (Rom 12:8). In Romans 12, it is distinguished from prophecy, ministry, teaching, encouragement, giving, and being merciful (12:6–8). Thus, possibly it refers more to governing or management and organization (a synonym of *kubernēsis*, 1 Cor 12:28) than to leadership in general, although it is also a type of leadership. Paul uses *proistēmi* as a term to describe all church leaders who serve a congregation: "respect those who labor among you, and *have charge* of you in the Lord and admonish you; esteem them very highly in love because of their work" (1 Thess 5:12–13 NRSV). In the Septuagint, *proistēmi* also connotes leadership synonymous with "steward" (*episkopos*)[242] or the overseeing of a household or an army troop.[243] When it comes to overseeing a household, Paul directs the younger widows to do so: to be the master or steward of the household.[244] The noun forms of *proistēmi* are *prostatēs* and *prostatis*.[245] *Prostatēs* has been used in the Old Testament for the chief officers and overseers for kings.[246] Josephus uses the term consistently for the leader of a nation, tribe, region, and even for God.[247] Phoebe, a "minister" of a specific church, Cenchreae, is an overseer or leader (*prostatis*).[248] Thus, the New Testament includes examples

---

240. See Titus 1:6.
241. Literally, "set over," or "stand before" (LSJ, 1482–83). See Titus 3:8.
242. See Titus 1:5–7.
243. 2 Sam 3:17; Amos 6:10; Prov 23:5;1 Macc 5:19.
244. 1 Tim 5:14 *oikodespoteō* (LSJ, 1204).
245. LSJ, 1526 defines *prostatēs* as "one who stands before," "leader, chief," "ruler," "president or presiding officer," "patron."
246. 1 Chr 27:31; 29:6; 2 Chr 8:10; 24:11.
247. See Spencer 1985: 115–17.
248. E.g., Rom 16:2 "overseer," NTME; "respected leader," CEV. Trebilco discovered that in some ancient communities, the *prostatēs* was probably the most important

of female overseers: not only Phoebe, but also the Apostle Junia, Elect Lady, the Elect Sister (2 John 1, 13), and coworkers Euodia, Syntyche, Prisca, and possibly also Stephana, Tryphaena, Tryphosa, Chloe, Lydia, Mark's mother, Nympha, and Apphia.²⁴⁹

Even though a household could include twenty to thirty people,²⁵⁰ Paul is most concerned for the overseer's relationship to the **children**, probably referring to minors. Are the children cooperative and supportive?²⁵¹ The cooperation is not done out of fear of the parents, but out of respect toward them. The same attribute (*semnotēs*, 3:4)²⁵² is used of the way the whole church should live in the world amidst the governing authorities (1 Tim 2:2), and the way "ministers" (*diakonos*) should act (3:8).

The goal of **managing** (*proistēmi*) one's household and God's household is further clarified by the synonym *epimeleomai* ("take care," 3:5).²⁵³ When Paul's friends provided him with food and provisions for his travel by sea, they too "took care" of him (Acts 27:3). In the same way as overseers are **hospitable** (3:2), treating guests as family, they also need to **manage** (3:4–5), treating family as guests. Care of the church and the home needs to be holistic, motivated by love (1:5).

Paul continues describing an ideal overseer: **(It is necessary the overseer to be) not newly planted, having been deluded, (s)he might fall into the condemnation of the devil** (3:6). A "neophyte" or "recent convert" is aptly described as someone **newly planted**.²⁵⁴ Paul's imagery is reminiscent of Jesus' parable of the sower where the seeds which fell on the rock "grew" (*phyō*) but then they withered because they had no moisture or the seeds which fell among thorns "sprouted forth" (*phyō*) but were later choked (Luke 8:6–7). These plants represent those who fall away in a time of testing or who get distracted by worries or wealth or pleasures (Luke 8:13–14). The danger in Ephesus is for these new con-

---

official (1991: 109).

249. See Spencer 1985: 109–19; Spencer 2005.

250. See Titus 1:6 on "household" and "children."

251. See *hupotassō* Titus 3:1. Belleville (2009: 69) renders as "a voluntary waiving of self-interest for the common good."

252. See also Titus 2:2; 1 Tim 2:2.

253. The good Samaritan "took care" of the person who was robbed, beaten, and left half dead, by being moved with compassion, approaching him, bandaging and medicating his wounds, bringing him on his own means of transportation to an inn, and paying for his care (Luke 10:33–35).

254. Thayer, 424; 661; BDAG, 669; LSJ, 1170.

verts to become **deluded** themselves (*typhoomai*) by the very teachings they are resisting.

Typhoomai (3:6 **delude**) comes from the root *typhō*, "raise a smoke" or "smoke," "consume in smoke, burn slowly."[255] The related *typhos* refers to "delusion" or "vanity."[256] The imagery suggests someone whose brain is filled with smoke and therefore the mind is unclear, "not knowing anything" (6:4). They may "fall into" the same danger as Hymenaeus and Alexander, who end up condemned (1:20). In the parable of the sower the devil "takes away the word from" the hearts of some so that they do not keep believing and do not end up saved (Luke 8:12). Possibly then the **condemnation** or judgment of the devil is one that keeps new converts from persisting in their Christian life. They will not definitely fall into the devil's condemnation, but they might **fall into** it (subjunctive mood). This idea is similar to the danger mentioned in 3:7:[257] **But, it is necessary also to have a good testimony from the outsiders, lest (s)he might fall into reproach and a trap from the devil**. This sentence summarizes the section (3:2–7) by repeating **it is necessary** (3:2) and repeating the concept of being **irreproachable** (3:2, *anepilēmptos*) in different words (**a good testimony from outsiders**).[258] Two things in this passage can make a believer vulnerable to falling: a new insufficiently strong faith (3:6) and a bad reputation from nonbelievers (3:7). A bad reputation might lead to being denounced or insulted by outsiders.[259] Since the devil is a liar,[260] false testimonies come ultimately from him. If at all possible, Paul wants the overseers to avoid such unnecessary persecution. These **reproaches** and condemnations do not come after lengthy warnings but are unexpected like snares or **traps** that suddenly catch animals such as birds,[261] unawares. The Lord can save believers from such traps, if the believers are pure themselves.[262]

Paul now omits an initial "it is necessary" (*dei*), thereby, connecting *diakonos* (**ministers**, 3:8) to the earlier "it is necessary," which introduced

---

255. LSJ, 1838; cf. Matt 12:20 *"smoldering* wick."

256. LSJ, 1838.

257. Also 1 Tim 5:14; 2 Tim 2:26.

258. See 1 Tim 3:2; Titus 1:6.

259. Of course, when the insults are on account of Jesus, they are to be received in joy (Matt 5:11–12; Luke 6:22–23; 1 Pet 4:14–16).

260. John 8:44.

261. Eccl 9:12; Prov 6:5; 7:23.

262. Pss 24:15; 30:4; 34:7 LXX.

the virtues for an "overseer" (3:2): **Likewise (it is necessary) the ministers to be honorable, not double-tongued, not devoting themselves to much wine, not fond of shameful gain, having the mystery of the faith in a clean conscience. And let these also be tested first, then let them serve, being not open to attack** (3:8–10). Paul also omits "it is necessary" before the "women" in 3:11, thereby also including them in the larger category of leadership of overseeing (*episkopē*, 3:1) and under the category of "ministers" (3:8). If they were only wives of male ministers, in this context a pronoun would be needed to indicate "wife" is intended.[263] Many female **ministers/deacons** have been discovered in the early church, as well as some elders and bishops.[264] *Diakonos* ("servant") signifies the one who renders personal service in obedience to Christ and for the edification of others. The New Testament refers to two kinds of **ministers** (1 Pet 4:10–11). The first is a minister of the "word" who equips Christians. These ministers are believers with the gifts of apostleship, prophesy, evangelism, pastoring, and teaching (Eph 4:11–12) who predominately use verbal skills. The use of **minister** builds on the literal "servant or minister" related to a ruler, someone who personally assists the ruler by making suggestions and implementing and delivering orders as the ruler's messenger (e.g., Rom 13:4). A second kind of **minister** or "minister of ministry" (Rom 12:7) predominately meets physical needs. The application of the term builds on the literal "servant or minister" who serves, pays for, and supplies food and drink, shelter and clothing, such as did Stephen and Dorcas.[265] Timothy, a **minister** (*diakonos*) would be a "minister of the word" because he is an evangelist (1 Tim 4:6; 2 Tim 4:5).

---

263. See 1 Tim 2:11 note. See also Belleville 2009: 75–76.

264. E.g., Phoebe, Rom 16:1. Two female "ministers" at Bithynia-Pontus in Asia Minor were tortured during Emperor Trajan's reign (A.D. 98–117) as the leaders in their congregation (Spencer 1985: 115). McKenna explains: "Throughout Asia Minor the deaconesses were a popular and important body of church women" (1967: 129). The fourth century *Const. ap.* 8.19–20 records a prayer for the ordination of deaconesses which recounts the great women of the Bible. See 1 Tim 3:15. See also Horsley 1987: 3–4; Pursiful 2001: 10–11; Morris 1973; *NewDocs* 1:121; Mounce 2000: 211–212. Many early church fathers, 65 inscriptions, and church canons refer to female deacons/ministers (Madigan 2005: 19–22, 28–96, 107–30, 203, 207–10); McKenna 1967: 54–56, 83–91. Only later did "deaconess" refer to the wives of male deacons (McKenna 1967: 131). Polycarp includes qualities from both the general "ministers'" list and the "women's" list: *diabolos* ("slanderer") and *dilogos* ("double-tongued") (3:8, 11) to show that he considers them one group (*Phil* 5:2).

265. E.g., John 2:5–9; Acts 6:1–6; 9:36–42; Spencer 1985: 113–14.

To what kind of minister does Paul refer here? As a basis to understand the function of a *diakonos*, what are the similarities and differences between the qualities needed for an overseer and a minister?

Comparison of Overseer (episkopos) and Minister (diakonos)

Overseer (*episkopos*) 3:2–7	Minister/deacon (*diakonos*) 3:8–10, 12	Women (3:11)
not open to attack**	not open to attack * 1. honorable***	honorable***
2. one-woman man*	7. one-woman men*	
3. sober*** 7. not given to getting drunk*	3. not devoting themselves to much wine**,***	3. sober**,***
4. wise*,***		
5. well behaved***		
6. hospitable*		
7. apt in teaching**, ***	5. having the mystery of the faith in a clean conscience**, ***	4. faithful in all **
8. not pugnacious*		
9. gentle		
10. not contentious**		
11. not loving money	4. not fond of shameful gain*	
12. managing own household well, having children in submission with all respectfulness**	8. managing well children and their own households **	
13. not newly planted	(6. tested)	
14. having a good testimony from the outsiders		
	2. not double-tongued	2. not slanderers***
*=same word as in Titus 1:6–9 for elder	**same concept as in Titus 1:6–9 for elder	***same word or concept as in Titus 2:2–3

Both the overseer and the **minister** are to be not open to attack, not loving money or fond of shameful gain, not given to getting drunk, one-woman men, not new converts or untested, managing well household and children.²⁶⁶ The **overseer** has almost twice as many required attributes as the minister (14 vs. 8). In addition, the overseer must be wise, well behaved, hospitable, apt in teaching, not pugnacious, gentle, not contentious, and having a good testimony from outsiders. Many of these qualities would help the overseer be well qualified to represent the church to the outside world.²⁶⁷ However, we can deduce that becoming an overseer required the ability to teach others and develop traits (having good behavior, hospitality, being gentle, and not contentious) that would be especially helpful in interacting with the heretics. *Diakonos* does not require the ability to teach others. Thus, it could refer to Christian leadership in general or to the "ministry of ministry" in particular.

The **women** (3:11) are required to have almost identical virtues as the **ministers** (3:8–10): **Likewise (it is necessary) the women (ministers) (to be) honorable,**²⁶⁸ **not slanderers, sober, faithful in all** (3:11). Not being slanderers and not being double-tongued (3:8) are very close in meaning, as also being faithful in all and having the mystery of the faith in a clean conscience (3:9).

Although in 1 Timothy 3 **overseer** is singular (3:2), while **minister** is plural (3:8, 12), in Acts 20:17, 28 a plural number of overseers (or elders) represent Ephesus. Philippi also had a plural number of overseers and ministers (Phil 1:1). Acts 14:23 also suggests a plural number of elders were selected "in each church" (or "corresponding to each church"). Paul seems to be using, therefore, the singular "overseer" in 1 Timothy 3:2 to be presenting a more abstract generic idea (not because Ephesus has only one overseer), while the plural "ministers" (3:8, 12) is more concrete.²⁶⁹

No clear role is mentioned for **ministers**, except, like the overseer, management (*proistēmi*) of children and household (3:12). Only the **minister** is not to be **double-tongued** (*dilogos,* 3:8), "insincere," "double in speech," "double-talking," "saying one thing with one person, another

---

266. See Titus 1:6.

267. Kelly (1963: 73, 76) notes also that the overseer had charge of the church's external relations and as its representatives entertained visiting Christians. See Titus 1:8 and 1 Tim 3:15.

268. See Titus 2:2.

269. The use of the singular in v. 2. follows the use of the singular in 3:1. Titus 1 also shifts from plural to generic singular (1:5–7) (Fee 1988: 84; Kelly 1963: 74).

with another (with intent to deceive)."[270] The focus is on the words said, whereas in "hypocrite" (*hypokritēs*, an actor or pretender), the focus is on the actions, acting in a way in order to deceive others.[271] In a context of heterodoxy (1:3), speaking differently to different groups of people might be one way to evade partisan contentious people. But, being **double-tongued** is not a means to genuine peace. Moreover, demonic teachings use "false words" to appear differently to different people (4:2). Only seared consciences can intend to deceive. The contrast to being **double-tongued** might be **having the mystery of the faith in a clean conscience** (3:9). **Conscience** (one aspect of the inward person that discerns good and evil) has been an important theme in 1 Timothy.[272] If one's conscience is pure, then one's words should have integrity. **Faith**[273] here resides in the context of a clean conscience. The **mystery of the faith** will be summarized in 3:16.

Slander (*diabolos*, 3:11) is also a problem with the female elders in Crete,[274] the young widows (1 Tim 5:13), and will continue to be a general problem in the "last days" (2 Tim 3:3). Like the devil, who is a liar, slander promotes lies or falsehoods about other people instead of faith, truth, peace, righteousness, and love. **Slander** is a *false* witness; Paul instead wants leaders to have a *good* (and true) witness (3:7). **Faithful in all** appears to be a summary referring to the content of faith and the behavior that follows from that content. The issue of faith will become particularly significant in the discussion of widows.[275]

First Timothy 3:12 (**Let ministers be one-woman men, managing well children and their own households**) appears to highlight specific requirements for the male ministers as **one-woman men** or faithful in their marital relationships and family oriented.[276] Similar to the summary (3:7) of the overseer discussion (3:2–6), Paul ends the discussion of **ministers** (3:8–12) with a summary statement: **For the ones having served well acquire a good foothold for themselves and much confidence in the faith, the one in Christ Jesus (3:13)**. **Serve** (*diakoneō*) was

---

270. BDAG, 250; LSJ, 431; Thayer, 151–52.
271. E.g., Matt 6:5; Luke 6:42; Thayer, 643; BDAG, 1038.
272. See 1 Tim 1:5.
273. See 1 Tim 1:19.
274. See Titus 2:3.
275. See 1 Tim 5:8, 12.
276. See 1 Tim 3:2, 4–5.

used already to describe what ministers do (3:10). The verb is not limited to those with the gift of serving physical needs (Acts 6:2; 2 Cor 8:19-20), as it also describes Timothy and Erastus' work with Paul (Acts 19:22). Peter uses it for both gifts in general and specifically for those who serve physical needs (1 Pet 4:10-11). The advantage of serving well in leadership helps the ministers in their Christian walk. It advances their faith (**acquire a good foothold**) and increases their confidence in the **faith** (3:13). A **foothold** (*bathmos*) is "a structured rest for the foot marking a stage in ascending or descending, *step*."[277] Jesus son of Sirach encourages: "If you discover anyone who is wise, rise early to visit him; let your feet wear out his *doorstep*" (Sir 6:36 REB). The "*steps* of his gate" (LXX) are symbolic of the way toward one's own wisdom. Therefore, does Paul refer to service as a way to progress in one's own faith or, instead, service as a means toward a "higher" ecclesiastical position, such as overseer? The text is unclear,[278] but my own preference is the former because the pronoun and the voice (middle) clarify the step is **for themselves**, in the present (not the future) tense, the standing is **good**, not "better,"[279] and the sentence ends with highlighting it is the faith **in Christ Jesus** toward which one is focused.

Paul concludes this section of his letter where he focuses on how godly overseeing helps the church advance the truth (3:1–16): **I am writing to you these things, while hoping to come to you shortly; but if I may delay, that you may know how it is necessary to behave in God's house, which is the church of the living God, pillar and support of the truth** (3:14-15).

Paul could have brought his teaching on these qualities for overseers and ministers in person rather than send them by letter since he planned to come soon to Ephesus from Macedonia (1:3). However, in case of delay, he wanted Timothy to understand mentally what kind of behavior is needed in those who lead God's **house** (3:14-15). A **house** (*oikos*)

---

277. BDAG, 162.

278. Commentators differ in their understanding of this phrase, e.g., "The ecclesiastical writers" "take it to be a higher grade or rank, but it is doubtful if Paul means that here" (Robertson 1931: 575); his "whole purpose is to enhance the value of the office" (citing Warfield, Mounce 2000: 206); "They who have discharged this ministry in a proper manner are worthy of no small honour" (Calvin: 2186); **Standing** probably refers to "their influence and reputation in the believing community, although it could refer to their *standing* with God" (Fee 1988: 89); it refers to an "excellent standing" in the church (Towner 2006: 268); *TLNT* 1:250–51.

279. Mounce 2000: 206.

could be an elaborate villa with a set of rooms or a single room or even a temple (Matt 12:4; 21:13),[280] but it would need stone **pillars** to support it. While Paul elsewhere has used a variety of images to describe the church, such as family,[281] body, a mature man,[282] a betrothed virgin,[283] a letter,[284] light/stars,[285] and a sanctuary,[286] **house** or "home" is a familiar familial image since believers have their own homes and households,[287] but they are also part of God's larger mansion (2 Tim 2:20-21). Most ancients lived and traveled in community.[288] Churches would meet in homes.[289] Being a faithful Christian has been described as being a faithful "steward" or manager of a household.[290] In the same way as **pillars** support a building, like the temple (e.g., 1 Kgs 7:15), the church should support the **truth**. Also, without truth the church cannot stand. Moreover, if God is a **living** God, then God's building is a "living" home. The goal of dwelling in the home is love (1 Tim 1:5), but love itself rejoices in the truth (1 Cor 13:6) because truth sets the perimeters of knowledge.

Paul summarizes that truth in 3:16: **And confessedly great is the godly mystery: who was manifested in the flesh, was declared righteous in the spirit, was seen by angels, was proclaimed among nations, was believed in the world, was taken up in glory.** The ancients celebrated many different mysteries (*mystēria*), which were syncretistic cults with secret initiation rites, hierarchical, and often sexually immoral. Such cults may have originated in Crete in the Mycenaean Age. Primarily women celebrated the mysteries of Dionysus and men the ones of Mithras.[291] In contrast, Paul writes here of the godly **mystery**. Mystery (*mustērion*) is a term Paul has used especially in 1 Corinthians, Ephesians, and Colossians. It refers to a certain truth that was once hidden,

---

280. Spencer 2005: 70.
281. E.g., 1 Tim 4:6; 2 Tim 4:21.
282. E.g., 1 Cor 12:12-27; Eph 1:22-23; 4:4, 12-16; Col 1:18.
283. 2 Cor 11:2.
284. 2 Cor 3:1-3.
285. 2 Cor 6:14; Eph 5:8-9; Phil 2:15.
286. 1 Cor 3:16-17; 6:19; 2 Cor 6:16; Eph 2:21.
287. 1 Tim 3:4-5, 12; 5:4, 13.
288. E.g., 2 Tim 1:16-17; 4:19; Titus 1:11; 1 Cor 16: 15-18.
289. E.g., Rom 16:5; 1 Cor 16:19; Col 4:15; Phlm 2.
290. *Oikonomia/oikonomos*, 1 Tim 1:4; Titus 1:7.
291. *OCD*, 695, 716. See critique by Clement of Alexandria, *Protr.* 2.

but has now been revealed,[292] especially by an apostle or prophet from God through the Spirit to believers often about Jesus Christ.[293] At times, **mystery** refers to specific information, an aspect of the gospel,[294] at other times it refers to the gospel as a whole entity, or to Jesus Christ as a synecdoche for the gospel.[295] The meaning of **mystery** may be summarized by King Nebuchadnezzar's discovery that Daniel's God "is the God of gods and the Lord of kings, the one revealing mysteries" (Dan 2:47). Daniel had told him that the interpretation that he had received was not one deduced by logic but only by revelation by the God in heaven (Dan 2:18–19, 27–30). Paul writes this confession to remind Timothy for the Christian leaders to teach and proclaim to others. It is written as a summary of the key events witnessed by a variety of sources to be presented to the larger public as well as the church. All these events have been recorded in the two volume work of Paul's companion Luke.

The **confession** (3:16) covers Jesus' whole life from the incarnation (**manifested in the flesh**), his life (**was declared righteous in the spirit**), resurrection (**was seen by angels**), early apostolic witness (**was proclaimed among nations**), response to apostolic proclamation (**was believed in the world**), and ascension (**was taken up in glory**). The confession is almost a perfect parallelism, each clause consisting of a verb, a preposition, an object.[296]

The concept of **mystery** is further communicated by the verb *phaneroō* (to **manifest** or "*to make manifest* or *visible* or *known* what

---

292. E.g., The message of the kingdom of heaven is given to disciples clearly to understand but explained in parables to the large crowds (Matt 13:10-11); prepared for those who love God (1 Cor 2:7-9), not revealed in the past but revealed now (Eph 3:5; Col 1:26-27).

293. 1 Cor 2:10; 13:2; Eph 3:3-5; Rom 16:25.

294. E.g., a hardening has come upon part of Israel (Rom 11:25); humans will be changed in a flash, the dead will be raised imperishable (1 Cor 15:51-52); the plan is to gather all things in God (Eph 1:9-10); Gentiles are fellow heirs (Eph 3:3-10; Col 1:26-27); two become one flesh (Eph 5:31-32).

295. Matt 13:11; 1 Cor 2:1-2, 7-8; Col 1:27; 2:2-3; 1 Cor 4:1; Eph 6:19. For an extended study of the meaning of *mustērion* from ancient to contemporary times, see Spencer 1992: 2-11.

296. However, **was seen by angels** has no preposition in the Greek. Therefore, this verse may be poetical, but it is not tight enough to call it a "hymn." Paul does not hesitate to cite when a phrase comes from another author, using *legō* ("said"), e.g., Titus 1:12; Acts 17:28. Fiorenza (1975: 19) points out that "no direct record of early Christian hymns . . . exists."

has been hidden or unknown," 3:16).²⁹⁷ For God to become incarnate would be incomprehensible to a Jew.²⁹⁸ How can God, who is a Spirit, become flesh? How could the immortal God become mortal? Philo aptly summarizes this Jewish perspective. In criticism of Emperor Gaius, who intended to have his statue placed in the temple of Jerusalem and who attired himself daily in the guise of different deities, Philo responds that the "Jews alone" opposed Gaius because they acknowledged the "one God who is the Father and Maker of the world." He adds that "deification" is "the most grievous impiety, since sooner could God change into a man than a man into God" (*Embassy* 16 [115, 118]). For some Gentiles, what would be remarkable is the assumption that the **flesh** was good enough for God to embrace because they would instead see matter as baser, as Plato explains: God constructed "things divine" but commanded mortal things to be made by "engendered sons" (*dēmiourgos*).²⁹⁹

Such a sentiment would be part of what would cause some at Ephesus to forbid marriage and demand abstinence because they would see flesh as evil (4:3–4; cf. 1 John 4:2). The Christian witness instead is that God in Christ Jesus (3:13, 15) "became flesh and dwelled among us."³⁰⁰ God had to become human flesh in order to atone for human sin.³⁰¹ His blood had to be shed as the perfect sacrifice for a perfect God.³⁰² It was in his flesh that the Messiah suffered.³⁰³ Consequently, it was in his **flesh** that Christ Jesus reconciled Jew and Gentile (Eph 2:14).

The next clause is difficult to understand since *pneuma* can refer to the Holy Spirit or the human spirit³⁰⁴ and *dikaioō* itself may be rendered in a variety of ways:

---

297. Thayer, 648.

298. See Titus 2:13.

299. *Tim.* 42D, 69C, 74E. Instead of being resurrected bodily, the person who lived his appointed time well returned again to his "abode in his native star" but whoever did not live well would be changed into a woman at the second birth (*Tim.* 42B, 90E).

300. John 1:14; Luke 1:31–33; 2:6–7.

301. E.g., 1 Tim 1:15; Rom 8:3; Phil 2:6–7.

302. Col 1:22; Heb 10:19–20.

303. Luke 24:26; 1 Cor 1:23; Heb 5:7; 1 Pet 3:18; 4:1.

304. In the Pastorals, *pneuma* can be used to refer to humans (2 Tim 1:7) and to God (1 Tim 4:1; 2 Tim 1:14; Titus 3:5).

- "vindicated in (the) spirit" (NRSV, NEB, REB);³⁰⁵
- "vindicated by the Spirit" (NIV, TNIV, NLT, ESV); "justified in the Spirit" (KJV); "vindicated in the Spirit" (NASB, RSV); "attested by the Spirit" (JB);
- "declared righteous by the Spirit" (CEB); "the Spirit proved that he pleased God" (CEV); "was shown to be right by the Spirit" (TEV).

In the Pastorals the word family of *dikaioō* is always a synonym of "holy," for example, holiness is a goal Timothy should seek.³⁰⁶ Jesus is always described as without sin or holy, the "Holy and Righteous One" (e.g., Acts 3:14). The centurion declared about Jesus after the three hour darkness and Jesus' death: "Surely this human was righteous!" (Luke 23:47). Thus, **declared righteous** (CEB) would be an appropriate translation. Then, if in the first clause in 3:16 the object is **flesh**, in contrast, in the second clause the object would be **spirit** referring, I think, to Jesus' human spirit. The **spirit** is that aspect of a human which searches one's self and knows oneself thoroughly (1 Cor 2:10–11; Prov 20:27). Therefore, the point would be that Jesus, even searched to his deepest spirit, was recognized as righteous.

Paul describes the ministry of apostles as witnessed by "the world and angels and humans" (1 Cor 4:9). **Angels** (3:16) are also mentioned later in 1 Timothy (5:21) as witnesses, together with God and Jesus Christ. Jesus' resurrection was also witnessed by angels, who reminded the women at the empty tomb that Jesus had taught them, even in Galilee, that he would be crucified and, on the third day, be raised again (Luke 24:4–8).

Human testimony is summarized in two parts: their **proclamation** and their **belief** (3:16). The book of Acts testifies to the post-resurrection acts of Jesus. Jesus, through the Holy Spirit, poured out the marvelous acts of Pentecost (Acts 2:1–4, 33) and was also present through the church (Acts 9:4–5). If the first three verbs (**manifested** [*phaneroō*], **declared righteous** [*dikaioō*], **was seen** [*horaō*]) give prominence to the visible (outward and inward), now Paul mentions the verbal. *Kēryssō* refers to the **proclamation** or preaching about Jesus.³⁰⁷ Paul called himself a

---

305. *DHH* renders "triunfó en su condición de espíritu."
306. 1 Tim 6:11. See Titus 1:8; 3:7.
307. See 1 Tim 2:7. A *kērux* was "a *herald, a messenger* vested with public authority, who conveyed the official messages of kings, magistrates, princes, military

"preacher" or "herald, especially to Gentiles."³⁰⁸ Timothy will be exhorted to "preach the word" in all circumstances and Paul would proclaim the *kērugma* ("proclamation," "message") in Rome (2 Tim 4:2, 17).

Ethnos (3:16) may refer to **nations** or more specifically "Gentiles," non-Jews. Elsewhere in the Pastorals, *ethnos* refers to Gentiles,³⁰⁹ but in the context of this confession the meaning may be broader, alluding to Jesus' great commission (Matt 28:19) and parallel to **world** (1 Tim 3:16). The goal of preaching is for listeners to believe in the One about whom one preaches (Rom 10:14). Paul and Timothy's travels throughout the ancient world, from Asia Minor to Macedonia, Greece, and Rome have been documented in Acts. The readers of the Pastorals in Asia Minor and Crete are believers of their message and part of the **world** Jesus came to save.³¹⁰

Paul concludes with the ascension of Jesus (**was taken up in glory**, 3:16). This event is only recorded in Luke and Acts when the disciples see Jesus "lifted up" and a cloud took him out of their sight.³¹¹ Key requirements for apostles were to have been with Jesus until he ascended (Acts 1:21–22). *Analambanō* (**to take up**)³¹² in the passive voice implies that Jesus did not ascend on his own power or initiative but **was taken**,³¹³ similar to "was raised" by God.³¹⁴ The verb literally often has a sense of movement from one place to another, as moving from land to a boat.³¹⁵ Often the resurrection and ascension of Christ is followed by a statement that God the Father caused Jesus to be seated at his right in a place of affirmation and authority.³¹⁶ Jesus is encased **in glory** in heaven.³¹⁷

---

commanders, or who gave a public summons or demand, and performed various other duties" (Thayer, 346).

308. See 1 Tim 2:7; 2 Tim 4:17.

309. 1 Tim 2:7; 2 Tim 4:17.

310. Titus 3:8; 1 Tim 1:15; 2:4.

311. Acts 1:9; Luke 24:51; Jesus foretells the event in John 6:62; 7:33; 14:28; 16:5–7; 20:17.

312. Thayer, 39; BDAG, 66.

313. Other verbs used for the ascension (*anapherō* ["was taken away"] and *epairō* ["was lifted up"]) are also used in the passive voice (Luke 24:51; Acts 1:9; cf. 1 Pet 3:22).

314. E.g., Rom 4:24; Acts 3:15; 10:40; 13:37; 1 Pet 1:21.

315. Acts 20:13–14; 23:31; also Acts 10:16; 2 Tim 4:11; Eph 6:13, 16.

316. E.g., Rom 8:34; Eph 1:20–22; 1 Pet 3:22.

317. Acts 7:55; Luke 24:26.

The other proclamations about the **godly mystery** (3:16) have been presented in chronological order: incarnation, righteous life, resurrection, proclamation, and response. The ascension occurred after the resurrection but before the proclamation. Why hold it until the end? Possibly, Paul concludes the confession with the ascension because thereby he highlights the positive conclusion of the confession (beginning with the incarnation, ending with glory) and **in glory** also alludes to Jesus' present position of authority and future return in **glory**.[318] **Glory** (*doxa*) reminds the reader of the glorious nature of the whole gospel and the glorious nature of the triune God.[319]

Fusing the Horizons: How to Use Leadership Lists

Much effort is spent on applying 1 Timothy 3:2–13 as a checklist from which to remove potential candidates for leadership. But instead it should be used as a guide to help Christians mature. We should all aspire to maturity, which also would make us good candidates for the teaching and ruling ministries. Do we live so that people do not have a justified reason to attack us? If married, are we focused totally on our spouse, rejoicing in him or her? Are we striving for self-control in all areas of our life, in moderating the use of wine or alcohol, in not being ruled by our sensual desires, in disciplining our use of and attitude toward money? Are we treating with kindness both strangers and members of our family? Are we working on how to teach others, being gentle and peaceable with them as opposed to slandering them or jumping swiftly to disagree? Are we trying to be wise and more mature in the faith? These are the characteristics that will help us lead others. A. J. Gordon in *How Christ Came to Church* exhorts his listeners to be used by the Spirit:

> As the wind pours through the organ pipes, causing their voice to be heard, albeit according to the distinctive tone and pitch of each, so the Spirit speaks through each minister of Christ according to his special gift, that the people may hear the word of the Lord. Is it not the most subtle temptation which comes to the preacher that he allow himself to be played upon by some other spirit than the Paraclete?

---

318. See Titus 2:13; 1 Cor 15:42–43. Kelly concludes that the phrase implies that Christ ascended and "has been taken up into the realm of the divine glory, there to reign with the Father" (1963: 92).

319. Glory is an important theme in the Pastorals. See 1 Tim 1:11, 17; 2 Tim 4:18.

The popular desire for eloquence, for humor, for entertainment, for wit, and originality, moving him before he is aware, to speak for the applause of men rather than for the approval of Christ?[320]

So many times we strive to appeal to others so they will approve us. Paul instead exhorts us to be mature Christians, which may or may not result in human affirmation.

---

320. Gordon 2010: 53.

1 TIMOTHY 4:1—5:2
Timothy Should Teach the Words of the Faith, Setting an Example

De (**but**, 4:1) introduces a contrast with the preceding verses: **But the Spirit expressly says that in later times some will depart for themselves from the faith paying attention to deceitful spirits and demonic teachings, as[1] hypocritical liars, their own conscience branded with a hot iron, forbidding to marry, to abstain from foods, which God created for reception with thanksgiving by the believers and those who have known fully the truth, since every created thing of God is good and nothing is rejected, being received with thanksgiving, for it is rendered holy (sanctified) through God's word and intercession** (4:1–5). After explaining various ways to help people to be saved and come to the knowledge of the truth (1:3—3:16), Paul now further explains the urgency of the matter. In chapter 1, Paul had highlighted heterodox teachings at Ephesus related to "myths and genealogies," misuse of the law, and misinformed teachers (1:4, 7–11). Now he describes what will happen and is happening in general.

HETERODOXY WAS PREDICTED BY THE SPIRIT (4:1–5)

Paul's source is the **Spirit**. Paul mentions the Holy Spirit in every one of his letters as one Person of the Trinity.[2] When Ananias prayed for him at Damascus, Paul was filled with the Holy Spirit and the Holy Spirit continued to dwell within him. In the midst of evil and persecution, the Holy Spirit's presence became intensive. During Paul's journeys, the Holy Spirit encouraged, led, testified to, and restrained Paul and his coworkers.[3] In Acts, the Holy Spirit also explicitly spoke to Peter, the church in

---

1. "As" or "in the form of" (BDAG, 329–30).
2. See Titus 3:4–7.
3. E.g., 2 Tim 1:14; Acts 9:17, 31; 13:9, 52; 16:6–7; 20:22–23; 21:4.

Antioch, and the prophet Agabus.[4] In 1 Timothy 4:1, the Holy Spirit is speaking explicitly about **later times**.

Have the **later times** (4:1) already begun, or are they future times? Normally, **later** (*hysteros*) by itself refers to some event that follows previous events (e.g., Luke 20:32). In 1 Timothy 4:1, Paul probably refers to "later times" after Jesus' "own times" (2:6) in contrast to the future time when Jesus would return (6:14-15). A synonymous term is used in 2 Timothy ("last days," *eschatē, hēmera*, 3:1), which, as in 1 Timothy 4:1-3, refers to activities which appear quite contemporary, such as "lovers of themselves, lovers of money . . .") (2 Tim 3:2). The "last day" in the singular normally refers to the very final day, the judgment day when Jesus returns.[5] The "last days" in the plural may refer to the days that began at Pentecost, fulfilling Joel's prophecy (Acts 2:17) or the days after Old Testament times that began with Jesus' incarnation and life.[6] Either way, these "last days" have already begun and are present. Calvin points out that "to us in the present day" the warning is "not less useful, when we perceive that nothing has happened which was not foretold by an express prophecy of the Spirit."[7]

How sad it is to learn that **some will depart for themselves from the faith** (4:1). Although they themselves are responsible for their actions,[8] others are also responsible, the ones who do the deceiving.[9] These are evil spirits, not humans, who ultimately are responsible for causing humans to wander away from the truth.[10] Eve is the archetypal human who wandered away from the truth because she was deceived.[11] Eve's weakness was that she listened carefully (**pay attention**, *prosechō*) to the wrong source: the devil disguised as a serpent.[12] In a similar way, the crowds in Samaria had listened with a receptive attitude to the magician Simon (Acts 8:10-11).

---

4. Acts 10:19; 11:12, 28; 13:2, 4; 19:6; 21:11.

5. John 6:39-40, 44, 54; 11:24; 12:48.

6. Heb 1:2; 1 Pet 1:19-20; 2 Pet 3:2-3; Jude 17-18.

7. Calvin, 2190.

8. Implication of middle voice (Robertson 1934: 809, 873). On "faith" see 1 Tim 1:19. Paul uses the future middle to indicate the predictive nature of the Spirit's message. Not all will depart but some.

9. See Titus 3:3; 1 Tim 3:16.

10. The opposite of deception is truth: Eph 4:14-15; 2 Pet 2:18; 3:17; 1 John 4:6. Jesus also predicted the future deception of believers (e.g., Matt 24:4-25).

11. See 1 Tim 2:14.

12. Gen 3:1-6; 2 Cor 11:3; Rev 12:9. See Titus 2:3.

Lydia, in contrast, in Philippi listened attentively and receptively, through God's help, to Paul's teachings (Acts 16:14). Timothy too will be exhorted to be attentive to good teaching (1 Tim 4:13). However, in Ephesus, some were listening carefully and receptively to deceitful spirits and demonic teachings. Later, Paul will clarify that "evil people" are the intermediaries between the spirits and the departing believers (2 Tim 3:13).

Evil **spirits** are mentioned numerous times in the gospels.[13] The Twelve and Seventy-two were empowered by Jesus to cast them out.[14] Paul himself cast out evil spirits at Ephesus (Acts 19:12, 15). Ephesus was known as a center for magic.[15] Even though some people might attempt to use magic to ward off evil spirits,[16] humans will always have a residue of evil.[17] These demons falsified the teachings (*didaskalia*) at Ephesus, which explains why true teachings are so important.[18]

Six aspects of those who depart are described by Paul: they will depart: (1) in the later times; (2) by paying attention to deceitful spirits and demonic teachings; (3) by means of false words; (4) by searing their own consciences; (5) by promoting the forbidding of marriage, and (6) by abstaining from certain foods (4:1–3). Those who promote the **demonic teachings** do so with false words: "They are esp. dangerous because they play a role (*en hypokrisei*) that puts their victims off the scent; like actors who play parts so well that their words have the ring of truth."[19] A *hypokrisis* (**hypocrite**) in ancient times was an actor on the stage.[20] Like Satan, who disguises himself as an angel of light (2 Cor 11:14), so too these false teachers have learned to disguise themselves by their effective acting.

Having a good **conscience** (4:2) is an important goal for Paul in 1 Timothy.[21] If the conscience is the interior faculty for the personal discernment of good and evil, here that faculty has been damaged by being **branded** or seared with **a hot iron**. *Kaustēriazō* includes the root ideas of

---

13. E.g., Matt 8:16; 12:43–45; Mark 1:23–27.
14. Matt 10:1; Luke 10:17–20.
15. Acts 19:19. See Introduction. Setting. Ephesus and Artemis.
16. E.g., Murphy-O'Connor 2008: 51.
17. See the study of effects of healing by "white witchcraft" by Koch 1965.
18. E.g., 1 Tim 1:3, 5; 2:12; 3:2, 16; 6:20–21.
19. BDAG, 1096.
20. LSJ, 1886.
21. See 1 Tim 1:5.

heat, lighting, burning, and branding.[22] A *kaustēr* was a cauterizing apparatus.[23] The perfect tense indicates that what was done to the conscience was done in the past but it has a long term effect. In a similar way, the deception of Eve entered her into a state of transgression (1 Tim 2:14). The ability to deceive and be deceived involved a hypocrisy enabled by blocking off the ability to discern good from evil.

Yet, what could appear more pious than asceticism? If a **conscience** (4:2) has been burned so that it no longer can discern good from evil, one would expect that that person would be like an Epicurean, or, like a Gentile, "living in licentiousness, passions, drunkenness, revels, carousing, and lawless idolatry," in "excesses of dissipation" (1 Pet 4:3-4 NRSV) or "wild" (Titus 1:6). However, these instead are ascetic, **forbidding marriage** and the eating of certain **foods** (1 Tim 4:3). Paul thus reminds us that a seared conscience can result in an ascetic as well as a dissolute lifestyle. A healthy conscience can discern subtlety and it can dialogue within itself and with others about more difficult questions of morality. For instance, although Paul might recommend to believers the benefits of being single, yet he allows the possibility of marriage (1 Cor 7:1-16). He encourages some widows to remain single, while others to marry (1 Tim 5:9-14).

This ascetic strain can be found both in some Jewish and Gentile communities.[24] Although most ancient Jews were strongly supportive of **marriage** because of God's command to humanity to "be fruitful and multiply" (Gen 1:28; 9:7) (exemplified by one order of the Essenes who thought that those who "decline to marry cut off the chief function of life, the propagation of the race"), other Essenes did not encourage marriage. For example, Josephus describes one order of the Essenes, whose diet was strict, also shunning "pleasures as a vice" and disdaining marriage. He said, they do not "on principle, condemn wedlock and the propagation thereby of the race, but they wish to protect themselves against women's wantonness, being persuaded that none of the sex keeps her plighted troth to one man." They thought only the soul is immortal and imperishable entangled in the "prison-house of the body." However, unlike the

---

22. E.g., *kaiō*: Matt 5:15; Luke 12:35; John 15:6; *kausoō*: 2 Pet 3:10, 12; LSJ, 932.
23. LSJ, 932.
24. See Titus 1:10-14.

Ephesians, the Essenes despised riches and, in contrast to Paul, usually prohibited presents to relatives.[25]

From a Gentile perspective, singleness and the **forbidding** of **marriage** would fit well with Artemis.[26] Artemis was a "virgin" unmarried goddess. Her priests were most likely celibate or castrated men.[27] A married woman was punished with death if she entered her temple.[28] Thus, the Gentile environment may have encouraged this ascetic strain in Anatolian Judaism. In the second century, about a hundred years later, the Montanists, arising from Phrygia in Asia Minor, also had restrictions on marriage and the promotion of rigorous fasting. The country people of Phrygia and Paphlagonia were known for their "natural puritanism," the "perfect climate for a rigorist church."[29] Montanists taught the "annulment of marriage." The prophetesses Maximilla and Prisca (Priscilla)[30] left their own husbands (Eusebius, *Hist. eccl.* 5.18). Jerome added that people who married a second time (even after the death of a spouse) were not to be allowed communion with the Montanist church.[31] Thus, we can see that the problems at Ephesus were to continue to develop in the later church. The deprecation of one's material self might appear pious, but often it assumes that additional sacrifice is necessary to complete the full efficacy of Christ's sacrifice. But the New Testament teaches that Jesus is the only mediator between God and humans, the perfect sacrifice for human sin done "once for all."[32]

---

25. Josephus, *J.W. II.* 8 [120–160]; Schürer 1979, 1:570, 578.

26. See Introduction. Setting. Ephesus and Artemis.

27. Gritz 1991: 39–41.

28. Wiedemann 1981: 196 citing Achilles Tatius, *Leukippe and Kleitophon* 7, 13.

29. Celibate ascetism had a great appeal in Anatolia (Mitchell 1993, 2:97, 114). See also *T. Isaac.* 4:1–4.

30. This heretical Priscilla is not to be confused with the faithful Jewish Christian teacher Priscilla who lived a century earlier.

31. Jerome 2010: 292–93. Jerome even calls Tertullian's view not to allow second marriages a heresy. In the same century some taught that "There is for you no resurrection unless you remain chaste and do not pollute the flesh" (*Acts Paul and Thecla* 12), and Irenaeus also notes that some Gnostics who preached abstinence from marriage and from animal food were thus "ungrateful to the God who made all things," while other Gnostics promoted promiscuity and plurality of marriages and ate foods sacrificed to idols (*Haer.* I, 28).

32. Heb 10:10, 12, 14, 18. See Spencer 2006.

Instead of holding themselves away from (**abstain,** *apechō*)[33] certain **foods**, God had clearly communicated to Peter and Paul and the other disciples that, even as Gentiles could be welcomed into the believing community, also all foods—clean and unclean—could be eaten.[34] Instead of an attitude of rejection, believers who **know** well the **truth** (*epiginōskō*) should receive with **thanksgiving**[35] everything **created** by **God** (4:3-4). The earth, its plant life, its lights, its animals, "everything" God has made was "very good" and blessed.[36] As David sings: "To the Lord belong the earth and everything in it, the world and all its inhabitants" (Ps 24:1 REB; 1 Cor 10:26). Flesh, in its literal sense, is good (1 Tim 3:16). The resurrection, too, would be a bodily one (1 Cor 15:44). Even food offered to pagan idols could be received if God is acknowledged as the Creator because in prayer God renders the food **holy** (4:5).[37]

A Good Minister (4:6-10)

Paul now directs his comments directly to Timothy: **Making known these things to the brothers and sisters, you will be a good minister of Christ Jesus, being nourished by the words of the faith and by the good teaching which you followed; but the godless and old-women's myths—decline; rather train for godliness; for bodily training for a little is profitable but godliness for all things is profitable, a promise having life for now and the future** (4:6-8). We are reminded that this is a letter from Paul, the mentor, to one person, Timothy, the mentored, about a church (in Ephesus, 1:3 vs. 6:21-plural "you"). We listen in as Paul clarifies what he wants Timothy to teach the Ephesians (1:3, 18). Throughout this letter, Paul intersperses personal comments directly to Timothy. Timothy too is in an environment of false knowledge and needs to guard his own process of salvation, sanctification, and knowledge of the truth. Already, he has exhorted Timothy to "fight with them the good fight having faith and a good conscience" (1:18-19) and, in order to help others, to "know how it is necessary to behave in God's home" (3:15). But now Paul has an extended section addressed directly to Timothy

---

33. Thayer, 57; BDAG, 103.

34. Acts 10:12-15; 11:6-12; Rom 14:14, 17; Gal 2:12-14; Col 2:16, 21-23; Heb 13:9; Mark 7:14-23.

35. See 1 Tim 2:1.

36. Gen 1:10, 12, 18, 21, 25, 28, 31.

37. 1 Tim 4:5; 1 Cor 10:30; Phil 4:6.

(4:6–5:2), ending with directions on how to treat widows (5:3). He will close the letter with two exhortations also addressed directly to Timothy (6:11–16, 20).[38] Thus, the term "Pastoral Letters or Epistles" brings out this aspect of the letters, Paul, a pastor, is writing to his coworkers, Timothy and Titus, to guide them as they pastor other Christians.

These two-pronged aspects of the letter may be seen in verse 6. Two things make a **good minister of Christ Jesus** (as opposed to a bad one): (1) **making known these things to the brothers and sisters** and (2) **being nourished by the words of the faith and by the good teaching** (4:6). One action is outward, the other is inward. Outwardly, Timothy is to supply (**make known,** *hypotithēmi*)[39] to his adopted siblings (**brothers and sisters**)[40] all that Paul has previously instructed in the letter. Simultaneously, Timothy needs to make sure he himself is **nourished** or trained and educated (*entrephō*).[41] He should regularly "feed" himself by two means: **the words of the faith** and **the good teaching** which he followed (4:6). These two phrases appear to be synonymous. Possibly, **words of the faith** refer specifically to summary creeds, such as in 3:16, and **teaching** is a broader term which includes all Timothy was taught and has done.[42] It would include, but not be limited to, "reading" the Scriptures (4:13; 2 Tim 3:14–17).

---

38. The second person singular is used for Timothy in his capacity as a leader overseeing the church (1:3; 3:14–15; 5:3, 7, 11, 19–22; 6:2, 17) and as a believer aiming to persevere in the faith (1:18; 4:6–5:2, 23; 6:11–14, 20).

39. Thayer, 645; BDAG, 1042.

40. *Adelphos* ("brother") in the plural is normally generic (LSJ, 20). The church has women as well as men (e.g., 1 Tim 2:8–15; 5:3–16). In Phil 4:1, Paul addresses *adelphos* (plural) followed closely by the names of women (Eudia, Syntyche) and a man (Clement) (4:2–3). Luke uses *adelphos* (plural) to describe Lydia, Paul, Silas, and others (Acts 16:40). "Brother" is a metaphor of equality (Josephus, *Ant.* 19.1.1 [4]). *Adelphos* in the plural is translated: "brothers and sisters" (NRSV, TNIV, NLT); "believers" (TEV, CEB, New Trans.); "followers" (CEV); "brothers" (NIV, JB, ESV); "brethren" (KJV, NASB); "brotherhood" (REB).

41. The root *trephō* is used of feeding birds (Matt 6:26; Luke 12:24) and humans (Matt 25:37; Luke 23:29; Acts 12:20; Rev 12:6, 14) and being reared (Luke 4:16); Thayer, 219; LSJ, 577.

42. Cf. Kelly (1963: 98): "diligently studied and perseveringly practiced"; Towner (2006: 304): Paul refers to "a body of tradition articulated in teachable doctrine" and "the gospel polemically as measurably superior to the false teaching"; Mounce (2000: 249): Paul distinguishes between "basic gospel message" and "the doctrinal teaching that comes out of it."

In contrast, he is to **keep declining** or refusing **godless and old-women's myths** (4:7). The very teaching Timothy is to exhort others to give up (1:3-4), he is warned himself to guard against (4:7).[43] These legends are **godless** or "profane" (*bebēlos*), unholy acts that lead to lack of piety.[44] The emphasis is on the unholy character of the legends.

These **myths** are also described as those of **old women** (4:7). *Graōdēs* has been translated as "*characteristic of an elderly woman* of speculative or legendary accounts that lack Christian pedagogical value,"[45] coming from *graus* ("an old woman") and *eidos* ("the external form").[46] Strabo uses *graōdēs* for creative old women who proclaim fictional legends (*muthologia*) for entertainment not for education (*Geogr.* I. 2.3. C16). Plato in his *Republic* mentions how philosophers, just to be polite, will agree with "old women" (*graus*) telling **myths**.[47] Thus, *graōdēs* appears to be an allusion to the fascination with telling myths at Ephesus (1:4) of which women were an active part (2:12-14; 5:13). In contrast, Paul encourages the female elders at Crete to teach (Titus 2:3), but not the entertaining tales that are neither instructive nor edifying (4:7). Paul's point is not that one must avoid the tales of elderly *women*, but that one must avoid speculative tales that may entertain but are not true, instructive, or edifying. Timothy will not mature spiritually if he relies on accounts that are unholy and false. But he did well to have learned true teaching from his grandmother Lois (2 Tim 1:5; 3:14).

Paul began and ends this extended sentence with positive exhortations: **Train for godliness** (4:7). He introduces a comparison between physical and spiritual activities through the common theme of exercise. The Greeks were known for their emphasis on physical exercise. Gardiner explains: "Athletics were to the Greek far more than mere recreation. To the Homeric warrior they were the means of training and maintaining the physical vigour and activity which he needed in a warlike age . . . the citizen might at a moment's notice be called upon to take the field and fight."[48] Emperor Augustus revived athletics even after the Greek

---

43. See 1 Tim 1:4; Titus 1:14; 3:9.

44. See 1 Tim 1:9.

45. BDAG, 207. Other translations are "from the older women" (CEB); "old wives' tales" (NRSV, NIV, NLT, REB); "old womanish" (NTME); "fit only for old women" (NASB, NEB); "silly" (ESV); "senseless" (CEV); "not worth telling" (TEV).

46. Thayer, 122, 172.

47. I. 22. 350E. See also Plato, *Gorg.* 527A.

48. Gardiner 1980: 28.

city-states were defeated. Every city had its gymnasium and stadium. In Ephesus itself a number of gymnasiums have been excavated.[49] A Greek boy from about the age of seven would spend a considerable portion of each day in the palaestra (a building for teaching wrestling) and gymnasium (an athletic ground for exercise, including a running track), exercising himself under trained supervision. The athletes would box, wrestle, or practice the pankration.[50] Most likely, Timothy's Greek father would have brought his son to the local gymnasium as part of his training.[51]

Paul acknowledges that such physical exercise has some benefit (for a brief time),[52] but spiritual exercise has much benefit for all times (4:8). **Training for godliness**, like training for war, should be a daily effort under supervision. Godliness is a way to live, dedicating oneself to please God in one's words and actions.[53] One's life is offered as worship to God. For example, Cornelius was a "godly" man who reverenced God, was generous, and prayed regularly (Acts 10:2). Paul is Timothy's supervisor, but only Timothy could do the work, "nourish," or train himself (4:6). Spiritual exercise would help Timothy now as he learned how and why to resist these ungodly storytellers and in the future to receive eternal salvation (4:7–8; Titus 1:1–2).

He could be sure of this promise because God is a living, saving God: **The word is trustworthy and worthy of all acceptance: for into this we labor and we strive, since we have hoped upon the living God, who is Savior of all people, especially of the faithful** (4:9–10). This is Paul's third authoritative accurate teaching from God in 1 Timothy expressed in a pithy statement that can be passed on to others as fully reliable.[54] As in 1 Timothy 1:15, the focus is on salvation. Whereas in 1 Timothy 1:15, Paul highlights the incarnate God and why Jesus was merciful with Paul, although he had persecuted Jesus' body on earth, the

---

49. Murphy-O'Connor 2008: 178.

50. Gardiner 1980: 46–47, 72, 84. The pankration is a type of wrestling where almost any means were allowed (212).

51. Ironically, during the era of Antiochus Epiphanes, promoting the building of a gymnasium in Jerusalem was one of the outrageous acts that spurred the Jewish rebellion (1 Macc 1:13–15; 4 Macc 4:15–20).

52. E.g., Jas 4:14; Thayer, 443.

53. See Titus 1:1; a way to live (1 Tim 2:2; Titus 2:12); a type of teaching or words (1 Tim 6:3); the opposite is "profane" (1 Tim 4:7). Godliness is not abstinence (1 Tim 4:3–4) but self-control (Kelly 1963: 99).

54. See 1 Tim 1:15; 3:1; Titus 3:8.

church (1:13-14), in 4:10, Paul highlights God as judge, encouraging Timothy to persevere in his desire to please God in his words and actions because Timothy's ultimate judge is God, who is living and a savior. Paul continues to use the imagery of exercise (**we labor** [*kopiaō*] **and we strive** [*agōnizomai*]). *Kopiaō* means **to labor** but especially "with wearisome effort."[55] Paul previously had exhorted the elders at Ephesus to follow his example and *to work hard* to supply their own physical needs and those of needy people.[56] Mary is another example of a hard worker (Rom 16:6). All coworkers should work hard because all ministry (like farming) is hard work.[57] Timothy should work hard, trusting God, because God his savior is reliable.[58]

Agōnizomai (**strive**, 4:10) is even more so a word for athletics signifying "*contend for a prize*, esp. in the public games" or "fight."[59] Greeks and Romans would exercise in order eventually to contend for a prize at a public festival.[60] Even before the contest, competitors had to arrive a month early having trained at least ten months before coming. But, Timothy's prize was not dependent on a severe mortal judge,[61] but on the merciful living Savior, who favored his own people.[62]

TIMOTHY SHOULD BECOME AN EXAMPLE (4:11—5:2)

Paul now provides an internal summary for Timothy: **Continue commanding these things and continue teaching** (4:11). *Parangellō* and *didaskō* are synonyms.[63] *Parangellō* signifies "*to transmit a message along from one to another*,"[64] bringing out the sense that what Timothy has learned from Paul he is to pass on (or transmit) to the church. *Parangellō* and its noun *parangelia*, as well as **command**,[65] may have the sense of

---

55. Thayer, 355; LSJ, 978. E.g., Matt 11:28; Luke 5:5; John 4:6; 1 Cor 4:12; Rev 2:3.
56. Acts 20:33-35; Eph 4:28.
57. 1 Cor 16:16; Phil 2:16; Col 1:29; 1 Thess 5:12; 2 Tim 2:6.
58. 1 Tim 4:10; 1 Cor 15:10; Col 1:29. Those who work at teaching should be recompensed extra for their labor (2 Tim 5:17).
59. LSJ, 18-19.
60. See 1 Cor 9:25; *OCD*, 28.
61. Gardiner 1980: 223-24.
62. 1 Tim 4:10. See 1 Tim 1:1; 2:3-4.
63. Thus they function as a pleonasm.
64. Thayer, 479; LSJ, 1306.
65. E.g., Matt 15:35.

"instruct" or "explain," as Jesus did, after commanding one leper to be healed, then giving him further instructions: "to tell no one. 'Go,' he said, 'and show yourself to the priest, and, as Moses commanded, make an offering for your cleansing, for a testimony to them.'"[66]

Teach (*didaskō*, 4:11) has a causative sense, to cause to learn.[67] It implies not only explanation but repetition because the ancients, including the Jews, taught mainly by repetition. In the mishnah stage of education (literally, "to repeat"), the Beth-Talmud, teachers would repeat aloud texts again and again (at least four times) and pupils would repeat again and again. For instance, Rabbi Eliezer ben Hyrkanos said: "A man's duty is to repeat (a passage) to his pupil four times" (*b. ʿErub.* 54b), and Hillel adds: "The man who repeats his chapter a hundred times is not to be compared with the man who repeats it one hundred and one times" (*b. Ḥag.* 9b). In the advanced talmud stage of "learning," the Beth Ha-Midrash, the student memorized texts and studied their meanings.[68] The same type of practice continued even with the early church fathers. Irenaeus observed how Polycarp "repeated" the words of John and others from "memory" and also "proclaimed" them in "complete harmony with Scripture" (Eusebius, *Hist. eccl.* 5.20.6). Thus, Timothy too was not simply to command the female and male believers at Ephesus but to instruct them and to teach them about wrong and correct doctrine and behavior.

Paul continues with advice for Timothy about how to live in a godly way as a leader among the believers at Ephesus. To begin, **let no one despise your youth, instead keep on becoming an example to the ones believing in word, in conduct, in love, in faith, in purity** (4:12). Paul commands Timothy that his youth is not to be **despised**.[69] He uses the same root (*phroneō*, "to form or hold an opinion") that he used with Titus.[70] However, in 1 Timothy he uses a different prefix (*kata*, "down," vs. *peri*, "around"). *Kata* clearly gives the verb a negative connotation:

---

66. Luke 5:13–14 NRSV. See also 1 Tim 1:3–5; 5:7; 6:13–17; Acts 1:4–5; Matt 10:5; 1 Cor 7:10–11; 11:17.

67. Verbs terminating in *-skō* generally are inchoative or causative (Robertson 1934: 150; see also 2:12).

68. For example, Resh Laqish went to Eleazar three days to repeat a tradition and three months to penetrate the meaning and usage of the material (*b. Yebam.* 72b). See Gerhardsson 1961: 115, 117, 134.

69. See 1 Tim 1:2 on "Timothy."

70. See Titus 2:15.

to hold a negative opinion, look down on, be opinionated against.[71] The cause (**your youth**)[72] of the negative opinion is emphasized by being placed before the verb (**despise**). Timothy may have been twenty-seven at this time.[73] According to the *Mishnah*, twenty was the age to pursue a calling and thirty for authority (*m. 'Abot* 5:21). *Neotēs* refers especially to youth of a "military or athletic age,"[74] which fits well with the previous athletic images (1:18; 4:7–8, 10). The manner of responding to negative opinions of his youth was not by speech (reprimanding such views) but by **example**. A *typos* was a pattern or model "in conformity to which a thing must be made," an archetype.[75] Paul had already referred to himself as an "example" or prototype (*hypotypōsis*)[76] of a sinner saved from punishment by Christ Jesus showing compassion toward him by forgiving him. Paul has used Timothy as a model in other letters: with himself, of believers who persevere despite suffering and who work.[77] Paul had sent Timothy to Corinth as a model of someone who shares in Christ's sufferings.[78] Even as an adolescent, Timothy saw Paul in his hometown of Lystra not only heal the sick but also be stoned and dragged outside the city by those supposing him to be dead. Probably Timothy, Eunice, and other disciples gathered around the "dead" Paul. What a profound example of the persecution Christians could receive as a result of believing in the crucified Messiah![79] And yet, Timothy agreed to accompany Paul and Silas in ministry when they later returned to Lystra (Acts 16:1–3).

Both Timothy and Titus were to be "models" (**example**, 4:12). Timothy was to be a model for all believers, first in orthodoxy (right doctrine), then conduct.[80] *Anastrophē* properly refers to "*walk*" or "*manner of life*,

71. Robertson 1934: 606–607, 617.

72. Goliath, the Philistine, disdained David because he was a youth, yet David was victorious because he fought in the name of the Lord of hosts (1 Sam 17:42–45).

73. Overstreet 2009: 561. Others round up his age to up to forty: Lock 1924: 52; Towner 2006: 314.

74. LSJ, 1170.

75. Thayer, 632; LSJ, 1835.

76. See 1 Tim 1:16.

77. Phil 1:1; 3:11–19; 2 Thess 3:7–12.

78. 1 Cor 4:10–17; Spencer 1989.

79. Acts 14:19–20; 1 Thess 1:1, 6–8; 1 Cor 1:23.

80. See Titus 2:7–8. Five nouns are listed in a perfect parallel anaphora structure using asyndeton. Asyndeton omits conjunction(s) in a series of phrases. In this anaphora *en* precedes every phrase (Spencer 1998b: 187–88). Although the repetition presents each quality as equal in importance to the other traits, **word** is listed first

behavior, conduct."[81] One's behavior may be a negative[82] or a positive[83] example. Here Paul wants Timothy to be a positive example. **Conduct** balances with **word**. **Conduct** is a general term that includes the more specific attributes to follow.[84] Living out of the faith is always important but especially in a situation where one is conscious of nonbelievers' potential criticisms.[85]

Why does Paul choose **love, faith,** and **purity**? **Love** is the trait first highlighted as the motivating goal of Paul's instructions.[86] **Faith** and love are intertwined together because love is a reflection of one's faith in Christ. **Purity** or "chastity" (*hagneia*) is highlighted for Timothy probably because he is a young man, possibly single, working with young women (1 Tim 5:2).[87] This same term and its corresponding verb (*hagnizō*) were used in the Old and New Testaments for ceremonial purification.[88] Although used to describe the purification of Levite priests[89] and the Israelite people in general,[90] it was also used of the Nazirite vow to be "set apart" for a specified time limit by abstaining from wine and all products of grapes, from haircuts, and from approaching any dead bodies (Num 6:2–8). Timothy himself seems to have abstained from wine (1 Tim 5:23). *Hagneia* was also used to describe the permanent purity which Jesus as the slain "lamb" brought and also holiness as the opposite of sin.[91] In 1 Timothy 4:12, *hagneia* might then serve as a summary attribute of the whole list encouraging Timothy to lead a purified and dedicated life which included purity of behavior (5:2) and self instruction

---

because heterodox teaching and learning is the primary problem at Ephesus that Paul left Timothy to address (1:3–4).

81. Thayer, 42; BDAG, 73.

82. E.g., Gal 1:13; Eph 4:22; 1 Pet 1:18; 2 Pet 2:7.

83. E.g., 1 Tim 3:15 (verb *anastrephō*); 2 Cor 1:12 (verb); Jas 3:13; 1 Pet 1:15; 2 Pet 3:11.

84. "Word" and "conduct" are placed together also in Heb 13:7 to refer to leaders, whom the readers are exhorted to imitate.

85. See 1 Tim 3:2; Titus 1:6; 1 Pet 2:12; 3:1–2, 16.

86. See 1 Tim 1:5.

87. See Titus 2:5.

88. E.g., Acts 21:24, 26; John 11:55.

89. Num 8:21; 1 Chr 15:12.

90. Exod 19:10; Num 11:18.

91. Jas 4:8; 1 Pet 1:19–22; 1 John 3:3. Sexual connotations may be found in the root *hagnos* "pure" (Titus 2:5; 2 Cor 11:2) (Mounce 2000: 260). See also 1 Thess 4:3–8; Matt 5:27–28.

(4:13, 16): **While I am coming, keep on occupying yourself in reading, in encouragement, in teaching** (4:13).

Paul again refers to time (**while I am coming**), as he did earlier ("while hoping to come to you shortly," 3:14, and "as I urged you to remain longer while I was going into Macedonia," 1:3). Apparently, Timothy was eager for Paul to join him there in Ephesus, but Paul had to encourage him to wait. In the meantime, Timothy must find a way to deal with some people at Ephesus who have been **occupying** themselves (*prosechō*)[92] in wrong ways: with myths and endless genealogies which give rise to speculations, drinking a lot of wine, with deceitful spirits and demonic teachings (1:4; 3:8; 4:1). In contrast, they should have been occupying themselves with "stewardship" of God's household (1:4). In 4:13, Paul presents three equally important ways for Timothy to occupy his time. The first way is to **read**. *Anagnōsis* (noun) and *anaginōskō* (verb) usually referred to the reading of the Old Testament, but it could include reading of an inscription (John 19:20) or of an authoritative letter.[93] It could be a public reading of Scripture in a service[94] or the recitation of Scripture (Luke 10:26) or a private reading of Scripture (Acts 8:28-33). The difference between public and private reading was slight since even private reading was done out loud.[95] Thus, in the context of 1 Timothy 4:11–12, **reading** probably refers to both private and public reading of Scripture, which might include Paul's letters.[96] Since Timothy was to be an example (4:12), he would want to exemplify what he will teach others to do (4:11).[97]

Encouragement (*paraklēsis, parakaleō*) is a regular part of the ministry of elders and pastoral leaders.[98] It can refer to appealing to (as opposed to commanding or rebuking)[99] someone to do something good or to change behavior. It can also include support of someone. Both in

---

92. See 1 Tim 4:1.
93. Acts 15:31; 23:34; 2 Cor 1:13; Eph 3:4; Col 4:16; 1 Thess 5:27; Rev 1:3.
94. Acts 13:15, 27; 2 Cor 3:14–15; Luke 4:16; Deut 31:11–12; Josh 8:34–35; Neh 8:7–8.
95. Philip could hear the Ethiopian treasurer reading Isaiah (Acts 8:30).
96. Col 4:16; 1 Thess 2:13; 5:27.
97. In 2 Tim 3:15–17 he will give a fuller description of the value of Scripture.
98. See Titus 2:15; Titus 1:9; 2:6; 1 Tim 6:2.
99. 1 Tim 5:1; 1 Cor 16:12.

4:13 and 6:2, it is distinguished from **teaching**,[100] although it is closely related to it.

Paul continues with another illustration of how to become an example to others: **Do not neglect the spiritual gift in you, which was given to you through prophecy accompanied by laying on of hands of the council of elders** (4:14). Most likely the council of elders prayed for Timothy to receive a **spiritual gift** (*charisma*) which (in his case) was the gift of evangelism (2 Tim 4:5). An evangelist, a minister of the word (Eph 4:11-12), was a messenger of God's good news of salvation who would preach, baptize, and instruct people in the basics of faith. The only other person called an evangelist was Philip.[101] In Acts we first see Timothy evangelizing as part of Paul's team of coworkers who join him as they fulfill God's vision to reach Macedonia.[102] *Charisma* has the same root as *charis* ("joy").[103] God as one who gives joy and delights in his children gives proofs or benefits of God's joy. These gifts give joy to others by strengthening them. They are given through the triune God to benefit the body.[104] Although two other spiritual gifts have been mentioned in 4:13 (encouragement [Rom 12:8] and teaching [1 Cor 12:28-29]), evangelism is Timothy's special gift. Every Christian may do some aspect of every spiritual gift, but he/she will be especially gifted in one or two areas. For instance, although Paul certainly proclaimed the good news,[105] he calls himself an "apostle" and "teacher" as well as "preacher" (1 Tim 2:7), but not an "evangelist." Therefore, he usually did not baptize people (1 Cor 1:14-17), as an evangelist would. In both 1 Timothy 4:14 and 2 Timothy 1:6 *charisma* are mentioned and the **laying on of hands**.[106] In 4:14,

---

100. See 1 Tim 4:11.

101. Acts 6:5; 8:4-12; 21:8.

102. Paul, Timothy, Luke, Silas (Acts 15:40-16:1, 9-10). In the N.T., the commission to preach good news goes back to the angel Gabriel sent by God, Jesus, and the Twelve (Luke 1:19; 4:18; 9:1-6; 20:1).

103. Thayer, 665, 667.

104. 1 Cor 12:4-11; Eph 4:7-12; 2 Tim 1:6; 1 Pet 4:10-11.

105. Acts 20:24; Rom 15:20; 1 Cor 15:1; 2 Cor 11:7.

106. Timothy himself would be **laying his hands** on others, but he is not to do so hastily (1 Tim 5:22). Laying on of hands was also a symbolic act during occasions for healing (Matt 9:18, 25; Mark 6:5; 7:32; 8:23, 25; Luke 4:40; 13:13; Acts 9:12, 17; 28:8), for blessing (Matt 19:13-15; Mark 10:16; Deut 34:9), and for asking for the indwelling Holy Spirit (Acts 8:17-19; 19:6, 17), but it was never magic. See Spencer 1985: 97-98. In the O.T., the people laid their hands on the Levites as a symbol of their being set aside to represent the people (Num 8:10-13). See also Irwin 2008: 125.

Paul commands Timothy not to **neglect** the gift, whereas in 2 Timothy 1:6, he is told to "rekindle" the gift. The difference though is whether the hands are those of the **council of elders** (1 Tim 4:14) or of Paul (2 Tim 1:6). Also, 1 Timothy refers to **prophecies** (4:14; 1:18) but 2 Timothy 1:6 does not. Does Paul, then, refer to the same or different events? It could be the same event[107] if Paul were part of the council of elders and for some reason he decides to highlight his personal part in the process in 2 Timothy.[108]

Paul further explains how Timothy is to be an example (4:12): **Keep on practicing these things, live among these, that your progress may be visible to all** (4:15). What Paul has urged Timothy to do, he must keep on **practicing** or "cultivating"[109] (as opposed to neglecting, 4:14). Paul states his commands in a positive way in 4:13 ("keep on occupying yourself"), in a negative way in verse 14 ("do not neglect"),[110] and again in a positive way (**keep practicing**, 4:15). Therefore, the positive is accentuated. Timothy is to take care (*meletaō*) to do all Paul has exhorted in 4:12–13 (become an example, pay attention to reading, encouragement, teaching, not neglect spiritual gift). This verb is "used by the Greeks of

---

107. E.g., Robertson 1931: 581 vs. Towner 2006: 325 (2 Tim 1:6 is an earlier event).

108. Normally, a church has a group of elders. Using a group of elders to lead has a long history in Judaism. (See Titus 1:5; 1 Tim 3:2.) The *presbuterion* continued at Ephesus even to the second century (Ignatius, *Eph.* 2:2; 4:1; 20:2). The Sanhedrin in Jerusalem (which consisted of high priests and scribes) was also called the **council of elders** (*presbuterion*) (Luke 22:66; Acts 22:5.) In the N.T., they dealt with judicial questions. Moses had 70–72 elders to help him with judicial questions in Israel. The **laying on of hands** was a symbolic act, accompanied by prayer, to commission people to a specific task (Acts 6:6; 13:3). When God commanded Moses to commission Joshua as his successor, Joshua already was indwelt by the Holy Spirit before the commissioning (Num 27:18–23). Joshua had previously been chosen by God as Moses' successor but the commissioning was now to be done before the congregation to indicate God's approval of Joshua's role. Also in Acts 13:2–3, the Holy Spirit commands Barnabas and Saul be set apart for a work before they are commissioned by prayer and the laying on of hands. When the elders commissioned Timothy, they asked God to give or to confirm his spiritual gift of evangelism as a blessing for his ministry.

109. Spencer 1998b: 126–27. Because of the close relationship between Paul and Timothy, Paul can use the imperative thirteen times in only eighteen verses or nine sentences. The imperatives are: "decline," "train," 4:7; "command," "teach," 4:11; "despise," "become," 4:12; "occupy," 4:13; "do not neglect," 4:14; "practice," "be," 4:15; "pay attention to," "persevere," 4:16; "appeal," 5:1. Even 5:3 begins with an imperative: "honor," 5:3.

110. E.g., Matt 22:5.

the meditative pondering and the practice of orators and rhetoricians."[111] But, it was also used for meditative pondering in the Old Testament, for example, "in his law *will he meditate* day and night" (Ps 1:2).[112] Wisdom "meditates, speaks, and practices" truth, not falsehoods.[113] Thus, *meletaō* in 4:15 includes an inward aspect of "meditative pondering" as well as practice. Paul intensifies this inward aspect in the next phrase, which literally is: "among these things—be" ("exist, **live**, stay," 4:15). Paul had told the Athenians at the Areopagus that God is not far from us because "in him we are living and we are moving and we are being" (Acts 17:28). In 1 Timothy, Paul wants Timothy not just to *do* what Paul asks, but to *be*, to have all these previous commands become a part of who he is, his very being.[114] Not that Timothy's example is perfect, but rather that he progresses in his spiritual life, becoming a model in word, conduct, love, faith, purity, reading, encouragement, teaching, use of spiritual gift (4:12-14). In a similar way, even Jesus as an adolescent **progressed** (*prokoptō*) in wisdom (Luke 2:52) and Paul "advanced" in Judaism (Gal 1:14).[115] What is inward will become outward or **visible to all** (4:6, 12, 15).

Paul then concludes this section of personal advice to Timothy: **Keep on paying attention to yourself and to the teaching, persevere in them; for doing this, also you will save yourself and the ones hearing you** (4:16). Timothy's focus should be dual: to himself and to the content and practice of Christian teaching. He is to **persevere** in these commands. The result will be dual: to **save** himself[116] and to save his listeners (4:16). Salvation is a major theme in this letter. God is the Savior who desires all to be saved, especially believers including Timothy and the church at Ephesus.[117] Will they remain on the narrow road that leads

---

111. Thayer, 396; e.g., Arrian, *Epict. diss.* II. 1.29.

112. See also LXX Pss 34:28; 36:30; 62:6; 70:24; 76:6, 12; 118:16, 47, 70, 117, 148; 142:5; Sir 6:37; 14:20.

113. Prov 8:7; 11:2; 24:2.

114. E.g., Exod 24:12 ("be" in God's presence); Prov 23:17 ("be" in fear of the Lord); Matt 2:13 ("be" in a place).

115. This same sense of maturing progress may be found in Phil 1:25; Col 1:28.

116. Also 1 Cor 9:27.

117. See 1 Tim 1:15; 2:3-4; 4:9-10; Titus 3:4-5.

to eternal life?[118] Even Timothy is not exempt from the temptation of the opponents.[119]

Fusing the Horizons: Progress in the Christian Life

In George MacDonald's novel, *The Princess and Curdie*, the Grandmother explains to Curdie:

> When you met your father on the hill to-night, you stood and spoke together on the same spot; and although one of you was going up and the other coming down, at a little distance no one could have told which was bound in one direction and which in the other. Just so two people may be at the same spot in manners and behaviour, and yet one may be getting better and the other worse, which is just the greatest of all differences that could possibly exist between them.[120]

Paul has urged Timothy to progress on becoming a positive model in right doctrine, conduct, love, faith, purity, reading, encouragement, teaching, and in use of his spiritual gift. How do contemporary pastors "progress" in their lives as Christians?

Rev. Dr. William David Spencer[121] uses reading the Bible and praying each morning as a framework to orient the rest of the day. Even a brief Bible reading, especially if systematic, affects one's ability to think more from God's perspective: "That is one thing we can learn from the Lord's prayer." It begins by focusing on God[122] ("Father, hallowed be your name. Let your kingdom come," Luke 11:2). Thus, "when you encounter daily experiences, the framework is set which colors the way one reacts."

Rev. Dr. Leslie McKinney[123] progresses in her Christian life by drawing support from community. This support base can be other pastors, a spiritual director, a group of women or men, or a few good friends. Among such people, pastors can share their hearts and those things with which they struggle: "It is really important to process feelings if you want to be healthy

---

118. Matt 7:13–14; 2 Cor 2:15–16.
119. Mounce 2000: 263.
120. MacDonald 1949: 66 (ch. 8).
121. Appreciation to the input of my colleagues in ministry. William David Spencer, interview with author, July 11, 2011.
122. See also Spencer 1990b: 34–35.
123. Leslie McKinney, telephone conversation with author, July 12, 2011.

and whole."¹²⁴ Inner issues need to be worked on so as to gain confidence in oneself to be better able to please God and not simply other people. Pastors need to protect themselves and be honest with themselves and, humbly, to seek help when necessary. Prayer and God's word are also important in order to draw close to God, to cultivate a listening ear for God's direction, and to live out God's word.

The Rev. Paul Bricker¹²⁵ cultivates his gift of evangelism by following the book of Jude because it teaches evangelism at its heart. For example, one must not "contend for the faith" (Jude 3) by being contentious. Rather, evangelists must keep themselves in the love of God (v. 21). Three participles explain how to keep oneself in God's love: "building yourselves up in your most holy faith," "praying in the Holy Spirit," and "waiting for the mercy of our Lord Jesus Christ for eternal life" (vv. 20–21). Out of this heart of love, the evangelist has mercy on those who are wavering and saves others by snatching them out of the fire, while even hating their "defiled tunics" (sins) (vv. 22–23).¹²⁶ The challenge to keep oneself in God's love includes battling against false thoughts. Jude, like Timothy, is trying to reach those who are apostate from the church. The evangelist is a host who offers God's love.

Paul continues with commands to Timothy but now more focused on his role as a pastor at Ephesus: **You should not chastise an elder but appeal to him as a father, younger ones (males) as brothers, elders (females) as mothers, younger ones (females) as sisters in all purity** (5:1–2). Paul concludes his personal admonitions to Timothy with observations on how to relate to others of different ages and gender. *Epiplēssō* has a basic physical significance (literally, *"to strike upon, beat upon"*), which developed into the metaphorical *"punish*, chastise, esp. with words, *rebuke, reprove"*¹²⁷ (5:1). Timothy should not reprimand but instead **appeal** to (*parakaleō*) (not command) people to do something good, to watch out for wrong teaching and behavior, and to change behavior.¹²⁸

124. See also McKinney 2008.
125. Paul Bricker, telephone conversation with author, July 12, 2011.
126. Zech 8:23 is another helpful passage showing that people are attracted to believers if they observe that "God is with you."
127. LSJ, 651; Thayer, 241; e.g., Rev 8:12.
128. See 1 Tim 4:13; Titus 2:15.

For ancient Jews, Greeks, and Romans, **elders** were highly esteemed.[129] *The Mishnah* recommends "at thirty for authority, at forty for discernment, at fifty for counsel, at sixty to be an elder" (*m. 'Abot* 5:21). According to Overstreet, an **elder** (*presbytēs*) is in the sixth of the seven stages of life when someone is fifty through fifty-six years of age, when gray hairs appear. A *gerōn* is in the final stage of life between sixty and eighty.[130] The elders are known for their good counsel (1 Kgs 12:6–15).[131] Being old is an esteemed stage of life: "Grey hair is a crown of splendor; it is attained in the way of righteousness."[132] Thus, an Old Testament law commanded: "Stand up in the presence of the aged, show respect for the elderly (*presbyteros*) and revere your God. I am the Lord" (Lev 19:32 TNIV). If Timothy was supposed to listen to the elders, as if they were his fathers and mothers (Prov 23:22), what should he do when they had to listen to him?[133] He was to treat them and all in the church with the deference and love he would use for his own father and mother and brother and sister.[134]

The **young** (*neos*, 5:2) would be people of the same age as Timothy,[135] probably between twenty-one to twenty-eight.[136] Thus, Timothy's greatest challenge would be relating to those definitely older than he and, most likely, in positions of authority (**elders**) and those of his own age who might not respect an equal. The metaphor of a family would fit all of them.[137]

---

129. See Titus 2:2. E.g., Plato, *Leg.* 9. 879B-C: "The view that should be held by everyone—man, woman and child—is this, that the older is greatly more revered than the younger . . . whosoever, man or woman, exceeds himself in age by twenty years he shall regard as a father or a mother" (Cicero, *Off.* 1.34.122).

130. Overstreet 2009: 545–46, 550, 563.

131. Job 32:4 vs. Lam 5:12.

132. Prov 16:31 TNIV. See also Prov 20:29.

133. *Presbuteros* is also used in Titus 1:5 and throughout 1 Tim 5:1, 2, 17, 19.

134. Children were to honor their own father and mother (Exod 20:12). Paul treated congregations as a father would his own children (1 Thess 2:11–12).

135. See 1 Tim 4:12 and Titus 1:5.

136. Overstreet 2009: 558.

137. See 1 Tim 4:6.

1 TIMOTHY 5:3—6:2
Church Leaders Should Be Honored and Justly Treated

Concluding on how to treat young women, Paul now returns again to the theme of church leaders but more specifically women ministering in the church.

TRUE WIDOWS AND YOUNGER WIDOWS (5:3–16)

Widows were potentially needy and potentially ministers in the church: **Keep on honoring widows, the ones truly widows** (5:3). With these words, Paul begins an extended discussion on widows (5:3–16=9 sentences), going back and forth between his explanations about those who are and are not "in reality" or **truly** widows so that the church may not be open to attack. Earlier Paul had implied that elders are to be respected and not chastised (5:1) Now he goes on to describe a more specific type of **honor** for elders—honoring them by showing their value in money.[1] *Timaō* is used in the Old and New Testaments for God's command to "honor your father and your mother."[2] **Honor** may refer to words of respect,[3] but it may also refer to actions[4] and these actions may also include physical provisions.[5] Since some widows were using the **honor** given them to live luxuriously, while their families were not providing for them (5:4, 6), **honor** in this passage includes providing for physical needs. The "real" widows were not simply being taken care of, they were also doing a job: praying (5:5), similar to the elders who were laboring in "teaching the word" (5:17). Jesus interpreted the Old Testament com-

---

1. *Timaō* (verb) means "*to fix the value*" and *timē* (noun) "*a valuing by which the price is fixed*" from *tiō* "to estimate, honor" (Thayer, 624).
2. E.g., Exod 20:12; Deut 5:16; Matt 15:4; 19:19; Mark 7:10; 10:19; Luke 18:20.
3. Matt 15:8; Mark 7:6; John 5:23; 1 Tim 1:17; 6:1; 1 Pet 2:17.
4. John 8:49; 12:26.
5. Matt 27:6, 9; Acts 4:34; 5:2–3; 7:16; 28:10.

mandment to **honor** one's parents to include taking care of them physically (Matt 15:3-6; Mark 7:9-13). Paul seems to follow this mandate: **But if some widow has children or grandchildren, let them keep on learning to show piety first to their own household and to keep on giving back to the parents; for this is pleasing before God** (5:4).

Taking care of one's **parents** is an aspect of "godliness" (**to show piety**, *eusebeō*), a way to live, dedicating oneself to please God in one's words and actions.[6] Here the object of such worship of God is shown in one's own **household**. How can one say one loves God, whom one has not seen, when one cannot love one's own family members, whom one can see (1 John 4:20)?

While Jesus and Paul insist that **children or grandchildren** (5:4) should take care of fathers and mothers or grandmothers as a way to thank them for having taken care of them, the Jewish rabbinic laws placed the responsibility on the heirs of the former husband, unless they reimbursed the widow her dowry. The heirs of the deceased husband legally were required to maintain the widow in the house they had inherited (*m. Ketub.* 4:12; 12:3-4). Jesus broadened all these teachings by having his disciple John "adopt" Jesus' mother Mary as his own mother (John 19:26-27). In this manner, Jesus created a new family of believers who would love one another, by being responsible for one another.

A **real** widow had no family to provide for her: **But the real widow who is also left alone has hoped on God and continues in prayers for needs and reverent prayers by night and by day, but the one living luxuriously has died** (5:5-6). The verb form (*chēreuō*) of **widow** (*chēra*) means "*to be without*."[7] In a patriarchal society, where a widow did not inherit her husband's property, she would be without sufficient financial resources.[8] Even those widows who had property were often robbed, even by religious leaders. Jesus denounced those scribes who, while seeking places of honor in synagogues and banquets, "devour widows' houses" (Luke 20:46-47). An early document recounts how Syrion of Thraso, the owner of a flock of sheep which the husband of Aurelia Artemis had tended, at the very funeral, burst into her house to seize the children's property and the sixty sheep and goats belonging to the deceased

---

6. See 1 Tim 4:7; 2:2; Titus 1:1.

7. LSJ, 1990.

8. One estimate is widows comprised 30% of women in the ancient world (Winter 2003: 124). In the third century in Rome, the church supported over 1500 widows and persons in distress (Eusebius, *Hist. eccl.* 6. 43 [11]).

husband.[9] The Old Testament has numerous laws and prophetic messages showing God's special concern for widows. Widows are an example of a group of people easily oppressed who should have justice. God who is "great and strong and awesome, who is not partial" "executes justice for stranger and orphan and widow" (Deut 10:17-18).[10] About thirty years earlier, the church had already been presented with the problem of needy widows (Acts 6:1-6). Tabitha (Dorcas) of Joppa had become renowned because she devoted herself to making clothing for the widows of her city (Acts 9:36-41). Paul's solution is to pay certain widows to do a prayer ministry, thereby resolving a financial need and creating an opportunity to advance God's kingdom.

These are the characteristics of a "real" versus a "false" widow:

Real Widow	*False Widow*
1. left alone, has hoped on God (5:5)	1. has children or grandchildren who should provide (5:4, 8, 16)
2. continues in prayers night and day (v.5)	2. lives luxuriously (v. 6) Cf. 1 Tim 3:3, 8; Titus 1:7
3. is not open to attack (v. 7) Cf. 1 Tim 3:2	3. some have turned away after Satan (v. 15)
4. 60+ years of age (v. 9) Cf. Titus 1:5, 7	4. younger than 60 (v. 9)
5. a one-man woman (v. 9) Cf. 1 Tim 3:2, 12	
6. bearing witness by good works (v. 10) (cf. Titus 1:8): Brought up children (cf. 1 Tim 3:4, 12), Showed hospitality (cf. 1 Tim 3:2), Washed feet of saints, Helped those being oppressed, Devoted herself to every good work	6. idle; goes around the households, speaking of that of which there is no need (5:13) (cf. 1 Tim 3:11; Titus 1:8)
7. made vow not to remarry (5:12)	7. might want to marry (5:11)

9. *NewDocs* 3:20.

10. David calls God the "Father of the orphans and judge of the widows," because God promises to protect, care, and vindicate them (Ps 67:5 LXX; Exod 22:22-24; Deut 14:28-29; 24:17-22; 26:12-13; 27:19; Ps 146:9; Ezek 22:7; Zech 7:9-10; Mal 3:5.) See Spencer & Spencer 1990b: 48-50. One of the reasons Israel and Judah were allowed by God to be defeated by Assyria and Babylon was because God's people did not "defend the orphan, plead for the widow" (Isa 1:17 NRSV). See also Isa 1:23; 10:1-2; Jer 7:5-7; 22:3.

Some of the attributes of a **real widow** were also required of overseers (*episkopos*) and ministers (*diakonos*), being: not open to attack, an elder, a one-man woman, bearing witness to good works, having brought up children, shown hospitality, not loving money, not slanderers, and having self-control.[11] Thus, a **real widow** has become a church leadership position, and, as such, was recognized by the later church, which recognized women deaconesses, widows, virgins, and elders.[12] McKenna summarizes: "The Order of Widows was the 'mother form' of the organized life of women in the service of the Church."[13]

The widows would devote themselves to **prayer** (5:5) of two types: prayer for needs (*deēsis*) and prayer devoted to God (*proseuchē*). The whole church is exhorted to include these types of prayers for everyone.[14] To be able to pray constantly, one would need to have the gift (*charisma*) of "faith," a faith exhibited in prayer.[15] In contrast to hoping on and praying to God is **living luxuriously**[16] (5:6), which proleptically has already resulted in not eternal life[17] but eternal **death**.

And these things command, that they may be not open to attack. But if any do not provide for their own and especially members of the household, (s)he has denied the faith and is worse than an unbelieving person (5:7-8). Timothy is to insist on the family's care of the widow

---

11. See 1 Tim 3:2. The overseer attributes that are missing are: being sober, wise, well-behaved, apt in teaching, not given to getting drunk, not pugnacious, gentle, not contentious, and not newly converted.

12. See 1 Tim 5:9. The positions of "virgin" and "monk" appear in the later church (Council of Chalcedon [A.D. 451], Canon 16); Ign., *Smyrn.* 13:1 "the virgins who are called widows" (Pol. *Phil.* 4.3). In *Const. ap.* (third to fourth century Syria) virgins, widows, and elders sat before the other women (2. 57). See also Belleville 2009: 96.

13. McKenna 1967: 35.

14. See 1 Tim 2:1. The Jewish community had a precedence in Anna the prophetess, a widow and an elder, who may have resided in the sector of the temple of Jerusalem where she "fasted and prayed (*deēsis*), worshiping night and day" (Luke 2:36-37). After seeing the child Jesus, she proclaimed Jesus as the Messiah to all who came (v. 38).

15. 1 Cor 12:9; Matt 21:21-22; Mark 11:22-24. See Spencer & Spencer 1990b: 92-94. The emphasis on prayer continued in the later church. Polycarp describes widows as "God's altar" who "pray unceasingly for everyone" (*Phil.* 4:3). Anna and Judith were also used as examples for widows in *Const. ap.* 3.7; 8.25.

16. The same verb is used of the wealthy landowners (Jas 5:5).

17. 1 Tim 4:8; 6:19. See Titus 1:2.

(5:7). Not only is it a godly act and an act of thanksgiving (5:4), but it is also one which will lessen attacks from outsiders (5:7).[18] Even non-Christian Greeks thought children should take care of their parents. For instance, Plato thought that citizens customarily treat parents "in awe and care and obedience" if they look for the favor of gods and humans (*Resp.* 5. 463D). **Denying the faith** is not only verbal, but it refers as well to action.[19] Widows, as a group of people who may be easily oppressed, are of special concern to God and serve as an apt synecdoche for the Christian faith. James, too, summarizes pure religion as "to look after orphans and widows in their distress, to keep oneself unstained from the world" (Jas 1:27).[20]

Paul now continues with positive specific attributes for a **real** widow: **Let a widow be enrolled having become no less than sixty years, a one-man woman, bearing witness by good works: if she brought up children, if she showed hospitality, if she washed the feet of holy ones, if she helped those being oppressed, if she followed after every good work** (5:9-10). At sixty, a woman would be well past the age for bearing children,[21] an "elder" according to the *Mishnah* (*m. 'Abot* 5:21) and for the Greeks and Romans in the final stage of life (*gerōn*).[22] The later church often fused the positions of widow (5:3) and deacon (3:11), requiring celibacy for both.[23] The ecumenical and generally recognized as authoritative Council of Chalcedon (A.D. 451) assumed a female "deaconess" not marry, but allowed her to be ordained at forty years of age (Canon 15). The Council in Trullo (A.D. 692) explained the reason for the lowering of the age was because the Council of Chalcedon "saw that the Church by divine grace had gone forth more powerful and robust and was advancing still further, and they saw the firmness and stability of the faithful in observing the divine commandments" (Canon 40).[24]

---

18. See 1 Tim 3:2, 7.

19. 2 Tim 2:12. See **honor**, 1 Tim 5:3.

20. See 1 Tim 5:5. The later church also highlighted concern for widows and orphans, the oppressed, as an important characteristic of orthodox believers (Ign. *Smyrn.* 6:2; *Barn.* 20:2).

21. Roman law encouraged the remarriage of young widows who were twenty to fifty (Winter 2003: 125, 137).

22. See 1 Tim 5:1-2, 5.

23. E.g., Basil defined the "catalogue of widows, that is, a deaconess being sixty years old" (Canon 24) (Mckenna 1967: 53).

24. In this canon, a **widow** is described as a "deaconess." *NewDocs* 2:144 notes an

Like the overseer and minister/deacon, the **real widow** was to be a **one-man woman** (5:9).²⁵ She, too, would have had to be faithful and devoted and focused only on her husband (not another man), when he had been alive. An ancient married man in his culture, unlike a married woman, was not considered an "adulterer" if he had sexual relations with a slave, concubine, or a prostitute. However, married women could be enticed into a lifestyle promulgated by some of the wealthy Roman society of the era of Emperor Augustus (after 44 B.C.) and later. Promiscuity was promoted by some poets and playwrights.²⁶ Ovid, for example, writes that a husband "is too countrified" who is hurt by an adulterous wife. Rome, he wrote, was founded on the adulterous practices of Mars, but Romulus and Remus were born without reproach. The husband should "cherish the friends your wife will bring."²⁷ Winter concludes that in Roman society "there was a pattern of sexual mores of women that openly defied the legislation on adultery and attendant issues."²⁸ Some in the later church questioned whether women should remarry at all after the husband's death.²⁹ In contrast, Paul assumes a wife can marry another man should her husband die (Rom 7:3; 1 Cor 7:39).

Although the Jews and Romans emphasized for women marriage and childrearing,³⁰ the ancients also had strong influences for being celibate or at least single. About ten years before 1 Timothy, Paul had encouraged widows and those who had never married to remain single, as he was. However, he explains, to marry is not sin (1 Cor 7:7–8, 28, 36, 40). Prayer warriors would certainly be needed during the forthcoming persecutions by Nero (A.D. 64–68) and the war in Jerusalem (A.D. 66–74). However, Paul summarized that remaining single is for the person who

---

epitaph for "Maria the deacon" which cites 1 Tim 5:10.

25. See 1 Tim 3:2, 12.
26. Winter 2003: 21–38, 129; Fantham 1994: 282–92.
27. Ovid, *Am.* 3.4.37–48; Winter 2003: 27.
28. Winter 2003: 30.
29. Montanists thought those who married a second time should be kept from communion of the church (Jerome 2010: 292). Tertullian decided that second marriages were a type of fornication (*Exh. cast.* ch. 9; *Const. ap.* 3.2). Jerome, however, called his *Mon.* "a heretical book about monogamy, which no one who reads the apostle will fail to know is contrary to the apostle" (Jerome 2010: 293). Tertullian wrote "We admit one marriage, just as we do one God," while the "heretics do away with marriages" (*Mon.* ch. 1). Even some Romans thought widows should not remarry (Pomeroy 1975: 161; Tertullian, *Exh. cast.* ch. 13).
30. Pomeroy 1975: 161, 164, 166.

"stands firm in his resolve, being under no necessity but having his own desire under control, and has determined in his own mind" to be single (1 Cor 7:37 NRSV). This four part set of conditions was not always adhered to when a young widow committed herself not to remarry. A subtle discussion of the benefits of being single in order to promote the Lord's affairs in a time of distress (1 Cor 7:26–34) was turned at Ephesus into always forbidding marriage (1 Tim 4:3).

A Greek or Roman woman might also think of the model of Artemis, renowned as the virgin goddess, lifting high the state of being single, but not necessarily of chastity. Sarah Pomeroy explains that Artemis and Athena "had never submitted to a monogamous marriage. Rather, as befits mother goddesses, they had enjoyed many consorts."[31] The Vestal Virgins in Rome, who tended the perpetual fire to Vesta, guardian of the hearth, were "the most severely disciplined, the most privileged, and the most highly honoured among Roman women."[32] These women who vowed to be virgins for thirty years were even exempt from the power of the *pater familias*. In the Greek pantheon, the most liberated goddesses were those not bound to male gods in a permanent relationship.[33] The widows of the church, although they had restrictions, also were "freed from the hierarchical dominance of either father or husband, freed from the demands of childbearing and rearing, freed even from pressing economic concerns."[34]

To restrict such enticements, Paul proposes four evidences of good actions (**good works**, 5:10)[35] toward her household, toward outsiders, toward the church, and toward society. *Teknotropheō* (5:10) (**to bring up children**) is the combination of *teknon* "child" and *trephō* (to nourish, attire, and nurse).[36] It includes providing for the physical and educational necessities for a child to mature. **Children** are a repeating theme in 1 Timothy. First, Paul calls Timothy his genuine **child** (*teknon*, 1:2, 18). Then, **The childbirth** (*teknogonia*) is the means for salvation (2:15). The treatment of one's own children becomes important as a helpful quality for leadership (3:4, 12). In chapter 5, the responsibility for children to

---

31. Pomeroy 1975: 6. See Introduction. The Setting. Ephesus and Artemis.
32. Scherer 1955: 67.
33. Pomeroy 1975: 150–54, 211–14.
34. Bassler 1984: 36.
35. See Titus 3:8, 14.
36. Thayer, 618; Matt 6:25–26; 25:37; Luke 4:16; 23:29; Acts 12:20.

take care of parents and grandparents is insisted upon (5:4). In contrast to the ascetic lifestyle, Paul normally promotes for the Christian a life of affirmation of marriage and food, receiving God's creational gifts with thanksgiving (4:3–4). Children, childbirth, marriage are all part of God's gifts that should be welcomed, since Paul's ultimate goal is to encourage the younger widows to go ahead and remarry (5:14), yet Paul as a single man also adopts, and is adopted into, the Christian household, childrearing and hospitality[37] being physical actions that demonstrate love for others. They are helpful to the outside community (5:7, 10), but they also are ways to worship God (be "godly" or show piety, 5:4). And, what about the widow who never could have children? Paul does not use the word for **bearing children** (*teknogoneō*, 5:14), but, rather, for **bringing up children** (*teknotropheō*, 5:10). Worshiping in a household church would afford opportunities to help all.

And, why must the **real widow** wash the feet of **holy ones** (5:10) or other believers? This passage appears to be a reference to Jesus' teaching to his disciples to imitate his own example when he washed their feet as a slave might have done (John 13:5–17). Washing of feet is a concrete example of humble service in the church.

Finally, even as a widow is an example of someone who might easily **be oppressed** (5:10), the widow herself should have been compassionate and helpful to others who have been oppressed: widows and orphans (Jas 1:27), Christians who have been persecuted,[38] including people such as Paul and Timothy, who greatly suffered when they ministered in Asia (2 Cor 1:4–9), Christians who have encountered difficulties in ministry (2 Cor 4:8; 7:5), and others who have suffered.[39]

For someone to dedicate their last years to continual prayer, their prayers would be more focused and empathetic if they had had a well-rounded life of service in the church and their commitment would have more integrity if they had become a mature Christian (and *not* "newly planted," 3:6). Paul closes this sentence by reiterating with emphasis that

---

37. See 1 Tim 3:2.

38. Matt 13:21; 24:9; John 16:33; Acts 11:19; 14:22; 20:23; Eph 3:13; 1 Thess 1:6; 3:3–4, 7; 2 Thess 1:4; Heb 10:33; 11:37.

39. Matt 24:21; John 16:21; Acts 7:10–11; Rom 5:3; 12:12; 1 Cor 7:28; 2 Cor 4:17; 6:4; 7:4; 8:2, 13; Phil 1:17; 4:14; Col 1:24. **Oppress** (*thlibō, thlipsis*), literally, refers to a "narrow" way or being crushed in a narrow way (Matt 7:14; Mark 3:9) and, metaphorically, to hardships, difficulties, persecutions, punishments (Rom 2:9), and internal (2 Cor 2:4) and external or general suffering.

the widow has not only done **good actions** witnessed by others, but has **followed after** ("devoted herself to") every **good work** (5:10).

In contrast to affirming mature Christian widows, Timothy needs to redirect younger widows: **But refuse younger widows; for when, wishing to marry, they might become arrogant against Christ, having condemnation, since they nullified the first promise; and, at the same time also, they learn to be idle, going around the households, and they learn to be not only idle but also talkers of falsehood and superstitious people, speaking the things of that of which there is no need** (5:11–13). In the same way as Timothy is to keep away from or guard against godless and old women's myths (4:7) and Titus is to keep away from divisive persons (Titus 3:10), Timothy is to keep widows younger than sixty from joining the widow's order of prayer (5:11). Otherwise, the ramifications could be serious. Paul provides two basic reasons: one has to do with breaking a vow (5:11–12), the second has to do with how the widows fill up the time, instead of constantly praying (5:13). Paul uses a rare word, *katastrēniaō* where the preposition *kata* ("down") intensifies the verb *strēniaō* ("to be wanton, to live luxuriously," "run riot," "of bulls running wild").[40] The younger widows exhibit a restlessness that becomes **arrogance** or "insolence" against Christ.[41] They had made a **promise** or "pledge"[42] not to marry again and by nullifying it are now condemned (5:12). Children who do not take care of parents deny the faith (5:8). Here the younger widows also deny their faith or **promise** made in trust (5:12).

Paul had told the Galatians that "no one can set aside or add to a human covenant that has been duly established" (3:15 NIV), but these widows were doing just that, setting aside the covenant they had made with Christ. Unlike the women (and men) who may have taken their vows lightly then (and now), for God, keeping a vow is very important: "Fulfill what you vow. It is better that you should not vow than that you

---

40. Thayer, 591; LSJ, 1654; BDAG, 949. *Const. ap.* 3.1 agrees the verb refers to not keeping a promise.

41. *Strēnos*, LSJ, 1654. *Katastrēniaō* (5:11) is often defined in physical terms (live luxuriously or sensually), "be governed by strong physical desire" (BDAG, 528), which may be the basis for the change of the younger widows now choosing to marry. However, since the object of the verb is **Christ**, the action is an offense against Christ, and is explained in the appositive clause **since they nullified the first promise** (v. 12), the definition of **arrogance** seems contextually appropriate or "to become or wax wanton" against someone (BDAG, 528).

42. LSJ, 1408.

should vow and not fulfill it. Do not let your mouth lead you into sin" (Eccl 5:5-6a NRSV) and "If you make a vow to the Lord your God, do not postpone fulfilling it; for the Lord your God will surely require it of you, and you would incur guilt" (Deut 23:21 NRSV). In the law, "every vow of a widow or of a divorced woman, by which she has bound herself, shall be binding upon her" (Num 30:9 NRSV). Paul himself claims he does not make his plans in a "fleshly" or "worldly" manner, "in the same breath" saying "Yes, yes" and "No, no" (2 Cor 1:17). The church cannot be **the pillar and bulwark of the truth** (1 Tim 3:15) if its members cannot be relied upon to keep their promises. God, who is the Truth, is fully reliable and thus those who obey God should be reliable as well.

The younger widows learn to be **idle** (5:13). They have no work to do. They are inactive (vs. 5:14). The "idle bellies" of the Cretans probably alludes to the pleasure-seeking Cretan lifestyle.[43] Inactivity is something the women **learn** by study (*manthanō*). It is not a natural instinct according to Paul. They **learn** how not to work as they go from house to house, in contrast to children who **learn** what it means to be godly as they take care of their parents (5:4), and in contrast to the women who **learn** in an affirmative manner about God the Savior (2:12)

Inactivity leads, then, to becoming **talkers of falsehoods** (*phluaros*, 5:13) **and superstitious people** or "workers of magic" (*periergos*).[44] *Phlyaros*, *phlyareō*, and *phlyarias* come from the root verb *phlyō* "'to boil up,' 'throw up bubbles' of water; and since bubbles are hollow and useless things, 'to indulge in empty and foolish talk.'"[45] The women are not so much talking in a "silly"[46] way, but rather in a non-productive manner, about an "empty" philosophy (4 Macc 5:10), without truth (like Diotrephes whose accusations against John and others were false and evil slander (3 John 10). Paul has already insisted that the female ministers not be slanderers but, rather, faithful (3:11), not women who do not keep their promises (5:12). Their talk should not be "devoid of truth."[47] That kind of talk is a "waste of time" (Titus 3:9).

Empty time and empty talk lead to curiosity about things **of which there is no need** (5:13). How can mere silliness and being a busybody

43. See Titus 1:12.

44. LSJ, 1371. "Workers of magic" is suggested by Kroeger 1992: 63, 203. See also Kelly 1963: 118.

45. Thayer, 655.

46. Cf., LSJ, 1946.

47. 1 Tim 1:6; Titus 1:10.

lead to **turning away after Satan** (5:15)? Most likely, the women were returning back to the addictive practice of magic. "Magic" (*periergos*) is the same Greek word in Acts 19:19 and 1 Timothy 5:13. As a plural noun, it refers to the "curious arts, magic."[48] Curiosity can be a positive or negative trait. It is negative when it leads inquiring minds[49] into searching out areas of which there is no necessity. The appeal of magic is to an unhealthy curiosity, a kind of spiritual meddling,[50] in contrast to the Magi whose study of the stars was a healthy and productive curiosity that led them to the incarnate God (Matt 2:1–11). At Crete there were also those who taught with words **devoid of truth** what was not **necessary** (Titus 1:10–11). Emptiness and curiosity can lead to Satan filling up the empty minds (5:15).[51] Were these women attracted to magic or were they actually practicing it? Verse 15 suggests that **some** but not all had **turned away after Satan**. Kroeger reminds us that "Magic spells, charms, enchantments, and curses were widely employed in the ancient world."[52] Possibly, the Jewish myths included some syncretistic version of the six Ephesian letters,[53] such as this prayer that combined elements of paganism, Christianity, and Judaism: "Of Jesus Christ, son of *Iaō*, quickly, quickly, heal! John, Son, Life."[54]

Paul ends with two summaries, one for the younger widows and one for the widows' family: **Therefore, I want younger ones to marry, to bear children, to rule their households, to give no occasion to the Adversary because of reproach; for already some have turned away after Satan. If any believer has widows, let her help them and not let the church be burdened, in order that it might help the real widows** (5:14–16). What can the younger widows do to keep from nullifying their vows, from being idle, and from being attracted to what is not necessary (5:11–13)? Paul recommends four interrelated actions to keep the women from condemnation from God and from the adversary. **Marrying** and having children are wholesome and to be affirmed as gifts from God. God blessed humankind by calling it to "bear fruit and become

---

48. LSJ, 1373.
49. LSJ, 1373.
50. Spencer 1995: 145.
51. See also Luke 11:24–26.
52. Kroeger 1992: 203.
53. Murphy-O'Connor 2008: 51.
54. Betz 1986: 323.

many and fill the earth and subdue it" (Gen 1:28). *Teknogoneō* (5:14) is the verb form of *teknogonia* (2:15). If salvation came through childbirth, then **bearing children** is a worthwhile activity. Paul is not requiring all women to get married and to bear children. Rather, those younger widows whose vow to pray has not worked need to be redirected to more fruitful activities. They are to **rule their households** (*oikodespoteō*).[55] The noun form (*oikodespotēs*) occurs several times in the Gospels, to refer to the owner of a farm (Matt 13:27), owner of a store (Matt 13:52), owner of a vineyard (Matt 20:1; 21:33), and person overseeing a household. The *oikodespotēs* has authority to hire laborers (Matt 20:1), to oversee tenants and servants,[56] to allow people in or out of the house (Luke 13:25), to receive guests,[57] and take responsibility for protecting the house (Matt 24:43). God (and Jesus) symbolically are *oikodespotēs*.[58]

Despotēs is a much stronger term than *kyrios*. A *despotēs* "denoted absolute ownership and uncontrolled power" and is "one who has legal control and authority over persons, such as subjects or slaves."[59] Hence, it is used for a human "master"[60] and metaphorically as a title for God.[61] Thus, the younger widows are indeed to become **rulers of their households**. "Keep house" (NASB)[62] or "take care of their homes" (TEV) are phrases not strong enough to translate this word. More accurate translations are "rule their houses" (NTME), "guide the house" (KJV), and "preside over a home" (NEB).[63] If women are explicitly told **to rule their households**, the interpreter has little exegetical basis to say 3:5, 12 supports male leadership and males being "heads" of households. Paul does not clarify exactly what is involved in the younger widows **ruling their**

---

55. *Oikodespoteō*, literally, is "to rule" (*despoteō*) "a house" (*oikos*). LSJ, 1204 renders *oikodespoteō* "to be master of a house or head of a family."

56. Matt 21:33; Luke 14:16–24.

57. Mark 14:14. Cf. 2 John 1, 10–11.

58. Matt 10:25; 20:1; 21:33–42.

59. Thayer, 130; BDAG, 220.

60. 1 Tim 6:1–2; Titus 2:9; 1 Pet 2:18.

61. Luke 2:29; Acts 4:24; Jude 4; Rev 6:10.

62. BDAG, 695.

63. "Manage their households" (CEV, NRSV) brings out some but not all of the aspects of being a "master."

households,[64] but Cohick summarizes: "Women did almost every type of work that was done by men."[65]

Who is the **Adversary**? Is it Satan or a human? Normally *antikeimai*, a verb used as a noun in the plural ("the ones opposing"), refers to human opponents of Jesus, Paul, and the disciples.[66] But, this reference in the singular may refer to the devil, since Satan is explicitly mentioned in 5:15 and the earlier reference seems to refer to the devil who condemns believers (3:6–7). Satan reproaches and then draws people away (5:14–15).

The **believer** (*pistē*, 5:16) has a feminine singular ending, as opposed to the plural in 5:4 for the believing children and grandchildren. Is this a feminine generic? Or, does it refer back to the woman who **rules her household** (5:14)[67] as the person responsible for alms (e.g., Prov 31:20)? One of the qualities needed to enter the widow's order was for the mature widow to have helped those being oppressed (5:10 has the same verb **helped,** *eparkeō*). Now, she who helped others is being helped by her own family. Financially caring for a widow is a "weight" (**burden,** 5:16) for a church to sustain. Paul therefore ends (as he began, 5:3) with the positive comment that it should be done for **real widows** (5:16).

Fusing the Horizons: Applying the Order of Widows to Today

The care of widows was a concern in ancient societies, but it still is a concern today even in industrialized societies. Women tend to live about seven years longer than men. In our local community, the planning board has to make decisions on whether to grant variances for construction. When having to choose between favoring the building of an apartment for a domestic employee or an apartment for an elderly mother, the latter is preferred and more easily granted. The order of widows appears to have developed into the Roman Catholic and Lutheran order of nuns in cloisters.[68] But, what about us in the Protestant church? Several aspects of the order of widows are pertinent: (1) should widows or elderly women who dedicate themselves to

---

64. See Titus 2:5.
65. Cohick 2009: 240. See ch. 7. See Titus 1:5.
66. Luke 13:14, 17; 21:15; 1 Cor 16:9; Phil 1:28. 2 Thess 2:3–4.
67. Robertson 1931: 587.
68. McKenna 1967: 111.

prayer be encouraged? (2) should they be paid? (3) should believers, women or men of any age, who dedicate themselves to prayer be paid?

Some traditional Korean churches invest in an apartment for widows who pray as a ministry and also oversee the upkeep of the entire church building. Originally, these widows were also the intermediaries between missionaries and the women.[69]

Today, in various African countries which are plagued by the devastation of men by the AIDS virus, widows are sometimes thrown out onto the streets, reduced to begging or, worse, prostitution. In response, some governments are pressuring Christian men to take on more wives to rescue such women, since Christian husbands are honest and moral and will provide for them. This official solution creates a great dilemma for Christian men. They want to obey the government and rescue these women, but both they and their churches oppose polygamy. In many countries, polygamous men are welcome to join Christian churches, but they may not hold office.

To this dilemma, reinstituting the order of widows speaks powerfully as a moral and viable solution. Together the entire church can provide for widows who may now serve the church as intercessors and ministers in their own right.[70] We are reminded that God can use believers no matter their age to advance God's kingdom. The church can take care of some physical needs while promoting prayer. If the prayer is a multidimensional one (for needs, worship, intercession, and thanksgiving) done in community, it can serve as a necessary aid to other ministry strategies.

Elders Leading Well (5:17–25)

Paul now moves on to a broader category of leadership (elders), but he still handles the issue of recompense: **The elders leading well—consider worthy of double honor, especially the ones laboring in teaching the word, for the Scripture says: "Do not muzzle a threshing ox" and "Worthy is the worker of his wages"** (5:17–18). So far Paul has dealt with three clear leadership groups: overseers (3:2), ministers (3:8, 11), and widows (5:3).

69. Chung Ho Lee, conversation with author, Nov. 17, 2011.

70. My husband, the Rev. Dr. William David Spencer, reached this solution after talking with many male and female African students at Gordon-Conwell Theological Seminary/Boston about the effects of the AIDS virus on various African churches and their mission.

Elders (*presbyteros, presbytera*) have been mentioned earlier as worthy of respect (5:1-2). "Elders" and "overseers" are synonymous terms.[71] Here Paul chooses the more Jewish term *presbyteros* (rather than *episkopos*, 3:2).[72] Elders have a governing or management and organization role.[73] If they do a good job, they should be financially honored,[74] and especially if they work at **teaching the word**.[75] Good teaching is especially important in a church with heterodoxy.[76] In addition, teaching requires preparation. **Honor** signifying recompense is clearly indicated by the two quotations that follow and explain the reason for paying teaching and ruling elders.

When Paul refers to **the Scripture** in the singular, he refers to specific quotations from the Pentateuch (Gen, Exod, Deut), historical narrative (1 Kgs), and the prophets.[77] In every reference, he treats the Old Testament as authoritative and reliable.[78] In 1 Timothy 5:18, he refers to two passages that have a similar message.[79] The first passage is Deuteronomy 25:4. Paul also cites it in 1 Corinthians 9:9 as a basis for paying wages to a Christian worker. *Bous* (**ox** or "cattle") were important for farming (e.g., Gen 26:14), pulling wagons (2 Sam 6:6), eating (e.g., Gen 18:7; Deut 14:4), and sacrificing.[80] Like humans, they were to rest on the Sabbath and those not one's own were not to be coveted (Deut 5:14, 21). Since an ox was strong (Prov 14:4), it was able to pull the **threshing** sled over the grain.[81] It could eat grass, straw, or stalks.[82] When an ox works, it should be fed, even if by feeding it, the ox would slow its work in order to nourish itself. Analogously, if elders were indeed working, they too should be nourished by being **honored** (5:17). Paul next cites **worthy is**

71. See Titus 1:5, 7; Acts 20:17, 28; 1 Pet 5:1-2.

72. *Const. ap.* 2.28 compares the teaching elders to the Sanhedrin.

73. See 1 Tim 3:4-5.

74. See 1 Tim 5:3.

75. Literally, "laboring in word and teaching," but the phrase may be better rendered as a hendiadys with *didaskalia* modifying *logos*.

76. See 1 Tim 3:2; Gal 6:6.

77. Rom 4:3; 9:17; 10:11; 11:2; Gal 3:8, 22; 4:30.

78. See 1 Tim 4:13; 2 Tim 3:16.

79. He appears to use similar reasoning to Hillel's "a main proposition from two scriptural passages" (Schürer 1979, 2:344).

80. E.g., Lev 1:2-3; John 2:14-15.

81. *IDB* 3:614; Mounce 2000: 310; Montague 2008: 113-14 vs. Marshall 1999: 615-the ox trampled the corn with its hooves.

82. Num 22:4; Ps 105:20 LXX; Isa 11:7.

the worker of his wages, taught by Jesus to the Twelve (Matt 10:10) and the Seventy-two disciples (Luke 10:7), but here Paul cites Luke word for word. Paul thereby treats the Gospel of Luke as **Scripture**, with the same authority as the Old Testament.[83] In the context of the gospel, **wages** for a worker includes room and board (Luke 10:7). In 1 Corinthians 9, **wages** is analogous to the salary of a soldier, the harvest of a farmer, and the sustenance for a priestly family (vv. 7, 10, 13). Workers for God's kingdom should not have to work at another occupation (v. 14).[84] Ministry is work. Worthiness merits a reward of **wages**. Elders are **worthy** because they **work**.

Paul continues with the topic of **elders**, but now about how to treat judicial cases (or elders who may have not led well): **Against an elder—do not accept a charge, except upon two or three witnesses. The ones continuing to sin—rebuke before all, in order that also the rest may keep on having fear. I charge before God and Christ Jesus and the elect angels, that you might keep these things without discrimination, doing nothing by partiality** (5:19-21). A **charge** is a formal, serious "accusation."[85] When Jesus was brought before Governor Pontius Pilate, he was charged by the chief priests and elders (Matt 27:11-13). Also, Paul was "accused" by the high priests and elders before governors Felix and Festus.[86] The charge could lead to death (Acts 25:11). Even Festus abided by the "Roman custom" to allow the accused (*katēgoreō*) (especially if a Roman citizen) to defend him/herself "face to face" against the accuser's charge (*katēgoros*, Acts 25:16). Paul warns Timothy not to "welcome" (**accept**, Acts 15:4) such an accusation except if more than one person makes it. Paul follows Jesus' teachings which were built on Old Testament law (Deut 19:15).[87] If another Christian does not listen when (s)he is shown

---

83. If 1 Tim is written between A.D. 62-64, then the Gospel of Luke must have been written earlier. Marshall (1999: 616) agrees that "a written source is surely required, and one that would have been authoritative."

84. Paul encouraged the Philippians to contribute financially to his own ministry (Phil 4:10-19; 2 Cor 11:9). In 1 Tim 4:10, Paul and Timothy describe their ministry as "work." *Const. ap.* 2.28 commands that a double portion of first-fruits be given by the laity to the elders who teach. Gifts should also be given to the pastors, elder women, deacons, readers, singers, and porters. The idea of 'double honor' could be built from Deut 21:17, the first-born receiving double.

85. See Titus 1:6; LSJ, 927.

86. Acts 23:26-30; 25:5.

87. Also Deut. 17:6; 2 Cor 13:1. The rabbis also used this O.T. law, e.g., *m. Sotah* 6:3.

a fault, "take with you one or two (people), so that, on (the) evidence of **two or three witnesses,** every word might stand" (Matt 18:16). Someone might unfairly accuse an elder (Deut 19:16–19). Although the church did not execute capital punishment, if the accusation were serious and accurate, the elder could be treated as an outsider by the church (Matt 18:17). Timothy did not want to encourage reprisals against the elders, especially possible in an environment of critical self-deprivation and heresy (1 Tim 1:3; 4:1–3). The Accuser (Rev 12:10) (who is opportunistic) might very well instigate accusations when demonic teachings were rampant (1 Tim 4:1).

In contrast, Paul commands Timothy to **rebuke** the people who **keep on sinning** (5:20). These are not people who sin and repent, because then everyone would always have to stand publically to confess their wrongdoings. The goal is to bring unrepented deeds out in the open for the sake of clarity and truth,[88] because if persistent sin is not discouraged, some may think it is encouraged. The goal is to discourage false accusations and unwholesome, sinful behavior.[89]

Paul encourages Timothy to watch that he is not partial: **without discrimination, doing nothing by partiality** (5:21). Timothy must not make a judgment before witnesses speak (*prokrima*, 5:19)[90] because he is inclined towards someone but inclined against another. Especially in the midst of heresy, leaders need to watch out for natural prejudices. God, in contrast, is always impartial, never judging a human by superficial criteria.[91]

Paul calls **God and** God-incarnate **Christ Jesus and the elect**[92] **angels** (5:21) as witnesses of Paul's **charge** and Timothy's actions. The angels and the Father are also witnesses to Jesus' acknowledgement of humans who have acknowledged Jesus.[93] The angels celebrate in heaven when a sinner repents (Luke 15:10) and grieve when worshipers of the beast suffer judgment (Rev 14:9–11). The angels will return together with

---

88. See Titus 1:13 vs. Gal 6:1.

89. Deut 17:13; 19:18–20; *m. Sanh.* 10:4.

90. A *prokrima* is in Latin a *praejudicium*, a preliminary hearing (LSJ, 1487).

91. E.g., Acts 10:34; Spencer 1995: 191–92.

92. *Eklektos* can indicate "special," or "precious," as in 1 Pet 2:4, 6, 9. The angels are special to God.

93. Mark 8:38; Luke 12:8–9; Rev 3:5.

Jesus at the second coming.⁹⁴ Being impartial is very important to the heavenly tribunal.

The next verse appears to continue the topic of judicial matters. **Do not lay hands hastily and do not share in another's sins; keep yourself pure** (5:22). In 4:14, **lay hands** is used to describe a symbolic act, when the elders commissioned Timothy, asking God to give or confirm his spiritual gift, as a blessing for his ministry. That event was done by the council of elders. But, this laying of hands is done only by Timothy. A consequence of laying hands quickly would be participating with sin, but Timothy must continue to guard his own **purity**.⁹⁵ In 5:22, the same word family for **sin** is used, as in 5:20 (*hamartia, hamartanō*). Thus, from the context, Paul appears to be summarizing his earlier discussion (5:19–21). Paul does not tell Timothy not to lay hands, but not to do so **hastily** or quickly or easily.⁹⁶ Since **laying hands** is a symbolic act with a variety of meanings,⁹⁷ being sure of the meaning that best fits this context is not easy. The most frequent understanding is that **lay hands** in 5:22 refers to commissioning or ordaining an elder to office.⁹⁸ The process of choosing and voting for elders (Titus 1:5; Acts 14:23) would be similar to the commissioning to a task such as received by Stephen and the other "deacons," Paul and Barnabas, or Joshua.⁹⁹ Although Timothy alone is mentioned, he might still work with others to do the actual commissioning. The reason to avoid **haste** would be to test an elder's character first (1 Tim 3:6, 10). Elders could be sinning still but their sin not be easily evident (5:24). By approving someone who later might be shown to be sinning either in behavior or teaching, Timothy would thus be partnering or **sharing** in their sin (5:22).

Paul then adds what looks to be homey advice to Timothy on his health in the midst of sentences that deal with sin but relates to Paul's command to guard his purity (5:22, 24–25): **No longer drink water, but use a little wine on account of the stomach and your frequent**

---

94. Matt 16:27; 25:31; Luke 9:26; 2 Thess 1:7. The three holy witnesses (God, Jesus, angels) balance the three human witnesses.

95. See Titus 2:5; 1 Tim 4:12; 5:2.

96. As in Gal 1:6; 2 Thess 2:2; BDAG, 992.

97. See 1 Tim 4:14.

98. Robertson 1931: 589; Kelly 1963: 127–28; Fee 1988: 131–32; Marshall 1999: 620–22; Mounce 2000: 316–18; Turner 2006: 373–75; Witherington 2006: 277; Montague 2008: 115.

99. Acts 6:6; 13:3; Num 27:18–23.

sicknesses (5:23). Apparently Timothy was drinking only water and not drinking any wine even though "water was relatively scarce and often polluted."[100] One ancient writer said: "it is hurtful to drink wine or water alone" while "wine mingled with water is pleasant" (2 Macc 15:39). Wine was a regular part of ancient life, used not only with meals, but also as part of some temple sacrifices,[101] and for disinfection (Luke 10:34). Jesus used wine as a positive image[102] and even turned water into fine wine as his first sign in Cana of Galilee (John 2:3-11; 4:46). Wine in itself is not considered evil in the Bible. God brings forth "wine to gladden the human heart, oil to make the face shine, and bread to strengthen the human heart" (Ps 104:15 NRSV). Solomon states: "wine gladdens life" (Eccl 10:19). Nevertheless, drunkenness was clearly discouraged because it led to wild living and not being filled by the Holy Spirit.[103] Titus and Timothy are warned not to choose leaders that drink too much wine.[104] The playwright Eubulus has Dionysus explain:

> Three bowls only do I mix for the temperate—one to health which they empty first, the second to love and pleasure, the third to sleep. When this is drunk up wise guests go home. The fourth is ours no longer, but belongs to violence; the fifth to uproar, and sixth to drunken revel, the seventh to black eyes. The eighth is the policeman's, the ninth belongs to vomiting, and the tenth to madness and hurling the furniture.[105]

A **little wine** would definitely fit under the first bowl, possibly a second bowl might "gladden the heart," but after that clearly more bowls were excessive.

Why might Timothy have been drinking only water? Possibly, he had made a Nazirite vow to abstain as a means to dedicate himself as **pure** (*hagneia*) to the Lord.[106] This vow could be made for a specified time period. However, he was hesitant to stop this vow early (cf. 5:12) even despite physical complications from the impure water.[107] Asceti-

---

100. *IDB* 4:851.

101. Lev 23:13; Num 15:5, 7, 10; 28:14.

102. Matt 9:17; Mark 2:22; Luke 5:37-39. Jesus himself drank wine with meals (Matt 11:19; Luke 7:34).

103. Titus 1:6; Eph 5:18.

104. See Titus 1:7; 2:3; 1 Tim 3:3, 8.

105. Branigan 1980: 186.

106. Num 6:2; 1 Tim 4:12; 5:2, 22.

107. Hippocrates mentions the health benefit of bread, boiled meat, and a little

cism had appeal in Ephesus.[108] Would Timothy's decision to drink wine have a negative impact with the congregation? Witherington explains: "The false teachers had been urging an inappropriate form of asceticism that involved food and drink, and Paul did not want Timothy to be caught in that trap."[109] Nevertheless, Paul commands Timothy to use a small amount of wine to prevent the physical illnesses that water was perpetuating.

Paul then summarizes this section on elders: **The sins of some humans are obvious, going before them into judgment, but to some humans also they follow; likewise also the good deeds of some humans are obvious, and those having their good deeds otherwise cannot be hid** (5:24-25). Paul makes an analogy between doing evil and doing good deeds. Some good actions, like evil actions, are **obvious** (*prodēlos*), while other good or evil actions are more hidden. Eventually, both will become as obvious as Peter's accent was a Galilean one (Matt 26:73). Jesus too told his disciples that the hypocrisy of the Pharisees hides their sins, but eventually their sins will become manifest: "Nothing is covered up that will not be uncovered, and nothing secret that will not become known. Therefore whatever you have said in the dark will be heard in the light, and what you have whispered behind closed doors will be proclaimed from the housetops" (Luke 12:2-3 NRSV). Thus, Timothy needs to be careful in prosecuting accusations (5:19) but also in approving people who may appear to be godly, but are not really (5:22).

---

wine, while raw wheat, raw meat, and water would cause "severe suffering" (*Vet. med.* 13 [10-23]). Sweet wine was used in medications that were drunk (*Liq.* 5 [129]); mild white Mendean wines served as laxatives (*Int.* 13 [200], 16 [206]; for fevers, old Thasian wine was diluted twenty-five parts water and one part wine (*Morb.* 3. 17 [160]). Wine in moderation can have health benefits for some people for cardiovascular health and other causes (*Consumer Reports* 1999: 10). Pliny also mentions the benefit of wine for cardiac disease. *Bion* (wine) was good for a "disordered stomach or a weak digestion, for pregnancy, faintness, paralysis, trembling, giddiness, colic, and sciatica." Some wines helped fatigue after military exercises (*Nat.* 23.25-26 [50-53]). Wine can also serve as a remedy against dyspeptic complaints (Kelly 1963: 129). Ancient physicians prescribed wine as a "remedy to facilitate digestion, combat anorexia, and suppress stomach-rumblings" (*TLNT* 3:298-99); Marshall 1999: 623-24; *NewDocs* 6:190. Timothy was probably not a "semi-invalid" (Robertson 1931: 590) because he exercised regularly (1 Tim 4:8) and traveled with Paul. He could have had intestinal or stomach problems (*TLNT* 3: 298).

108. See 1 Tim 4:3. The "pious" might even point to priests being required to abstain from wine while serving at the temple (Josephus, *Ag. Ap.* I [199]; Lev 10:9; Ezek 44:21.

109. Witherington 2006: 277.

Slaves (6:1-2)

Paul now moves from widows and elders to slaves: **As many are slaves under the yoke regard their own masters worthy of all honor, lest God's name and the teaching may be slandered. But the ones having faithful masters do not despise, since they are brothers and sisters, but more serve, since they are faithful and beloved, the ones devoting themselves to good deeds** (6:1-2a). Unlike Aristotle, who addresses only masters, Paul in 6:1-2 and in Titus 2:9-10 addresses only **slaves**, probably household slaves.[110] Possibly, the slaves' attitudes were affected by the general rancor against masters and enslavement. In ancient times, people became slaves in different ways: instead of capital punishment, they might serve a penal service, exposed children were forced into slavery,[111] captives of war,[112] pirates, and debtors. Many slaves labored in domestic and mining areas. Some estimate that one-third of urban residents were slaves. Manumission was more common in domestic and urban employments than in mining. Some Roman slaves were given a *peculium* (money or property) from which the slaves eventually bought their freedom. Slaves were of any race, often encouraged to be educated, could own property, and were often emancipated.[113] Many slaves were acquired by slave-traders, whom Paul includes among the lawless and godless (1:10). The most famous organized ancient slaving system was based in southwestern Asia Minor. Ephesus itself was a major slave-market for at least four hundred years.[114] Strabo describes the pirates from Cilicia as exporting slaves because of the profit. The main market was Delos, which could admit and export ten thousand slaves on the same day. An ancient proverb noted the quick sale of slaves: "Merchant, sail in, unload your ship, everything has been sold" (Strabo, *Geogr.* 14.5.2 [C668-69]).

---

110. See Titus 2:9; cf. Eph 6:5-9; Col 3:22-4:1. Towner 2006: 382. While Stoic philosophers addressed their peers about equality, Christian teachers addressed the slaves directly "in their own right." Christianity offered its adherents "an equality of religious opportunity" previously unknown (Bradley 1994: 145, 150).

111. Cohick (2009: 40-42) observes that more females than males were exposed. Jews, on the other hand, condemned exposure of infants.

112. Just from the Jewish war of A.D. 66-70, the Romans enslaved 130,230 Jews (Bradley 1994: 40).

113. Montague 2008: 119. Augustine said it was the practice of Christian communities to redeem as many of the kidnapped slaves as possible (Bradley 1994: 37, 81).

114. *OCD*, 994-96; Cohick 2009: 257-68; Pomeroy 1975: 191-93; Bradley 1994: 32-42; Herodotus, *Hist.* 8. 105.

Slaves (6:1-2)

Paul describes the slaves as **under the yoke** (*zygos*), a negative image he uses for slavery.[115] A **yoke** was a wooden or iron frame placed over the necks of two oxen or other cattle and humans when taken captive.[116] Thus, Paul sympathizes with the slaves with this introductory image. However, instead of insisting on harming of the master,[117] he wants the slave to regard his/her own master with **honor** or respect. Paul's overriding concern is to promote all to be saved and come to knowledge of the truth. If Christian slaves were disrespectful (*timēe*) of their masters,[118] God—who is the Savior of all—and Christian teaching would be slandered.[119]

Some of the slaves had Christian **masters** and understandably might hold a negative opinion[120] of them because they were their equals in Christ.[121] Instead of despising them, the slaves are to **serve** them (6:2). Previously, Paul had encouraged slaves to serve their masters as they would Christ and masters to treat slaves fairly and equally (Eph 6:5-9). All Christians were to serve each other and honor everyone.[122] Jesus and, later, Paul commanded Christians to resist evil by overcoming evil with good actions.[123] Paul reminds the slaves that as **brothers and sisters** the masters are **faithful and beloved,** themselves devoted to **good deeds.**[124]

Paul internally summarizes: **These things—keep on teaching and encouraging**[125] (6:2b), probably referring back to 5:3—6:2, his directions about different categories of people in the church at Ephesus (widows, elders, and slaves).[126]

---

115. Gal 5:1; Acts 15:10.

116. *IDB* 4:924-25.

117. Slaves attacked the masters regularly (Bradley 1994: 112-16).

118. See 1 Tim 5:3. The same root (*despotēs*) is used for women ruling their households (*oikodespoteō* [5:14]).

119. See 1 Tim 3:7; 5:14; Titus 2:5, 10; Rom 2:24; Isa 52:5; Ezek 36:20-21.

120. See 1 Tim 4:12.

121. Phlm 16; Gal 3:28; Col 3:11.

122. Gal 5:13; 1 Pet 2:17.

123. Matt 5:39-41; Rom 12:18-21.

124. Since the last phrase is an appositive to the **masters,** I think that the masters, together with the slaves, are doing good deeds, i.e., furthering the faith. Others think the slaves do the good deeds (Kelly 1963: 132; Marshall 1999: 632-33; Towner 2006: 385-88).

125. See 1 Tim 2:12; Titus 2:15.

126. Towner (2006: 379) begins the section at 5:1.

1 TIMOTHY 6:3-21
Timothy Should Fight His Own Fight of the Faith

Paul then moves to the final section of his letter, explaining that heterodox teaching should be fled because it robs the truth (6:3-10), but Timothy instead should seek righteousness, fighting the good fight of the faith, guarding the commandment, not open to attack until Jesus returns (6:11-16), encouraging the rich to rely on God, not riches (6:17-19), and Paul summarizes that Timothy should guard the deposit, turning away from false knowledge (6:20-21a).

HETERODOX TEACHING VERSUS PIETY WITH CONTENTMENT (6:3-10)

If any keep on teaching a different doctrine and do not draw near to healthy words, the ones about our Lord Jesus Christ, and the godly teaching, they are deluded, nothing knowing, but ailing for arguments and word-battles, from which comes envy, contention, slander, evil suspicions, constant irritations among humans corrupted in mind and robbed of the truth, thinking godliness to be a means of gain (6:3-5). Paul continues the topic of teaching (6:2b) and recalls the initial topic of heterodoxy.[1] After emphasizing the conditional clause (**if any keep on teaching a different doctrine and do not draw near to healthy words, the ones about our Lord Jesus Christ, and the godly teaching,** 6:3) by placing it first in the sentence, he describes persons who hold such beliefs (**they are deluded, nothing knowing, but ailing for arguments and word-battles,** 6:4) and finally describes the derivative behavior that results (**from which comes envy, contention, slander, evil suspicions, constant irritations,** 6:4-5). The heterodox teachings at Ephesus were not **healthy** (wholesome)[2] about Jesus,[3] nor **godly**. Rather, the teachers

---

1. See 1 Tim 1:3, 10. See Titus 1:10.
2. See Titus 1:13.
3. The phrase in 6:3 can be a subjective genitive (**words from our Lord Jesus**

were **deluded**, their minds were "clouded with smoke" and, therefore, unclear, consequently they would not **know anything**.[4] In contrast to affirming **healthy** words, some at Ephesus were **ailing** (*noseō*). They were "sick" or "diseased."[5] In their diseased state,[6] instead of desiring health, they desired **arguments** (*zētēsis*) **and word-battles** (*logomachia*). *Zētēsis* refers to vigorous **arguments** that might or might not be over a search for the truth.[7] In 6:4, since the teachers' minds are clouded with smoke and thus diseased, the arguments become ends in themselves, not searches for truth.

Logomachia (**word-battles**, 6:4) and *logomacheō* ("to fight about words," 2 Tim 2:14) are composite words made of *logos* ("word") and *machomai* ("fight") or *machē* ("battle, combat").[8] Paul uses many of the same words or concepts in 1 Timothy 6:4–5 to describe the heresy in Crete about worthless battles related to genealogies.[9] In the New Testament, *machē* and *machomai* always have negative connotations. Paul described the difficulties in Macedonia as external **battles** that caused lack of rest and afflictions (2 Cor 7:5) and James says **battles** are caused by sinful desires to want something that cannot be obtained (Jas 4:1). Thus, at Ephesus some desired to battle using words (and about words) (6:3–4). **Arguments and word-battles** is a pleonasm accentuating by repetition the main idea that this heterodoxy was promoting fighting, not "righteousness, godliness, faith, love, perseverance, gentleness" (6:11).

Five harmful behaviors result from the **arguments**. *Phthonos* is "*ill-will* or *malice*, esp. *envy* or *jealousy* of the good fortune of others."[10] Pilate observed that the chief priests had handed Jesus over to him "out of

---

Christ) or objective genitive (**words about our Lord Jesus Christ**). Probably the latter fits this context better since it modifies **healthy words** which is parallel to **godly teaching** (6:3).

4. See 1 Tim 3:6; 1:7. Recent converts in particular can be **deluded** (3:6).

5. BDAG, 678; LSJ, 1181. The noun form *nosos* was used for physical illness. Jesus' own commission and that of the Twelve includes healing diseases (Matt 4:23–24; 8:17; 9:35; Mark 1:34; Luke 4:40; 6:18; 7:21; 9:1; 10:1). Even Paul healed the sick at Ephesus (Acts 19:12). Paul continues Jesus' commission to the apostles to bring healing physically and spiritually.

6. See also Wis 17:8.

7. See Titus 3:9.

8. Thayer, 380. Literally, *machē* referred to armies in single combat (LSJ, 1085).

9. **Arguments** (*zētēsis*), **contentions** (*eris*), battles (*machē*) (Titus 3:9).

10. LSJ, 1930.

jealousy" of Jesus' popularity.[11] **Envy** describes what non-Christians may feel (Titus 3:3), one result of not worshiping the Creator (Rom 1:28–29), and one of the works of the flesh (Gal 5:18–20, 26).[12] Battles result in envy or malice towards others, not gentleness (1 Tim 6:11). *Eris* (**contention**)[13] is a synonym for **arguments** (*zētēsis*) highlighting the inciting to battle. One of the devious means to win battles is **slander** (*blasphēmia*, 6:4), to insult and speak falsely.[14] **Slander** thus is very close in meaning to **evil suspicions** or "evil opinions." Jesus ben Sirach thinks an **evil suspicion** can overthrow one's judgment (Sir 3:24). *Paratribō*, the root stem of *diaparatribē* (**constant irritations**), signifies "*rub beside* or *alongside.*" Heightened by *dia* ("through"), *diaparatribē* refers to attacks of "constant argumentativeness" that "rub" or "clash against" one another and therefore are "irritating."[15]

All this fighting occurs among people described in three phrases (**corrupted in mind and robbed of the truth, thinking godliness to be a means of gain, 6:5**). *Diaphtheirō* (**corrupted**) refers literally in the New Testament to the physical destruction of an outer garment (Luke 12:33), of a human body (2 Cor 4:16), and of ships (Rev 8:9). Here the **mind**, "*the faculties of perceiving and understanding* and those of *feeling, judging, determining*,"[16] has been destroyed. *Apostereō* signifies to **rob** by committing fraud, not paying a debt, or doing another breach of confidence perpetuated for profit.[17] Thus, the truth was not simply rejected, it was deceitfully taken away from them. The current enticement for the teachers is thinking that **godliness**[18] is **a means of gain**, a means of livelihood, a way to earn a living, or procure money.[19]

---

11. Matt 27:18; Mark 15:10. The devil, according to the author of the Wisdom of Solomon, was envious of humanity being created immortal in God's image (2:23–24).

12. Gal 5 also mentions **contention** (*eris*), anger, quarrels, and drunkenness (vv. 20–21).

13. See Titus 3:9.

14. See 1 Tim 1:13.

15. BDAG, 235; LSJ, 1328; Robertson 1931: 592; Marshall 1999: 641.

16. Thayer, 429.

17. LSJ, 219; 1 Cor 6:7–8.

18. See Titus 1:1; 1 Tim 1:3–4, 6–7; 4:7.

19. LSJ, 1450. Financial gain is the same motivation in Crete (Titus 1:10–11).

Excursus: Heresy in 1 Timothy

In summary, what kind of heresy was there at Ephesus as described in 1 Timothy?[20] We can inductively draw out some of its features by assessing Paul's answers and emphases in the letter. Christology normally affects soteriology. The heterodox male and female teachers had inadequate teaching about Jesus Christ (6:3). Most likely they did not agree that Christ Jesus, a human, was the one mediator between God and humans sufficient for all people (2:5–6). Therefore, all humans could not be fully saved by God's mercy. Thus, God as the Savior was emphasized in many places in Paul's letter,[21] as well as the desire to present a positive influence to the larger community by godly behavior.[22] The teaching focused in two contrasting areas: legalism with asceticism and promotion of wealth. When Christ is seen as insufficient to save, people create laws to make up for Christ's insufficiency. The legalistic or "unlawful" use of the law included using the law for the salvation of the righteous, not the unrighteous (1:8–11) and forbidding marriage and certain foods (4:3). The promotion of this legalism was done by argumentation and verbal battles about myths and genealogies (1:4, 6; 6:4–5). The men even argued during prayer (2:8). The demonic and magic were included (4:1; 5:13). Truth was abandoned for slander.[23]

This legalism was concurrent with a desire for wealth and luxury. Instead of living for their Savior, they lived for themselves. The women flaunted their wealth even during prayer (2:9). The young widows were living in luxury while families were not supporting the older widows (5:6, 8). Those who deserved to be paid were not (5:17–18). Godly behavior was not the result (4:7). Possibly, the "hypocritical liars" (4:2) were leaders who taught asceticism while they themselves lived in luxury. Or, they lived an ascetic lifestyle for financial benefit.[24] Some wanted to become wealthy at the expense of others.

---

20. See Titus 1:10–14.
21. 1:13–16; 2:3–4, 15; 4:10, 16.
22. 6:3; 3:2–3, 7, 10; 5:7, 14.
23. 6:5; 1:19; 3:6, 11.
24. Kelly (1963: 135) thinks they exacted fees for their instruction; Marshall 1999: 643.

For a Christian to be free from legalism, a healthy, working conscience and healthy teaching are needed.[25] If Christ fully saves someone, then legalistic use of laws is not needed for salvation. Instead of judgment, faith, love, truth, mercy, purity, and mutual respect should be emphasized.[26] All should be prayed for (2:1; 5:5). Paul is promoting the way of affirmation, but not of excess: marriage to one person, childrearing, household management, food, leadership preparation are affirmed.[27] Christ was manifested in the *flesh* (2:5; 3:16). Teaching and learning are emphasized for all but especially those who are ignorant.[28] Progress, not perfection, is the standard (4:15).

Paul redefines means of gain (6:5): **But godliness with contentment is a great means of gain; for we brought nothing into the world, for neither are we able to take out anything; but with these we will be satisfied—having food and clothing** (6:6–8). Godliness is a way to live, dedicating oneself to please God in one's words and actions.[29] **Contentment** (*autarkeia*) was a virtue of Stoics and Cynics, "self-sufficiency" or "independence," "the state of one who supports himself without aid fr. others."[30] Paul redefines "self-sufficiency" to the Corinthians as a means to support, not just oneself, but primarily others (2 Cor 9:8). Although Paul is thankful to the Philippians for their gifts for his ministry, he still explains that he can remain "strong" or content whether he is in need or plenty (Phil 4:10–11). Thus, Paul uses *autarkeia* to focus on being satisfied with what one has. Godliness is a wholesome way to live when combined with an attitude of contentment.

Paul gives several explanations of why this is true. First, he alludes to Job ("I myself came forth naked from my mother's womb, and naked shall I return there" [1:21]) or Ecclesiastes ("As he came forth naked from

25. 1:5, 19; 3:9.
26. 1:5, 13–14, 16, 19; 2:15; 3:15; 4:12; 5:1–3, 17; 6:11–12, 14.
27. 3:1–2, 4, 12, 15; 4:3–4; 5:9–10, 14.
28. 1:7; 2:11–12; 3:2; 4:13, 16; 5:17.
29. See Titus 1:1; 1 Tim 4:7.
30. BDAG, 152. *Autarkeia* is composed of *autos* ("self") plus *arkeō* ("to be strong") (Thayer, 73, 85). For instance, Epictetus, the Stoic philosopher, encourages his students "to be self-sufficient (*arkeō*), to be able to commune with oneself; even as Zeus communes with himself, and is at peace with himself . . . so ought we also to be able to converse with ourselves, not to be in need of others" (*Ench.* 3.13.7).

Heterodox Teaching versus Piety with Contentment (6:3-10)

his mother's womb, he shall return back as he came" [5:14 LXX]).[31] Paul contrasts **we brought into** (*eispherō eis*) with **we take out** (*ekpherō*). Both at the entry and departure points do humans possess nothing.[32] Second, he reminds Timothy to be **satisfied** (*arkeō*) with **food**[33] **and clothing** (6:8).

Skepasma (**clothing**) is literally "a covering." The noun can refer to provisions of clothing and house.[34] Paul is thereby reminding Timothy that the basic necessities of food, clothing, and shelter should serve to leave one satisfied. Jesus had taught that "life is more than food (*trophē*) and the body (more than) clothing" (Luke 12:23). For this reason, the Father takes care of these necessities in the disciples so that they can concentrate on promoting God's kingdom.[35]

Then Paul goes on to describe the dangers of pursuing the procuring of money for its own sake: **But the ones desiring to be rich fall into temptation and a trap and many foolish and harmful desires, which drag humans to the bottom into ruin and destruction** (6:9). After having explained why godliness with contentment is the right way to live (6:6-8), Paul returns to those who use godliness as a means of financial enrichment (6:3-5), but now he focuses only on the financial aspect. These people will include the false teachers (6:3-5), but also anyone who keeps on desiring to be rich.

What does it mean to be **rich**? Joseph of Arimathea, called **rich**, owned his own tomb. As a member of the Sanhedrin he was most likely aristocratic.[36] The **rich** are able to reciprocate another's dinner invitation (Luke 14:12). They own property and could hire a manager to oversee

---

31. Eccl. 5:14 LXX has *exerchomai* and *epistrephō*.

32. He uses the aorist tense to describe the punctiliar action of birth, but the present tense to describe the linear action of continually trying (*dunamai*) to take possessions with us at death.

33. *Trophē* tends to refer to **food** in the N.T. *Diatrophē* (**food**) appears to be an intensive form of *trophē*. For example, John the Baptist lived on locusts and wild honey (Matt 3:4). *Trophē* can also refer more broadly to money, food, and clothing (Matt 10:9-11). The more intensive aspect of *diatrophē* (Robertson 1934: 581) is shown when Bethsura had insufficient food to resist an army because they were in the midst of a sabbatical year (1 Macc 6:49).

34. It comes from *skepazō* ("to cover") and *skepē* ("shade"). *Skepazō* refers to providing security, protection, and shelter (BDAG, 927); "clothing" (Aristotle, *Pol.* 7.15 [1336a. 17]).

35. Luke 12:28-31; Matt 6:25-33.

36. Matt 27:57-59; Mark 15:43; Luke 23:50-51; *IDB* 4:216..

it (Luke 16:1). They could dress in expensive clothing, have extra food, and donate generously.[37] They were called rich even before they had surplus crops (Luke 12:16–21). They could afford to bring someone to court (Jas 2:6). Zacchaeus, a chief tax collector, was rich (Luke 19:2). Ephesus itself was renowned as a place of wealth.[38] The Temple of Artemis was the general bank of Asia. Worship of Artemis brought much wealth to the area. The Ephesians were known as being devoted to luxury. As the greatest metropolis of Asia, the gateway to Rome and Asia, the Ephesus area would entice many to value wealth.

Paul does not simply speak to the rich, he also speaks to the poor who desire to be wealthy. He warns them the rich **fall** (not walk) **into three unexpected things: temptation, a trap, foolish and harmful desires** (6:9). **Temptation**[39] can be things that occur from the outside ("trials") or from within (**temptations**). Paul had told the Ephesian elders that he endured hardships ("trials") when he was persecuted by some Jews (Acts 20:19). Sometimes people try to entice one to sin by presenting opportunities (temptations) that could resonate with internal propensities to sin.[40] At other times, the temptations are internal sinful desires (Jas 1:13–15). The desire to be rich appears to be itself a temptation, however, theoretically, if someone were to desire to acquire wealth in order to use it for distribution to the needy that would be a worthwhile activity. They would then be "rich in good works" and "generous" (1 Tim 6:18). Nevertheless, many who desire even to distribute their wealth, or use it for moral purposes, instead get "choked" and their faith does not "mature" (Luke 8:14). Wealth can limit the growth of faith like thorns that choke a new plant (Luke 8:7). What is the temptation? Is it to prize the wealth over God (Luke 16:13–15; 18:18–25)? Is it to depend on the security of the wealth rather than the security of God (Luke 12:16–21)? Is it to prefer comfort over the cost of discipleship (1 Cor 4:8–13)? Any one of these temptations could lead to a **trap**.[41] A trap is sudden, unexpected,

---

37. Luke 16:19–21; Mark 12:41.

38. See Introduction. Setting. Ephesus and Artemis; Trebilco 2004: 25–26.

39. *Peirasmos* (noun) and *peirazō* (verb).

40. For example, the devil tried to entice Jesus to sin by encouraging him to live for the material, to worship the devil in order to obtain the glory and power of the world's kingdoms, and to test the Lord (Luke 4:2–13). Jesus, though, did not succumb (Heb 2:14–18).

41. *Pagis* is a device used to catch animals (BDAG, 747). Literally, "that which holds fast," from *pēgnymi* ("to make fast"), of "snares in which birds are entangled and

Heterodox Teaching versus Piety with Contentment (6:3-10) 151

and destructive (Luke 21:34-35). An animal might fall unawares into a pit because it was covered by a camouflaged net (or **trap**) (Job 18:8). A bird, attracted by the bait, might "fly into" a net, which entraps it (6:9). The temptation is the bait.

Desires refer to strong feelings and passions turned upon something. A desire can be good and wise (like desiring to be an overseer [1 Tim 3:1]) or **foolish** and harmful.[42] Since **desires** can include wanting or coveting what belongs to another,[43] possibly desires to be wealthy include wanting more than one's due, like the rich farmer who wanted to keep more than his share of the crop (Luke 12:16-20). These desires are **foolish** and **harmful**. These desires drag the entrapped humans to the bottom of the pit into **ruin and destruction**.[44] **Ruin** (*elethros*) can refer to painful experiences, like labor pains and even hell, the total removal of God's presence.[45] **Destruction** (*apōleia*) can also refer to hell and judgment, the opposite of salvation and life.[46]

Paul further explains why desiring to be rich is harmful: **For the**[47] **root of all kinds of evils is the love of money, by which some, reaching after, have been led astray from the faith, and pierce themselves through by many sorrows** (6:10).[48] This trap began with an underground **root** which grows into a shoot.[49] A root goes deep and sustains a plant.[50] If the root is not holy, the branches are not holy.[51] This root is not Jesus Christ.[52] It is **the love of money**, the love of "silver" (*argyros*).[53] Silver was

---

caught" (Thayer, 472). Prov 6:5; 7:23; Eccl 9:12. See *IDB* 4: 688. One **trap** has to do with reproach from outsiders (1 Tim 3:7).

42. See Titus 2:12; 3:3 and 2 Tim 2:22; 3:6; 4:3.
43. Rom 7:7; Exod 20:17; Deut 5:21.
44. Ruin and destruction is a pleonasm—two synonyms that highlight one point.
45. 1 Thess 5:3; 2 Thess 1:9.
46. Matt 7:13; Phil 1:28; 3:19; 2 Thess 2:3; Heb 10:39; 2 Pet 3:7.
47. According to Colwell's rule, although **root** has no article, it is definite.
48. See novel by McKinnery, *Abracadaver*, where the motive for murder is greed. The murderer dies by a spike as in 1 Tim 6:10.
49. BDAG, 905-6.
50. Matt 13:6; Rom 11:18.
51. Cf. Rom 11:16.
52. Rev 5:5; 22:16.
53. Thayer, 72, 653.

valuable.[54] Coins were made of silver.[55] Silver is a shiny god[56] one can see, not an invisible one (6:16). While at Ephesus, Paul's coworkers Gaius and Aristarchus had been attacked by the mob because Demetrius and the other silversmiths had been threatened when they observed that less people were buying their silver shrines of Artemis (Acts 19:24-29). Paul had made a point of telling the Ephesian elders that he had not coveted or desired their silver (Acts 20:33).[57] The root of love of money sprouts forth **all kinds of evil. The love of money,** when it becomes the goal one **reaches after,** has two results: it **misleads** (*apoplanaō*) and **pierces** (*peripeirō*) (6:10). Silver looks attractive, secure, and brings many worldly pleasures and power but in reality silver eventually perishes (Jas 5:3). It does not save; only Christ's blood saves (1 Pet 1:18-19). It does not satisfy (Eccl 5:9). It leads people away from truth. Meat can be **pierced** or "run through" with skewers on a spit.[58] In 1 Timothy, those who love money end up piercing themselves by many pains or **sorrows**. At the bottom of the pit, the trap pierces them. It does not lead to "righteousness, godliness, faith, love, perseverance, gentleness" (6:11).[59]

Pursue Righteousness (6:11-16)

Paul offers a two-pronged solution to Timothy: **But you, O**[60] **person of God, flee these things; rather pursue righteousness, godliness, faith, love, perseverance, gentleness** (6:11). Timothy is to **keep fleeing** false teaching, the desire to be rich, and the love of money (6:3-5, 9-10), because he is **God's person.**[61] Instead, he is to **keep pursuing** God's attributes (most of which have been mentioned already in the letter). Jesus who is fully holy or **righteous** is a model for Timothy.[62] The whole message about Jesus is summarized as **godliness** (3:16), a way to live,

54. Matt 25:27; 28:12; 1 Cor 3:12; 2 Tim 2:20.
55. Luke 9:3; Acts 7:16; 8:20.
56. Acts 17:29; Rev 9:20.
57. Cf. Judas, Ananias, Sapphira (John 12:4-6; Matt 26:14-16; Acts 5:1-11).
58. LSJ, 1355, 1382.
59. Rhetorician Longinus, a later contemporary of Paul, sees the danger of the love of money because evils accompany it, lives are ruined, the material or mortal is overly valued, and people live for financial gain (*Subl.* 44.6-10).
60. See 1 Tim 6:20.
61. See also 2 Tim 3:17.
62. 1 Tim 3:16. See also Titus 1:8; 3:5.

dedicating oneself to please God in one's words and actions.[63] Paul had several times exhorted Timothy to be godly, rather than ungodly.[64] The battle at Ephesus is all about **faith** and **love**. Christ's faithfulness and love are reflected in Christ's followers.[65]

Hypomonē (**perseverance** or "patience") is also a trait that comes from God. It is the ability to persevere until the end.[66] It is itself strengthened by hardships.[67] The elders in Crete, like Timothy, had to learn faith, love, and perseverance (Titus 2:2). Paul himself modeled faith, love, and perseverance (2 Tim 3:10). **Gentleness**[68] is also an attribute of Christ, by which Paul had exhorted the Corinthians (2 Cor 10:1).

Paul connects these six attributes in a running stream sequence.[69] He begins with two attributes that are almost synonyms. **Righteousness** and **godliness** both highlight being set apart from others, even in the midst of being with others. **Faith** and **love** center on Christ Jesus, whom one trusts and from whom one is strengthened. **Perseverance** and **gentleness** are outward manifestations of the previous four attributes.[70] If Timothy is holy, godly, faithful, and loving, he will be more able to be persevering or patient and humble with others around him, especially in a climate of dissension and argument (e.g., 6:4–5).

Paul then rephrases this same point more urgently in the next two sentences: **Keep on fighting for yourself the good fight of the faith, grasp for yourself eternal life, into which you were called and you confessed the good confession before many witnesses** (6:12). Paul uses two parallel verbs signifying active participation to persevere as a Christian (6:11): to **fight** and to **grasp** (6:12). Paul has used **fight** (*agōnizomai*) earlier to describe how Paul and Timothy (and other believers) actively prepare and contend for a prize from the merciful living Savior (4:10). Here that prize is explicit: **eternal life** (6:12). *Agōnizomai* and *agōn* describe

63. See Titus 1:1; 2:12; 1 Tim 4:7–8.
64. 1 Tim 4:7–8; 6:6.
65. See 1 Tim 1:5, 14; 2 Tim 2:22.
66. Luke 8:15; 21:19.
67. Rom 5:3; 2 Cor 1:6.
68. See Titus 3:2; 2 Tim 2:25.

69. He uses asyndeton ("and" is omitted between a series of words, phrases, or clauses) (Spencer 1998b: 188). Cf. 6:9 has polysyndeton.

70. Mounce (2000: 354) and Bernard (1922: 97) also arrange the virtues in three groups. Lock (1924: 71) writes that righteousness, godliness, faith are virtues "towards God," while love, patience, gentleness are virtues "towards men."

athletes who contend for a prize in the public games, including running and boxing.[71] Since athletes exercised as preparation for war, *agōnizomai* also refers to armed combat (John 18:36). Paul does use the metaphor to describe his own Christian life.[72] Nevertheless, athletic and military images are so repeatedly used in 1 and 2 Timothy when Paul directly exhorts Timothy that Paul could very well be using an extended image to appeal to Timothy's own interests.[73] At least he would have to be athletic to resonate with all the athletic images. Possibly, his father had him training to be a soldier at Lystra (which was a Roman colony).

Here are some of the athletic/military metaphors in 1 and 2 Timothy:

- **Order** or **charge** (1 Tim 1:3, 5, 18; 4:11; 5:7; 6:13, 17, *parangelia, parangellō*—can refer to a military order)[74]
- May fight (1 Tim 1:18, *strateuō*) **with them the good** fight (*strateia*—a military campaign)
- Train **for godliness** (1 Tim 4:7, *gymnazō*)
- **Bodily training** (1 Tim 4:8, *gymnasia*) **for a little is profitable**
- **We labor** (1 Tim 4:10, *kopiaō*) **and we strive** (*agōnizomai*)
- **Let no one despise your youth** (1 Tim 4:12, *neotēs*—military age—literal) **in conduct** (*anastrophē*—used of soldiers)[75]
- **Your progress** (1 Tim 4:15, *prokopē*)[76]
- **Guard the deposit** (1 Tim 5:21; 6:20; 2 Tim 1:12, 14; 4:15, *phylassō, parathēkē*)
- **Guard** (1 Tim 5:22; 6:14; 2 Tim 4:7, *tēreō*)
- **Pursue** (1 Tim 6:11, *diōkō*)
- **Keep on fighting for yourself** (1 Tim 6:12, *agōnizomai*) **the good fight** (*agōn*) . . . **grasp** (*epilambanō*)
- **Command** (1 Tim 6:14, *entolē*)[77]

71. See 1 Tim 4:10.
72. 1 Cor 9:24–27; Col 1:29—2:1; 2 Tim 4:7.
73. See also 1 Tim 1:2.
74. LSJ, 1306. Of the 36/37 occurrences of the word family in the N.T., 7 are in 1 Tim (19% of N.T. references), while 1 Tim is only slightly over 1% in length of the N.T.
75. LSJ, 122, 1170.
76. LSJ, 1486.
77. LSJ, 576.

- Some... missed the mark (1 Tim 6:21, *astocheō*)
- **Join in suffering as a good** soldier (2 Tim 2:3-5, *stratiōēs*) **of Christ Jesus.** No one serving as a soldier (*strateuō*) entwines himself in affairs of life, in order that, by the one having enlisted him, he will accommodate himself. But if also someone may compete in a contest, (s)he is not crowned unless (s)he might compete according to the rules (lawfully).
- **The good fight**—(2 Tim 4:7, *agōn*) **I fought for myself** (*agonizomai*), **the race course—I finished**
- Crown (2 Tim 4:8, *stephanos*) **of righteousness**

As he does in 4:7-8, Paul reinterprets the appealing imagery of athletics for the Christian life, **the good fight of the faith** (6:12). Whatever was being taught at Ephesus must have been quite enticing for even Timothy as a Christian leader to be warned and exhorted numerous times.[78] Paul had already described many ways for Timothy (and the church) spiritually to "exercise."[79] Jesus too had used the same verb (*agōnizomai*) to describe the effort needed to enter the narrow door (Luke 13:24).

Grasp or "lay hold of, seize"[80] (*epilambanō*, 6:12) continues the athletic imagery. **Fight** and **grasp** use the middle voice to highlight the effort Timothy needs to take. Salvation is granted by the Savior (4:10), but simultaneously the thankful believer must cooperate with that grace. The believer should put as much effort as Jesus did when he seized drowning Peter out of the Sea of Galilee (Matt 14:31).

Eternal life[81] comes from an **eternal** God (1:17; 6:16). The only way to have eternal life is to be acceptable to the eternal God. Jesus defines eternal life as knowing God, the only true God, and Jesus Christ whom God sent (John 17:3). Jesus came to give life and that abundantly (John 10:10). Thus, eternal life or "heaven" can be experienced now with personal knowledge of God that affects one's mind, heart, and actions. Eternal life is grasped now as a preview, but fully received in the future.

Timothy had been **called** (by God) to have eternal life, but also he **confessed** his faith before **witnesses** (6:12). Being **called** into fellowship

---

78. See 1 Tim 6:4.

79. 1 Tim 1:5, 18-19; 2:1; 4:3-7, 12-16; 5:1-2, 19-23; 6:6, 8, 11.

80. LSJ, 642.

81. *Aiōnios* gives "prominence to immeasurableness of eternity" (LSJ, 26; Thayer, 21). See Titus 1:2.

with God is a continual theme of Paul's.[82] Paul had previously exhorted those in the larger area of Ephesus to "lead a life worthy of the calling to which you have been called" (Eph 4:1 NRSV). Part of reaching for eternal life includes the acknowledgement of one's faith in Christ Jesus[83] in public (**confession**), to be "of one mind,"[84] not hypocritical, saying one thing but doing another (vs. 4:2; Titus 1:16). Jesus teaches that, if humans will acknowledge or commit themselves to him publically, he too will acknowledge those humans before the Father (Matt 10:32–33). Paul had told the Romans that confessing Jesus is Lord before others is indispensable to salvation (Rom 10:9–10). Apparently Timothy himself had confessed his faith in Christ Jesus before many **witnesses** (6:12).

Paul now summarizes his appeal to Timothy: **I charge, before God, the one giving life to all things, and Christ Jesus, the one having witnessed to Pontius Pilate the good confession, you guard the commandment, spotless, not open to attack, until the appearing of our Lord Jesus Christ, which in his own time will reveal the blessed and only ruler, the ruler of the ones ruling and lord of the ones being lords, the only one having immortality, dwelling in unapproachable light, whom no one among humans saw, neither is able to see, to whom be honor and power forever, amen** (6:13–16). Paul again employs a word family (**charge**) used previously for Timothy "to pass on or transmit"[85] to others, but, when it has a stronger sense of a command[86] issued to Timothy, it implies his "orders" as a "soldier" of Christ Jesus (2 Tim 2:3–5). God and Jesus are Paul's witnesses. The earlier charge had to do with being impartial (5:21). This charge has to do with keeping the commandment of being **not open to attack** (6:14).[87] Paul picks one quality each to describe God and Jesus. God is described as **the one giving life to all things** (6:13). God as Creator gave life to all beings (4:4). God also will give life to humans at the resurrection. Only God can provide eternal life.[88] The quality by which Jesus is described (**the one having witnessed to Pontius Pilate the good confession**) fits nicely in the context as a

---

82. Rom 8:30; 9:24; 1 Cor 1:9; Gal 1:6; 5:8, 13; 1 Thess 2:12; 4:7; 5:24; 2 Thess 2:14; 2 Tim 1:9.

83. See 1 Tim 3:16.

84. *Homologeō*: BDAG, 708.

85. See 1 Tim 4:11; 1:3; 5:7; 6:17.

86. 1 Tim 1:5, 18; 6:13. See also 5:21.

87. *Anepilēmptos*; 1 Tim 3:2; 5:7.

88. 1 Tim 1:16; 4:8; 6:12.

model for Timothy himself.[89] Paul earlier had reminded Timothy of his own confession (6:12).[90] Timothy, as Jesus before him, had made **good confessions** before witnesses.[91]

As a "soldier" of Christ Jesus, Timothy is to **guard** (6:14). Is the **command spotless** and **not open to attack**[92] or is Timothy being commanded to be **spotless** and **not open to attack**?[93] Probably the latter fits better in the context. **Spotless** and **not open to attack** are adjectives and most likely refer to Timothy's own manner of guarding. **Spotless** (*aspilos*) alludes to the previous references to purity (4:12; 5:2). Jesus is **spotless**, a lamb "without defect" (1 Pet 1:19). *Spilos* is a type of sin that contaminates and spreads.[94] Timothy, like elders and widows, should not become discredited from within or outside the church (**not open to attack**).[95]

Perseverance is needed until Christ returns in the time God has chosen (6:14-15).[96] Whom Jesus Christ reveals is described in an extended clause with three parallel subjects:[97] (1) **the blessed and only ruler**, (2)

---

89. In 1 Tim 2:6, Jesus is described as "the witness to his own times."

90. *Homologia* (v. 12) is the same word as in v. 13.

91. *Martyria* (v. 12), *martyreō* (v. 13). The Gospel of John records the event to which Paul alludes (John 18:33-38). As instructive to Timothy, Jesus describes his own kingdom as not having armed combat (*agōnizomai*). See 1 Tim 6:12. Jesus picks up on Pilate's statement that Jesus is a king (John 18:37; 1 Tim 6:15). Jesus also tells Pilate that he came to witness to the truth, an important theme in 1 Tim (2:4, 7; 3:15; 4:3; 6:5). Pilate also represents a Greco-Roman non-Christian listener (e.g., 2:1-2; 3:2, 7; 5:7-8, 10, 14).

92. Both adjectives are in the accusative case, the same case as **command** (Lock 1924: 72; Kelly 1963: 145; Mounce 2000: 359-60).

93. Marshall 1999: 665; Towner 2006: 415; Lock 1924: 72. In Matt 19:17 keeping the commandments results in life.

94. Jas 3:6; Jude 23; Spencer et al. 2009: 90.

95. 1 Tim 3:2; 5:7; Titus 1:6. What **command** does Paul have in mind? In Titus 1:14, Paul refers to Jewish myths as human commandments. Does Paul, in contrast, in 1 Tim 6:14 refer to God's principles: **stewardship of God's household, the one in faith**, the goal of this **order is love from a clean heart and a good conscience and a genuine faith** (1:4-5)? Or does he refer to the previous sentence: **keep on fighting for yourself the good fight of the faith, grasp for yourself eternal life** (6:12) or to another earlier command to Timothy (4:16)? (Fee 1988: 151-52); charge given at baptism (Lock 1924: 72; Kelly 1963: 144); entire Christian gospel (Marshall 1999: 664-65; Montague 2008: 129); or entire letter (Mounce 2000: 359). Most likely he refers to 1:4-5 since he had also described those words as an **order** (*parangelia*), comparable to the **charge** (*parangellō*) in 6:13.

96. Matt 24:36-39; 25:13; Acts 1:6-7.

97. Each phrase begins with an article. The relative pronoun *hēn* (**which**, 6:15)

the ruler of the ones ruling and lord of the ones being lords, (3) **the only one having immortality, dwelling in unapproachable light** (6:15). Paul has begun and ended the letter with a doxology (1:17). The first one was in a response of gratitude to what Christ did in Paul's life, the second one was as a motivator for Timothy, the One with whom Timothy would spend eternal life, who is worthy of Timothy's "good fight of the faith" (6:12) and serves as a contrast to rich humans (6:17). God gives life to all (6:13) and therefore also is the source of eternal life (1:16; 6:12). The doxologies in both passages may be compared:

Doxologies

1:17	6:15–16
The ruler (*basileus*) of the ages (*aiōn*),	The blessed and only (*monos*) ruler (*dynastēs*);
	The ruler (*basileus*) of the ones ruling and
	Lord (*kyrios*) of the ones being lords,
Imperishable (*aphthartos*),	The only one (*monos*) having immortality (*athanasia*),
Invisible (*aoratos*), only (*monos*) God,	Dwelling in unapproachable light, whom no humans saw and no one is able to see
Response: Be honor (*timē*) and glory forever (*aiōn*) and ever, amen.	Response: To whom be honor (*timē*) and power forever (*aiōnios*), amen..

Both passages appear to describe Jesus at first because of the antecedents (1:14–16; 6:14) but then conclude appearing to describe God the Father ("invisible" [1:17] **whom no one among humans saw, neither is able to see** [6:16]). Both describe the triune God first as the unique **ruler** or sovereign. The closing doxology emphasizes how God is unique (**only ruler**), particularly in comparison to human rulers. Humans are currently ruling, but God always will be **the ruler**. Three synonyms are used

---

agrees with its antecedent *epiphaneia* (**appearing**, 6:14), thereby suggesting the passage refers to Jesus Christ (6:14). However, Jesus was seen by angels and humans (3:16 vs. 6:16), suggesting the doxology refers to God the Father. **Reveal** appears to be the key connection. Jesus **will reveal** fully the nature of the unseen God the Father (cf. John 1:18; 6:46; 14:9). See also Marshall 1999: 654.

to describe God's sovereignty (*dynastēs, basileus,* and *kyrios,* 6:15). All these terms may be used of God and of humans.[98] The human sovereigns are those for whom the church and Timothy should pray (2:2). *Dynastēs* emphasizes God as being able or powerful.[99] *Basileus* emphasizes God as reigning, the **ruler**.[100] *Kyrios* (**lord**) emphasizes God as "*he to whom a person* or *thing belongs, about which he has the power of deciding,*" the "*owner,*" God as having "*dominion over.*"[101] In 1 Timothy, the stronger term *despotēs* is used of only humans: slave masters (6:1–2) and women ruling their households (*oikodespoteō,* 5:14). Trench suggests that generally a *despotēs* "exercises a more unrestricted power and absolute domination" than the *kyrios,* who has authority "owning limitations—moral limitations it may be."[102] Paul sets in perspective the confession Timothy has made and will need to continue to make.[103] If ever he is intimated, Timothy should remember that the ultimate source of his life, God the Trinity, has power, reign, and ownership over all human rulers. **Lord** (*kyrios*) in 1 Timothy is used only of Jesus Christ, the One who strengthens and appoints (1:12), the One whose grace produces faith and love (1:14), the One their message is centered around (6:3), who will return again revealing the full nature of God's kingship (6:15). *Kyrios* is also used of God in the Old Testament (e.g., Gen 2:4), the "Lord of lords" (Deut 10:17), and in the New Testament of Jesus as God incarnate (John 20:28).

The only one having immortality, dwelling in unapproachable light, whom no one among humans saw, neither is able to see, to whom be honor and power forever, amen appears to refer to God the Father but also describes Jesus the Son. *Athanasia* (**immortality,** 6:16) is a synonym of *aphthartos* ("imperishable," 1:17). While *aphthartos* signifies not liable to *decay, athanasia* signifies not liable to *death* (*thanatos*).[104] Humans, at

---

98. E.g., about humans *dynastēs*: Luke 1:52; Acts 8:27; *basileus*: 1 Tim 2:2; *kyrios*: Eph 6:5.

99. E.g., Rom 14:4; 2 Cor 9:8; 13:3; Thayer, 160.

100. See 1 Tim 1:17; Thayer, 98.

101. Thayer, 365.

102. Trench 1880: 96.

103. 1 Tim 6:12, 14; 2 Tim 1:8.

104. See 1 Tim 1:17. Paul uses the two terms synonymously in 1 Cor 15:53–54: "For the perishable must clothe itself with the imperishable (*aphtharsia*), and the mortal with immortality (*athanasia*). When the perishable has been clothed with the imperishable, and the mortal with immortality, then the saying that is written will come true: 'Death has been swallowed up in victory.'"

the resurrection, will have new bodies that do not die because God is a God over whom death is not master. Jesus did die, but he was resurrected.

Light (*phōs*, 6:16) is a significant aspect of Paul's life. His life was turned around when suddenly, as he journeyed to Damascus, to persecute Christian men and women, "a light from heaven flashed around him," blinding him.[105] Only by God through Ananias could Saul be healed.[106] This light was "brighter than the sun" (Acts 26:13). Paul's ministry then came to be to "enlighten" others.[107] Humans can not directly look into the sun without eventually becoming blind. Paul thus describes God the Trinity as dwelling in **unapproachable** light. Like a shining fortress encompassed by deep, dark valleys[108] is God. Light is a frequent metaphor for righteousness.[109] God created light.[110] Metaphorically, God is light. Jesus "was the true light, the one giving light to all people."[111] In the New Jerusalem, no "great lights" (sun or moon) will be needed because the Lamb will be the lamp.[112] God is so awesome that what blinds humans is to God merely a robe that serves as a garment to cover oneself (Ps 103:2 LXX).[113] No one is able to see God and live (Exod 33:20) but, yet, by God becoming flesh, humans could then see God.[114] Paul closes this doxology, as he did the other one (1:17), blessing God with **honor**[115] and also **power** or strength (6:16).

---

105. Acts 9:3, 8–9; 22:6, 11.

106. Acts 9:15, 17–18; 22:13.

107. Acts 13:47; 26:18.

108. Josephus, *J.W.* 7.8.2 [280].

109. E.g., 1 John 1:5–7; Prov 4:18.

110. Gen 1:3–5; Jas 1:17. **Light** can refer to lamps, candlesticks, and fire (Exod 27:20; 35:16; Lev 24:2; 2 Chron 4:20; Isa 50:11; Jer 25:10; Mark 14:54), or to the sun, moon, and stars, the "great lights" (Ps 135:7–9 LXX; Isa 13:10; Jer 4:23; 38:35).

111. John 1:9; 3:19; 8:12; 9:5; 12:35–36, 46; 1 John 1:5. At the transfiguration, Jesus became as "white as the light" (Matt 17:2).

112. Rev 21:23; 22:5.

113. See also Exod 24:17, where the glory of the Lord was like burning fire and Acts 2:3, where the Holy Spirit appeared "as fire."

114. 1 Tim 3:16; John 1:14; 1 John 1:1.

115. See 1 Tim 5:3, 17; Rev 5:13.

THE RICH (6:17-19)

Paul adds an admonition directly for the rich as a group (vs. 6:9-10 is addressed to Timothy about wealth), as he did for overseers, ministers/deacons, widows, and slaves: **To the rich ones in the now age—charge not to be haughty and not to hope upon the uncertainty of riches but upon God, the one supplying to us all things richly to enjoy, to do good, to be rich in good works, to be free to give, to be ready to share, storing up for themselves a good foundation for the future, in order that they might grasp the real life** (6:17-19). Paul wants Timothy to instruct[116] the wealthy[117] in six ways: **not to be haughty, not to hope upon the uncertainty of riches**, but, rather, to **hope upon God, to do good, to be rich in good works**, and **to be free to give.** How can anyone be **haughty** after comparing oneself with "the blessed and only ruler, the ruler of the ones ruling and lord of the ones being lords, the only one having immortality, dwelling in unapproachable light, whom no humans saw and no one is able to see" (6:15-16)? *Hyphēlophroneō* (**haughty**, 6:17), literally, is "*to be high-minded*" since *hyphēlos* is "*high; lofty.*"[118] *Hyphēlos* may refer to a very high mountain (Matt 4:8; 17:1). Ancients would build their fortresses often on top of high mountains for protection. A pile of wealth, too, can serve for protection. But only God is "the Majesty on high" (Heb 1:3). The rich believers are not to be like the Gentiles who think they are superior (*hyphēlos*) to the Jews because they have replaced some unbelieving Jews in God's kingdom (Rom 11:20). Rather, the rich should think they are the same as others, not thinking themselves to be superior, but rather to associate with the lowly (Rom 12:16).

In contrast to relying upon riches, the rich are to rely upon **God**.[119] God has already been described as "the one giving life to all things" (6:13). In 6:17, God is **the one supplying to us all things richly to enjoy**. Paul had already explained that God supplies many material gifts, such as marriage and foods, which should be enjoyed in a thankful manner (4:3-4). Ecclesiastes similarly states it is good "to eat and to drink" since that is "God's gift" to those whom God has given "wealth and possessions" to enjoy (Eccl 5:17-18 LXX). However, "if wealth should flow in, set not your heart upon it" (Ps 61:10 LXX).

116. See 1 Tim 4:11.
117. See 1 Tim 6:9.
118. Thayer, 646.
119. Ps 51:7 LXX.

The reason God blesses materially is so that people can then "share abundantly in every good work" (2 Cor 9:8). Paul had illustrated by example to the Ephesians that by working they could help those who were less strong, citing Jesus' own words: "It is more blessed to give than to receive" (Acts 20:34–35). Giving helps others, but also oneself (1 Tim 6:9–10). Paul uses four synonymous phrases to describe this same point. The first verb is the most general: **to do good** (6:18). For instance, when Tabitha (Dorcas) made clothing for the widows, she did good works (Acts 9:36–39). Wealthy women at Ephesus were already encouraged to dress with "good deeds" rather than flaunting their wealth in finery during worship (2:9–10). A true widow also must have done many good deeds (5:10). Paul had explained this message to King Agrippa: "I was proclaiming (to Jew and Gentile) to repent and to turn to God, doing works worthy of repentance" (Acts 26:20). The second verb is metaphorical: **to be *rich* in good works** (6:18). As God provides **richly** to humans physically and spiritually (6:17), so too humans should provide richly for others (6:18), but these "riches" are good deeds.[120] The third phrase has two parts: **to be free to give, ready to share** (6:18). These two adjectives are more concrete.[121]

The last adjective (*koinōnikos*, **share**, 6:18) summarizes the list of exhortations to the rich. A *koinōnos* was a business partnership, such as the fishing partnership of James, John, and Simon Peter (Luke 5:10). A *koinos* or *koineion* could refer to a religious, professional, or social association or club. These clubs would provide benefits for their members, including some social services, such as burial sites and banquets.[122] The Christians in Jerusalem as a religious group went further—they had all things in common (Acts 2:44). Paul had already encouraged the elders who taught to be given honorariums (1 Tim 5:17–18). Hospitality is another way to **share** (Rom 12:13).[123] By the rich sharing their riches, they

---

120. See Titus 3:5; Acts 14:17.

121. *Eumetadotos* signifies "to share well" or to be "*ready* or *free to impart; liberal*," "*generous*" (Thayer, 256, 260, 404; BDAG, 409). One reason for former thieves to work and not steal was to "share" (*metadidōmi*) with those having needs (Eph 4:28). Jesus had taught his disciples to "share" extra food and clothing with others (Luke 3:11).

122. *NewDocs* 2:49; LSJ, 968.

123. Hebrews exhorts Christians to "not neglect the doing of good and sharing (*koinōnia*), for such sacrifices God finds pleasing" (13:16). The Philippians were a unique congregation Paul allowed to contribute regularly financially to his own ministry (Phil 1:5; 4:10–18).

would now be contributing to a different kind of bank account,[124] one that truly helped for the future in order that **they might grasp the real life** (6:19). **Eternal life** (6:12) is **the real life** (6:19). Effort must be made so as to obtain it in its fullness.[125]

Fusing the Horizons: Living with Wealth

Few people consider themselves "rich." However, statistically, most of us in "developed" countries are "rich," if we consider that at least 80% of humans live on less than $10 U.S./day.[126] If we begin with this basis, then we are indeed "rich." So what should we do about it?
1. Maintain a balance of thanksgiving and generosity. Enjoy God's gifts of marriage and material blessings, while working out a budget to assist others to enjoy these too.
2. Be satisfied with the basic necessities of food, clothing, and shelter. Beware of simply wanting what others have or others expect you to have.
3. Work on getting your security from God, not wealth, and seek to please God in words and actions.

GUARD THE DEPOSIT (6:20–21)

Paul summarizes the letter as he leaves Timothy with a final exhortation and a closing salutation: **O Timothy, guard the deposit, turning away from the godless empty talk and contradictions of the falsely called knowledge, with which some, professing concerning the faith, missed the mark. Grace be with you** (6:20–21). Paul addresses Timothy with an exclamation of anguish and depth of feeling (**oh!**)[127] and then focuses on what Timothy has to guard—**the deposit** (6:20).[128] Paul is most likely

---

124. *Apothēsaurizō* signifies "to treasure away" (Thayer, 61) or "laying up in store" (Robertson 1931: 596). See also Luke 12:33; 18:22.

125. See 1 Tim 6:12.

126. Shah 2010, para. 1.

127. LSJ, 2029.

128. *Parathēkē* may refer to money or a valuable item. A **deposit** is "*a trust or thing consigned to one's faithful keeping*" (Thayer, 482). *Parathēkē* may refer to a message that

alluding back to 1:5 ("the goal of the order is love from a clean heart and a good conscience and a genuine faith"), from which the heterodox teachers had deviated (1:6).[129] In 2 Timothy, Paul will exhort Timothy to find others upon whom to rely (2:2). As a good soldier of Christ Jesus (2 Tim 2:3), Timothy needs to emulate the good tribune Claudius Lysias, to whom was entrusted the prisoner *Paulos* of Tarsus. He used a detachment of 200 heavily armed soldiers, 70 cavalrymen, and 200 spearmen to bring Paul through the night from Jerusalem to Caesarea in order to keep him alive (Acts 23:23–35).

Timothy needs a strategy that faces two ways: one is proactively guarding what has been entrusted to him, the other is proactively resisting (**turning away from**) what could mislead him.[130] This false teaching is summarized as **empty talk and contradictions** (6:20). *Kenophōnia* (**empty talk**) appears to be a synonym of *mataiologia*. *Mataiologia* are words that have no value because the content is not true.[131] They are satanic. *Kenophōnia* are sounds (*phōnē*) that are empty (*kenos*), without a truthful, real goal,[132] therefore, they deceive (Eph 5:6). These **empty** sounds are unholy, leading to acts that lack piety (**godless**, *bebēlos*).[133] Study of the truth is protection against them (2 Tim 2:15–16).

Talk without value is a synonym for **contradictions** (*antithesis*). According to Aristotle, an *antithesis* is a syllogism in which contraries are placed side by side, for example, "The wise are unsuccessful, while fools

---

is only to be revealed to someone trustworthy (Herodotus, *Hist.* 9.45). For example, the priests in Jerusalem were entrusted with four hundred talents of silver and two hundred talents of gold for the relief of widows and orphans (2 Macc 3:10, 15). One sin in the law was to steal a deposit entrusted to one. This item had to be restored to the owner (Lev 6:2–4). The comparable verb *paratithēmi* in the middle voice, signifying "*to deposit; intrust, commit to one's charge*" (Thayer, 486) was used by Paul at the start of the letter ("This order *I am entrusting* to you, child Timothy," 1:18).

129. In the closing of 6:20–21, Paul uses a number of words that allude back to the start of the letter creating a well-rounded message. Some of these words reappear in 2 Tim: *parathēkē* vs. *paratithēmi* (1:18); *astocheō* (1:6; 2 Tim 2:18); *ektrepō* (1:6; 2 Tim 4:4); *bebēlos* (1:9; 2 Tim 2:16); *pistis* (1:4; 2 Tim 1:13); *kenophōnia* vs. *mataiologia* (1:6); *pseudōnymos* and *pseudologos* (4:2). Others think that the **deposit** is the whole letter (Fee 1988: 161) or the whole of the apostolic teaching (Marshall 1999: 675–76; Witherington 2006: 298; Towner 2006: 431).

130. *Ektrepō* is otherwise used in a negative way of the heterodox **turning** or twisting away from the true order. See 1:6; 5:15; 2 Tim 4:4.

131. See 1:6; Titus 1:10.

132. 1 Cor 15:4; 2 Cor 6:1; Gal 2:2; Phil 2:16.

133. See 1 Tim 1:9.

succeed" or "Some of them perished miserably, others saved themselves disgracefully." Aristotle explains that "this kind of style is pleasing" (*Rhet.* 3.9.7–9). There is nothing inherently wrong with *antithesis* or **knowledge**, however, what was at Ephesus was false, not real, true knowledge.[134] But, possibly *antithesis* indicates some of the appeal of the false teachers who were playing with words that engage the mind but do not lead to truth. Those who **profess** this content, declaring themselves adherents who will carry it out, **miss the mark** (*astocheō*). Their aim is bad or amiss.[135] Possibly, **the mark** could refer to the goal (*skopos*) or post toward which a runner ran (Phil 3:14).[136] The false teachers were missing the true mark: "love from a clean heart and a good conscience and a genuine faith" (1:5).

Paul closes his letter with his brief farewell.[137] He uses the plural **you** (6:21), which shows that, although he writes to Timothy (1:2), he does so in the context of the whole church.[138] Paul ends his letters frequently referring to **grace**.[139] In this letter, it is a reminder of the grace of the Lord that overflowed with faith and love in Paul's own life resulting in his own grace or thankfulness (1:12, 14). Therefore, Paul prays that Timothy and the church "experience God's gracious presence among them."[140]

---

134. Irenaeus (A.D. 180) entitled his work referring to 6:20 *Refutation and Overthrow of Knowledge Falsely So-Called* (Eusebius, *Hist. eccl.* 5.7.1). In contrast, Marcion entitled his heretical work *Antetheses* (A.D. 150) (Kelly 1963: 151).

135. LSJ, 262, 1650; BDAG, 356.

136. Gardiner 1930: 135.

137. 1 Tim 6:20 has the same closing as 2 Tim 4:22 and Col. 4:18. See Titus 3:15.

138. Paul intends the letter to be read in church(es): Fee 1988: 162; Kelly 1963: 152; Montague 2008: 134; Witherington 2006: 299.

139. 2 Tim 4:22; Titus 3:15; 2 Cor 13:13; Gal 6:18; Eph 6:24; Phil 4:23; Col 4:18; 1 Thess 5:28; 2 Thess 3:18; Phlm 25.

140. Towner 2006: 435.

Bibliography

Arnold, Irene Ringwood. 1972. "Festivals of Ephesus." *AJA* 76: 17–22.
Aune, David E. 1987. *The New Testament in Its Literary Environment*. LEC. Philadelphia: Westminster.
Balch, David L. 1981. *Let Wives Be Submissive: The Domestic Code in 1 Peter*. SBLMS 26. Chico, CA: Scholars.
Baring-Gould, S. 1897–98. *The Lives of the Saints*. 16 vols. London: John C. Nimmo.
Barrett, C. K. 1963. *The Pastoral Epistles in the New English Bible*. Oxford: Clarendon.
Bassler, Jouette M. 1984. "The Widow's Tale: A Fresh Look at 1 Tim 5:3–16." *JBL* 103.1: 23–41.
———. 1996. *1 Timothy, 2 Timothy, Titus*. ANTC. Nashville: Abingdon.
Belleville, Linda L. 2005. "Teaching and Usurping Authority: 1 Timothy 2:11–15." In *Discovering Biblical Equality: Complementarity without Hierarchy*, edited by Ronald W. Pierce and Rebecca Merrill Groothuis, 205–23. 2nd ed. Downers Grove, IL: InterVarsity.
Belleville, Linda L., Jon C. Laansma, and J. Ramsey Michaels. 2009. *Cornerstone Biblical Commentary: 1 Timothy, 2 Timothy, Titus, Hebrews*. Carol Stream, IL: Tyndale.
Bennett, Florence Mary. 1967. *Religious Cults Associated with the Amazons*. New York: AMS.
Bernard, J. H. 1922. *The Pastoral Epistles*. CGTSC. Cambridge: Cambridge University Press.
Betz, Hans Dieter, editor. 1986. *The Greek Magical Papyri in Translation*. Chicago: University of Chicago Press.
Bradley, Keith. 1994. *Slavery and Society at Rome*. Cambridge: Cambridge University Press.
Branigan, Keith, and Michael Vickers. 1980. *Hellas: The Civilizations of Ancient Greece*. New York: McGraw-Hill.
Brooten, Bernadette J. 1982. *Women Leaders in the Ancient Synagogue: Inscriptional Evidence and Background Issues*. Brown Judaic Studies 36. Chico, CA: Scholars.
Bruce, F. F. 1990. *The Acts of the Apostles: Greek Text with Introduction and Commentary*. 3rd ed. Grand Rapids: Eerdmans.
Calvin, John. N.d. *Calvin's Commentaries 10: John-Acts*. Wilmington, DE: Associated Publishers and Authors.
Campbell, Constantine R. 2008. *Basics of Verbal Aspect in Biblical Greek*. Grand Rapids: Zondervan.
Caragounis, Chrys C. 2004. *The Development of Greek and the New Testament: Morphology, Syntax, Phonology, and Textual Transmission*. WUNT 167. Tübingen: Mohr Siebeck.
Cohick, Lynn H. 2009. *Women in the World of the Earliest Christians: Illuminating Ancient Ways of Life*. Grand Rapids: Baker.
Consumer Reports on Health. 1999. "Wine and Health" (Nov) 10.

Cox, Benjamin D., and Susan Ackerman. 2009. "Rachel's Tomb." *JBL* 128:1 (Spring) 135–48.
Dibelius, Martin, and Hans Conzelmann. 1972. *The Pastoral Epistles*. Hermeneia. Translated by P. Buttolph and A. Yarbro. Edited by H. Koester. Philadelphia: Fortress.
Donelson, Lewis R. 1986. *Pseudepigraphy and Ethical Argument in the Pastoral Epistles*. Tübingen: J. C. B. Mohr.
Ellicott, Charles J. 1865. *A Critical and Grammatical Commentary on the Pastoral Epistles*. Andover, MA: Warren F. Draper.
Erdemgil, Selahattin. 2009. *Selçuk Ephesus*. Istanbul: Net Turistik Yayinlar.
Fantham, Elaine, Helene Peet Foley, Natalie Boymel Kampen, Sarah B. Pomeroy, and H. Alan Shapiro. 1994. *Women in the Classical World: Image and Text*. New York: Oxford University Press.
Fee, Gordon D. 1988. *NIBC: 1 and 2 Timothy, Titus*. Peabody, MA: Hendrickson.
Gardiner, E. Norman. 1980. *Athletics of the Ancient World*. Chicago: Ares.
Gerhardsson, Birger. 1961. *Memory and Manuscript: Oral Tradition and Written Transmission in Rabbinic Judaism and Early Christianity*. Lund: C. W. K. Gleerup.
Goodwater, Leanna. 1975. *Women in Antiquity: An Annotated Bibliography*. Metuchen, NJ: Scarecrow.
Gordon, A. J. 2010. *How Christ Came to Church: The Pastor's Dream A Spiritual Autobiography*. Grand Rapids: Kregel.
The Greek Anthology. Translated by W. R. Paton. 5 vols. LCL. New York: Putnam, 1915.
Grenz, Stanley J. 1995. *Women in the Church: A Biblical Theology of Women in Ministry*. Downers Grove, IL: InterVarsity.
Gritz, Sharon Hodgin. 1991. *Paul, Women Teachers, and the Mother Goddess at Ephesus: A Study of 1 Timothy 2:9-15 in Light of The Religious and Cultural Milieu of The First Century*. Lanham, MD: University Press of America.
Groothuis, Rebecca Merrill. 1997. *Good News for Women: A Biblical Picture of Gender Equality*. Grand Rapids: Baker.
Guthrie, Donald. 1990. *The Pastoral Epistles*. TNTC. Downers Grove, IL: InterVarsity.
Hanson, A. T. 1982. *The Pastoral Epistles*. NCBC. Grand Rapids: Eerdmans.
Harris, Murray J. 1992. *Jesus as God: The New Testament Use of Theos in Reference to Jesus*. Grand Rapids: Baker.
Harris, R. Laird. 1969. *Inspiration and Canonicity of the Bible: An Historical and Exegetical Study*. 2nd ed. Grand Rapids: Zondervan.
Harrison, P. N. 1964. *Paulines and Pastorals*. London: Villiers.
Hawkes, Jacquetta. 1968. *Dawn of the Gods*. New York: Random House.
Heine, Ronald E. 2002. *The Commentaries of Origen and Jerome on St. Paul's Epistle to the Ephesians*. Oxford Early Christian Studies. Oxford: Oxford University Press.
Hemer, Colin J. 1986. *The Letters to the Seven Churches of Asia in Their Local Setting*. JSNT 11. Sheffield: JSOT.
Hillard, A. E. 1919. *The Pastoral Epistles of St. Paul*. London: Rivingtons.
Hood, Sinclair. 1971. *The Minoans: The Story of Bronze Age Crete*. New York: Praeger.
Horsley, G. H. R. 1987. "Early Evidence of Women Officers in the Church." *Priscilla Papers* 1:4 (Fall) 3–4.
Hull, Gretchen Gaebelein. 1987. *Equal to Serve: Women and Men in the Church and Home*. Old Tappan, NJ: Fleming Revell.

Humphreys, A. E. 1895. *The Epistles to Timothy and Titus*. Cambridge: Cambridge University Press.
Hurley, James B. 1981. *Man and Woman in Biblical Perspective*. Grand Rapids: Zondervan.
Ilan, Tal. 1996. *Jewish Women in Greco-Roman Palestine*. Peabody, MA: Hendrickson.
Irwin, Brian P. 2008. "The Laying on of Hands in 1 Timothy 5:22: A New Proposal." *BBR* 18.1: 123–29.
Jeremias, Joachim. 1969. *Jerusalem in the Time of Jesus: An Investigation into Economic and Social Conditions during the New Testament Period*. Philadelphia: Fortress.
Johnson, Luke Timothy. 1996. *Letters to Paul's Delegates: 1 Timothy, 2 Timothy, Titus*. The New Testament in Context. Valley Forge, PA: Trinity.
Keener, Craig S. 1992. *Paul, Women, and Wives: Marriage and Women's Ministry in the Letters of Paul*. Peabody, MA: Hendrickson.
Kelly, J. N. D. 1963. *A Commentary on The Pastoral Epistles (1 Timothy, 2 Timothy, Titus)*. HNTC. New York: Harper and Row.
Koch, Kurt E. 1965. *Christian Counseling and Occultism*. Translated by Andrew Petter. Grand Rapids: Kregel.
Kohlenberger, John R., III, Edward W. Goodrick, and James A. Swanson. 1995. *The Exhaustive Concordance to the Greek New Testament*. Grand Rapids: Zondervan.
Kroeger, Catherine Clark. 1995. "God/dess of the Past." In *The Goddess Revival*, edited by Aída Besançon Spencer, Donna F. G. Hailson, Catherine Clark Kroeger, William David Spencer, 57–74. Grand Rapids: Baker.
———. N.d. "Who Are the Individuals Whose Conduct the Apostle Paul Deplores in 1 Cor 6:9–11?" Hamilton: Gordon-Conwell Theological Seminary. Photocopy.
Kroeger, Richard Clark, and Catherine Clark Kroeger. 1992. *I Suffer Not a Woman: Rethinking 1 Timothy 2:11–15 in Light of Ancient Evidence*. Grand Rapids: Baker.
Kubo, Sakae. 1975. *A Reader's Greek-English Lexicon of the New Testament*. Grand Rapids: Zondervan.
Lanham, Richard A. 1991. *A Handlist of Rhetorical Terms*. 2nd ed. Berkeley: University of California Press.
Lea, T. D. 1991. "Pseudonymity and the New Testament." In *New Testament Criticism and Interpretation*, edited by David Alan Black and David S. Dockery, 535–59. Grand Rapids: Zondervan.
LiDonnici, Lynn R. 1992. "The Images of Artemis Ephesia and Greco-Roman Worship: A Reconsideration." *HTR* 85:4 (Oct) 389–415.
Liefeld, Walter L. 1999. *1 and 2 Timothy, Titus*. NIVAC. Grand Rapids: Zondervan.
Lightfoot, J. B. 1913. *St. Paul's Epistle to the Philippians*. Grand Rapids: Zondervan.
Lock, Walter. 1924. *A Critical and Exegetical Commentary on The Pastoral Epistles*. ICC. Edinburgh: T. & T. Clark.
MacDonald, George. 1949. *The Princess and Curdie*. New York: E. P. Dutton.
Madigan, Kevin, and Carolyn Osiek, editors, translators. 2005. *Ordained Women in the Early Church: A Documentary History*. Baltimore: Johns Hopkins University Press.
Maloney, Linda M. 1994. "The Pastoral Epistles." In *Searching the Scriptures I*, edited by Elisabeth Schüssler Fiorenza, 361–80. New York: Crossroad.
Marshall, I. Howard. 1999. *A Critical and Exegetical Commentary on The Pastoral Epistles*. ICC. Edinburgh: T. & T. Clark.
Marxsen, Willi. 1970. *Introduction to the New Testament: An Approach to its Problems*. Translated by G. Buswell. Philadelphia: Fortress.

McKenna, Mary Lawrence. 1967. *Women of the Church: Role and Renewal*. New York: Kenedy.

Meinardus, Otto F. 1979. *St. Paul in Ephesus and the Cities of Galatia and Cyprus*. New Rochelle, NY: Lycabettus.

Mitchell, Stephen. 1993. *Anatolia: Land, Men, and Gods in Asia Minor*. 2 vols. Oxford: Clarendon.

Montague, George T. 2008. *First and Second Timothy, Titus*. Catholic Commentary on Sacred Scripture. Grand Rapids: Baker.

Moo, Douglas. 1991. "What Does It Mean Not to Teach or Have Authority over Men? 1 Timothy 2:11–15." In *Recovering Biblical Manhood and Womanhood: A Response to Evangelical Feminism*, edited by John Piper and Wayne Grudem, 179–93. Wheaton: Crossway.

Morris, Joan. 1973. *The Lady Was a Bishop*. New York: MacMillan.

Mounce, William D. 2000. *Pastoral Epistles*. WBC 46. Nashville: Thomas Nelson.

Murphy-O'Connor, Jerome. 2008. *St. Paul's Ephesus: Texts and Archaeology*. Collegeville, MN: Liturgical.

Neil, James. 1920. *Everyday Life in the Holy Land*. New York: MacMillan.

Ngewa, Samuel. 2009. *1 and 2 Timothy and Titus*. African Bible Commentary Series. Grand Rapids: Zondervan.

Nilsson, Martin P. 1971. *The Minoan-Mycenaean Religion and Its Survival in Greek Religion*. 2nd ed. New York: Biblo and Tannen.

Overstreet, R. Larry. 2000. "The Greek Concept of the 'Seven Stages of Life' and Its New Testament Significance." *BBR* 19:4: 537–63.

Payne, Philip B. 2009. *Man and Woman, One in Christ: An Exegetical and Theological Study of Paul's Letters*. Grand Rapids: Zondervan.

Plummer, Alfred. 1922. *A Critical and Exegetical Commentary on the Gospel According to S. Luke*. ICC. 5th ed. Edinburgh: T. & T. Clark.

Pomeroy, Sarah B. 1975. *Goddesses, Whores, Wives, and Slaves: Women in Classical Antiquity*. New York: Schocken.

———. 1984. *Women in Hellenistic Egypt: From Alexander to Cleopatra*. New York: Schocken.

Porter, Stanley E. 1992. *Idioms of the Greek New Testament*. Biblical Languages: Greek 2. Sheffield: Sheffield Academic Press.

———. 1995. "Pauline Authorship and the Pastoral Epistles: Implications for Canon." *BBR* 5: 105–23.

Pursiful, Darrell. 2001. "Ordained Women of the Patristic Era." *Priscilla Papers* 15:3 (Summer) 7–13.

Quinn, Jerome D., and William C. Wacker. 2000. *The First and Second Letters to Timothy*. ECC. Grand Rapids: Eerdmans.

Ramos, Marcos Antonio. 1992. *I y II Timoteo y Tito*. Comentario Bíblico Hispanoamericano. Miami: Editorial Caribe.

Ramsay, W. M. 1895. *The Cities and Bishoprics of Phrygia*. 2 vols. Oxford: Clarendon.

———. 1908. *The Cities of St. Paul*. New York: A. C. Armstrong.

———. 1927. *Asianic Elements in Greek Civilisation*. New York: AMS.

———. 1994. *The Letters to the Seven Churches*. Edited by Mark W. Wilson. Peabody, MA: Hendrickson.

———. 2001. *St. Paul: The Traveler and Roman Citizen*. Edited by Mark Wilson. Grand Rapids: Kregel.

Random House Webster's Unabridged Dictionary. 2001. New York: Random House.
Robertson, A. T. 1930–31. *Word Pictures in the New Testament.* 6 vols. Nashville: Broadman.
———. 1934. *A Grammar of the Greek New Testament in the Light of Historical Research.* Nashville: Broadman.
———. 2005. *Word Pictures in the New Testament II: The Gospel According to Luke.* Revised by Wesley J. Perschbacher. Grand Rapids: Kregel.
Scheck, Thomas P., translator. *St. Jerome's Commentaries on Galatians, Titus, and Philemon.* Notre Dame: University of Notre Dame Press, 2010.
Scherer, Margaret R. 1955. *Marvels of Ancient Rome.* New York: Phaidon.
Scherrer, Peter, editor. 2000. *Ephesus: The New Guide.* Translated by Lionel Bier and George Luxon. Turkey: Graphis.
Schreiner, Thomas R. 2005. "An Interpretation of 1 Timothy 2:9–15: A Dialogue with Scholarship." In *Women in the Church: An Analysis and Application of 1 Timothy 2:9–15,* edited by Andreas J. Köstenberger and Thomas R. Schreiner, 85–120. 2nd ed. Grand Rapids: Baker.
Schürer, Emil. 1979. *The History of the Jewish People in the Age of Jesus Christ (175 B.C.—A.D. 135).* 4 vols. Edited by Geza Vermes, Fergus Millar, and Matthew Black. 2nd ed. Edinburgh: T. & T. Clark.
Schüssler Fiorenza, Elisabeth. 1975. "Wisdom Mythology and the Christological Hymns of the New Testament." In *Aspects of Wisdom in Judaism and Early Christianity,* edited by Robert L. Wilken, 17–42. Notre Dame, IN: University of Notre Dame.
Shah, Anup. 2010. "Poverty Facts and Stats." *Global Issues* (September). No pages. Online: http://www.globalissues.org/article/26/poverty-facts-and-stats.
Sider, Ronald J. 2005. *The Scandal of the Evangelical Conscience: Why Are Christians Living Just Like the Rest of the World?* Grand Rapids: Baker.
Spencer, Aída Besançon. 1985. *Beyond the Curse: Women Called to Ministry.* Grand Rapids: Baker.
———. 1990a. "God's Order Is Love." *Brethren in Christ History and Life* 13 (April) 39–50.
———. 1991. "Romans 1: Finding God in Creation." In *Through No Fault of Their Own? The Fate of Those Who Have Never Heard,* edited by William V. Crockett and James G. Sigountos, 125–35. Grand Rapids: Baker.
———. 1998b. *Paul's Literary Style: A Stylistic and Historical Comparison of 2 Corinthians 11:16—12:13, Romans 8:9–39, and Philippians 3:2—4:13.* Lanham, MD: University Press of America.
———. 2001. *2 Corinthians.* The People's Bible Commentary. Oxford: BRF.
———. 2005. "'El Hogar' as Ministry Team: Stephana(s)'s Household." In *Hispanic Christian Thought at the Dawn of the 21st Century: Apuntes in Honor of Justo L. González,* edited by Alvin Padilla, Roberto Goizueta, and Eldin Villafañe, 69–77. Nashville: Abingdon.
Spencer, Aída Besançon, Donna F. G. Hailson, Catherine Clark Kroeger, and William David Spencer. 1995. *The Goddess Revival: A Biblical Response to God(dess) Spirituality.* Eugene, OR: Wipf and Stock.
Spencer, Aída Besançon, and William David Spencer. 1990b. *The Prayer Life of Jesus: Shout of Agony, Revelation of Love, A Commentary.* Lanham, MD: University Press of America.
———, editors. 1998a. *The Global God: Multicultural Evangelical Views of God.* Grand Rapids: Baker.

Spencer, Aída Besançon, William David Spencer, Steven R. Tracy, and Celestia G. Tracy. 2009. *Marriage at the Crossroads: Couples in Conversation about Discipleship, Gender Roles, Decision Making and Intimacy.* Downers Grove, IL: InterVarsity.
Spencer, William David. 1989. "The Power in Paul's Teaching." *JETS* 32:1: 51–61.
———. 1992. *Mysterium and Mystery: The Clerical Crime Novel.* Carbondale: Southern Illinois University Press.
———. 2006. "Global Views of the Messiah." *Doon Theological Journal* 3:1: 21–41.
Strauss, Mark. 1998. "Linguistic and Hermeneutic Fallacies in the Guidelines Established at the 'Conference on Gender-Related Language in Scripture.'" *JETS* 41: 239–62.
Strelan, Rick. 1996. *Paul, Artemis, and the Jews in Ephesus.* Beihefte zur Zeitschrift für die neutestamentliche Wissenschaft und die Kunde der älteren Kirche 80. New York: Walter de Gruyter.
Swidler, Leonard. 1976. *Women in Judaism: The Status of Women in Formative Judaism.* Metuchen, NJ: Scarecrow.
Thomas, Christine. 1995. "At Home in the City of Artemis: Religion in Ephesos in the Literary Imagination of the Roman Period." In *Ephesos: Metropolis of Asia, An Interdisciplinary Approach to Its Archaeology, Religion, and Culture,* edited by Helmut Koester, 81–118. Valley Forge, PA: Trinity.
Towner, Philip H. 2006. *The Letters to Timothy and Titus.* NICNT. Grand Rapids: Eerdmans.
Trebilco, Paul R. 1991. *Jewish Communities in Asia Minor.* SNTSMS 69. New York: Cambridge University Press.
———. 1994. "Asia." In *The Book of Acts in Its First Century Setting, Volume 2: The Book of Acts in Its Graeco-Roman Setting,* edited by David W. J. Gill and Conrad Gempf, 291–362. Grand Rapids: Eerdmans.
———. 2004. *The Early Christians in Ephesus from Paul to Ignatius.* Grand Rapids: Eerdmans.
Trench, Richard C. 1880. *Synonyms of the New Testament.* 8th ed. Grand Rapids: Eerdmans.
Webb, William J. 2001. *Slaves, Women and Homosexuals: Exploring the Hermeneutics of Cultural Analysis.* Downers Grove, IL: InterVarsity.
Westcott, Brooke Foss. 1896. *A General Survey of the History of the Canon of the New Testament.* 7th ed. New York: Macmillan.
Wiedemann, Thomas. 1981. *Greek and Roman Slavery.* Baltimore: Johns Hopkins University Press.
Winter, Bruce W. 2003. *Roman Wives, Roman Widows: The Appearance of New Women and the Pauline Communities.* Grand Rapids: Eerdmans.
Witherington, Ben, III. 2006. *Letters and Homilies for Hellenized Christians.* Vol. 1. *A Socio-Rhetorical Commentary on Titus, 1–2 Timothy and 1–3 John.* Downers Grove, IL: InterVarsity.
Wood, J. T. 1877. *Discoveries at Ephesus.* London: Longmans, Green.
Yamauchi, Edwin M. 1980. *New Testament Cities in Western Asia Minor: Light from Archaeology on Cities of Paul and the Seven Churches of Revelation.* Grand Rapids: Baker.
Zahn, Theodor. 1953. *Introduction to the New Testament.* 3 vols. Minneapolis, MN: Klock & Klock.
Zinserling, Verena. 1972. *Women in Greece and Rome.* New York: Abner Schram.

Subject Index

abuse. *See* violence.
Acts of Paul, 4
Adam, 34, 51, 67–72, 74. *See also*
    Eve.
adelphos (brother), 108n
adultery, 32, 81–83, 127
Agrippa, 5, 48, 162
aidōs (respect), 55–56
Akabya ben Mahalaleel, Rabbi, 41
Alexander, 13, 25, 42, 44–45, 49, 89.
    See also Hymenaeus.
Alexander, the Great, 29
Amazon(s), 14–15, 17, 29, 65
analogy, 68, 76, 141
Ananias, 52, 102, 160
Androchus, son of Codrus, 14
anaphora, 113n
angel(s), 98, 138
anger, 54
Antioch, 23, 36, 103
Antiochus II, 14
Antipater, 15, 63
Apollos, 13, 61
apostle(s), 21, 49, 52, 78, 88, 90, 96,
    98–99, 116, 145n
Apostolic Constitutions, 9
Appian, 63
Aquila, *See* Prisca.
Aristarchus, 13, 80, 152
Aristotle, 64, 142, 164–65
arsenokoitēs, 33
Artemidorus, 50
Artemis, 14–18, 24–25, 30, 33, 41,
    50, 57, 65, 75, 85, 106, 128,
    150, 152. *See also* magic.
ascetism, 25, 105–106, 129, 140–41,
    147–48

Asia, 10, 13–14, 16, 24, 29, 57, 90n,
    106, 129, 142, 150. *See also*
    Ephesus.
asyndeton, 113n, 153n
Athenaeus, 16
athletics. *See* soldier(s).
Attalus Philometor, 14
Augustus. *See* Octavius Augustus.
Aurelia Artemis, 123–24
autarkeia. *See* contentment.
authenteō (domineer), 62–67, 69.
    See also authority.
authority, 63–70, 113, 121, 133, 137,
    159. *See also authenteō*.
authorship, 2–11
baptism, 9–10
Barrett, C. K., 2, 7
Basilides, 42
Baur, F.C., 4
Berger, Adolf, 82
Bernard, J.H., 10
bishop, 8–9. *See also* elder(s).
blasphemy/slander (*blasphēmeō*),
    19, 26, 32, 35, 45, 91–93,
    100, 125, 146–47
boast (*kauchaomai*, *kauchēsis*), 7
Bricker, Paul, 120
calling, 155–56
charge, 137–38, 154, 156
child(ren), 22, 69–70, 80, 82, 84–88,
    91–93, 123–32, 142. *See also*
    youth; childbirth.
childbirth (*teknogonia*),
    childrearing, 73–76, 127–29,
    133–34, 148
Christmas, 41–42
church, 92, 94–95, 117n, 131,
    134–35, 138

Subject Index

Claudius Lysias, 58, 164
Clement of Rome, 3, 5, 10, 108n
clothing, 55–57, 75, 77, 85, 90, 124, 148–50, 162–63
Cohick, Lynn, 134
compassion (*makrothymeō*), 42, 88n, 129. See also Jesus; mercy.
conduct (*anastrophē*), 27, 113–14, 118–19, 154
conscience (*syneidēsis*), 26–27, 43–45, 56, 84, 86, 91–93, 104–5, 148, 157n, 164–65
contentment (*autarkeia*), 148–49
Conzelmann, Hans. See Dibelius.
Corinth, 11, 23, 44, 67, 77, 113
Cornelius, 59, 110
council(s), 9, 33, 116–17, 125–26, 139
coworker(s), 13, 24–25, 39, 61, 88, 102, 108, 111, 116, 152
Crete, 2, 11, 25, 28–29, 61, 86, 93, 95, 99, 109, 131–32, 145, 153
Cybele, 15, 50
Cynic(s), 148
David (King), 70, 107, 113n, 124n
deacon (minister) (*diakonos*), 8–9, 79–80, 87–94, 124–26, 131, 137n, 139
deception (delusion), 16, 70–73, 89, 93, 103, 105, 145–46
Demas, 4–5
Demeter, 15, 50
Demetrius, 13, 16, 152
Demosthenes, 82
desire(s), 18, 32, 77–78, 100, 128, 130n, 145, 150–52
Diana. See Artemis.
Dibelius, Martin, 6, 10
Didache, 6–8
Diodorus, 63
Dionysus, 50, 95, 140
Diotrephes, 131
disease. See sound (healthy).
docetism, 10
doctrine, 8, 18, 25–26, 77, 85, 108n, 112–13, 119. See also education.

Domitian, 5n, 24
Dorcas, 90, 124, 162
doxology, 37, 40, 158–60
drinking, 17n, 25, 86, 115, 140. See also wine.
dynastēs (ruler), 6, 158–59. See also ruler(s).
education, 29–31, 40, 45, 58–60, 65, 68, 70–73, 76, 108–9, 112, 116, 131, 136, 148. See also women.
elder(s) (presbyter), 8–9, 29, 43, 57, 61, 66n, 78–94, 109, 115–17, 121–22, 125–26, 135–39, 141, 150, 152–53, 157, 162
Elohim, 49–50. See also God, the Father.
encouragement (*paraklēsis*), 87, 115–19
Ephesus, 11, 13–14, 16–18, 23–24, 28–30, 32, 40–41, 43–44, 48–50, 52, 53–55, 57, 61, 65, 67, 71–74, 77–85, 88–89, 92, 97, 102, 104, 106, 109–10, 115, 117n, 128, 141–47, 150, 153, 155–56, 162, 165. See also Artemis.
Erastus, 23, 94
Essene(s), 15, 105–6
Eunice, 22, 29, 113. See also Lois.
Euripides, 15, 17n
eusebeia. See godliness.
Eusebius, 3–5, 42, 106, 112, 123n
evangelist, 43, 52, 90, 116, 120
Eve, 34, 58, 65, 67–74, 103, 105. See also Adam.
faith, 26–27, 36–37, 44–45, 76–77, 93–94, 114, 126, 153
Felix, 27, 137
Festus, Porcius, 5, 58, 77, 137
First Timothy, outline, 18–19
food(s), 74–75, 85, 90, 104–7, 129, 141, 147–50, 161, 163
Gaius (Caligula), 5, 97, 152
Gaius (coworker), 13, 80
Gamaliel, Rabbi, 30, 58
gar (for), 67n–68n
Gardiner, E. Norman, 109

Subject Index   175

genealogy, 25–26, 74, 115, 145, 147.
　　See also word-battle(s).
genuine (*gnēsiōs*), 22, 27
glory (*doxa*), 96, 99–100
Gnosticism, 9, 11
God, the Father, 40–41, 44, 49–50,
　　54, 68, 85, 96, 99, 111, 118,
　　131, 149, 156, 158–60. See
　　also savior/salvation; God,
　　the Trinity.
God, the Trinity, 49–50, 73, 116,
　　158–60
God-breathed, 2
godliness (*eusebeia*), 6–7, 10, 44–45,
　　48, 77, 109–10, 123, 145–46,
　　148–49, 152–54
Gordon, A.J., 100–101
grace, 9–10, 21–22, 35–37, 75, 155,
　　165. See also peace; Jesus.
Greek, tense, 61n-62n, 72
Grenz, Stanley, 67
hands, laying on of, 43, 116–17, 139
Hanson, A.T., 5n, 7–8, 10
haustafel (household codes), 6
heart, 26–27, 44
hendiadys, 57, 66n, 136n
herald, 52, 98n-99
heresy. See teacher(s) (teaching),
　　false.
Herod, 82
Hermogenes, 4
hetairai, 82. See also adultery.
Hillard, A.E., 7
Hillel, Rabbi, 112, 136n
holy/holiness (*hagiasmos*), 48, 74,
　　76–77, 98, 114, 129, 139
Homer, 15
hope. See Jesus.
hospitable (loving strangers,
　　philoxenos), 79, 85–86, 88,
　　91–92
household, 6, 26, 29, 36, 64, 75,
　　79, 82, 84, 86–88, 91–95,
　　115, 123–24, 128–34, 142,
　　148, 159. See also *haustafel*;
　　steward(s).
hygiēs (sound), 6, 33n. See sound.

Hymenaeus, 25, 28, 44–45, 49, 89.
　　See also Alexander.
Hypatia, 29
hypocrite (*hypokrinomai*), 27, 93,
　　104–5, 156. See also genuine.
Hyrkanos, Rabbi Eliezer ben, 112
Iconium, 23, 36, 43
Ignatius, 3, 5n, 9, 26, 74
Ilan, Tal, 83
Irenaeus, 4, 106n, 112
Isis, 50, 57
Jerome, 16, 57, 106, 127n
Jesus, 21–22, 26, 36–42, 44, 47, 50–
　　52, 85–86, 96–97, 113–14,
　　118, 129, 147–48, 152–53,
　　156–59
Jesus, son of Sirach, 39, 94, 146
Job, 51, 122, 148
Joseph, of Arimathea, 62, 149
Josephus, 31, 33, 54, 63, 87, 105
Jude, 22, 120
Justin Martyr, 4n, 53
Kroeger, Catherine, 65–66, 132
Kubo, Sakae, 6
law, 9–10, 28, 30–34, 36, 43, 45, 55,
　　69, 72, 79, 82–83, 102, 118,
　　123–24, 137, 147–48. See
　　also teacher(s) of the law.
leadership, 27, 48, 51, 63, 67, 69,
　　78–79, 83–84, 87, 90, 92, 94,
　　100–101, 125, 128, 133, 135,
　　148. See also elder(s).
learn (*manthanō*), 58, 69, 131. See
　　also education.
life, eternal, 21, 40, 77, 120, 125,
　　153, 155–58, 163
light, 158–61
Linus, 4
Lois, 22, 29, 109. See also Eunice.
love, 26–27, 36–37, 44, 76–77, 114,
　　153
Luke, 1–2, 5, 96, 137
Lydia, 86n, 88, 104, 108n
Lysimachus, 14
Lystia, 23, 36, 43, 113, 154
MacDonald, George, 119
McKenna, Mary Lawrence, 90n, 125
McKinney, Leslie, 119–20

Subject Index

magic, 16–18, 103–4, 116, 131–32, 147
Maloney, Linda M., 11
makarios (blessed), 6
Marcion, 4, 10, 165n
marriage, 30, 32, 50, 64, 74–75, 80–85, 97, 104–6, 127–29, 132–33, 147–48, 161, 163
Marshall, I. H., 65–66, 137n
Marxsen, Willi, 4, 6, 8–10
Mary, 59, 74–75, 111, 123
master(s), 64, 87, 133, 142–43, 159
mediator, 10–11, 21, 50–51, 74, 106, 147. See also Jesus.
Meir, Rabbi, 31
mercy (*eleos*), 12, 21–22, 34, 38–40, 42, 58, 69, 73, 76, 120, 147–48. See also compassion; Jesus.
minister(s). See deacon.
Mithras, 95
money/wealth, 9–10, 16, 25, 27, 78, 85, 91–92, 100, 103, 105, 122–23, 125, 136–37, 142, 146–47, 149–52, 161–63
Montanist(s), 106, 127n
Moses, 31, 34, 39, 49, 62, 68, 85, 112, 117n
Muratorian Canon, 3
mystery, 7, 9, 91–93, 95–100
myths, 25, 32, 43, 102, 109, 115, 130, 132, 142, 157n
Nebuchadnezzar, 96
Neil, James, 57
Nero, 5, 33, 41n, 48, 127
Nerva, 24
Nicholas, Barry, 82
Octavius Augustus, 41, 43, 50, 109–10, 127
Onesimus, 26
Onesiphorus, household, 4
order (*parangelia*), 4, 43–44, 46, 62, 67, 85, 130, 134–35, 139n, 154–56, 157n, 164
Origen, 4–5, 42
overseer. See elder(s).
Overstreet, R. Larry, 121
Ovid, 127

ox(en), 136, 143
paronomasia, 68n
Pastoral Epistles, 1, 11–12, 60n, 98, 108
Paul, 22, 24, 34–37, 51–53, 102, 113, 116, 160, 164–65
Pausanias, 15–16
peace (*eirenē*), 22, 45–46, 52–54, 65, 78, 85–86, 93, 100, 148n
Perictione, 29
permit (*epitrepō*), 62
Philemon, 3–5, 7
Philetus, 28
Philip, 116
Philo, 27, 52, 63, 70, 97
Phoebe, 87–88
Pilate, Pontius, 40, 43, 62, 137, 145, 156–57
plassō (form), 68–70
Plato, 69, 74, 97, 109, 126
pleonasm, 46, 66n, 145, 151n
Polybius, 25
Polycarp, 3–4, 6–8, 90n, 112, 125n
polygamy, 82–83, 135, 148
Pomeroy, Sarah, 128
pornos/porneia (sexual immorality), 26, 32–33, 55, 71, 76–77, 81–82, 95, 127. See also adultery.
Potamiaena, 42
prayer(s), 40, 46–48, 53–55, 57, 62, 77–78, 86, 90n, 107, 117n, 119–20, 124–25, 127, 129–30, 132, 135, 147–48. See also hands, laying on of.
presbyter. See elder(s).
Prisca, and Aquila, 13, 23, 61, 88
Procksch, Otto, 77
prophecy/prophet(s), 43–44, 87, 96, 117
protevangelium, 74
prototype (*hypotypōsis*), 34, 38–40, 45, 69–72, 113–15, 117
psychē (life), 6
quiet/silent (*hēsychios, hēsychia*), 48, 57–59, 62, 66–67. See also women.
Quintilian, 39–40

ransom. *See* Jesus.
resurrection, 28, 48, 98–100, 106n-7, 156, 160
rich. *See* money.
Robertson, A.T., 63n, 66–68, 94n
ruler(s), 6, 40–41, 48, 53–54, 63, 74, 90, 133–34, 158–59, 161. *See also* Jesus; God, the Father; *dynastēs*.
Sanhedrin, 26–27, 41, 117n, 136n, 149
Satan (satanic), 25, 28, 45, 71, 73–74, 89, 93, 103–4, 124, 132, 134, 138, 164
savior/salvation, 5–7, 16, 21, 34, 38, 46, 73, 75, 110–11, 118–19, 143, 147, 153, 155. *See also sōtēr*; God, the Father; Jesus.
Sceva, 14
Schleiermacher, F., 4
Scripture(s), 25, 29–31, 53–54, 58, 108, 112, 115, 136–37
semnos (character), 6
Septimus Severus, Emperor, 42
Silas, 23, 26, 39, 80, 108n, 113
silence. *See* quiet.
Simon Magus, 103–4
slander. *See* blasphemy.
slave(s), 127, 129, 133, 142–43
Smyrna, 3, 14
soldier(s), 42–45, 109–11, 113, 137, 153–57, 164
Solomon, 53, 140
some (*tis*), 25
sophia (wisdom), 6, 56–57, 67, 76–77, 85–86, 94, 118
sōphrosynē (self-control), 6
sōtēr (savior), 6–7, 48–49. *See also* savior.
soul, 105
sound/healthy (*hygiēs/hygiainō*), 33n, 145
Spain, 5, 11
Spencer, William David, 119, 135n
Spicq, Ceslas, 27, 56
Spirit, Holy, 35, 43, 47, 97–98, 100, 102–3
spirit(s), 103–4

spiritual (*pneumatikos*), 7, 28, 43, 116
Stephen, 90, 139
steward(s), stewardship, 26, 79, 87, 95, 115
Stoic(s), 142n, 148
Strabo, 14, 16, 109, 142
synagogue, 13, 29, 31, 36, 52–54, 123
synecdoche, 22, 39, 44, 75, 96, 126
Tacitus, 49
teacher(s) (teaching), false, 9, 25, 27–28, 43–44, 49, 55, 61, 65–67, 71–72, 74, 85–86, 104, 144–48, 164–65
teacher(s) (teaching), true, 33, 52, 61, 86, 108, 113
teacher(s) of the law, 28, 30–31. *See also* law.
temptation(s), 59, 150–51
Tertullian, 4, 82n, 106n, 127
thanksgiving (*eucharistia*), 47–48
theosebeia (religion), 6
times, last, 103
Timothy, 13, 22–25, 38–39, 43–44, 90, 94, 104, 107–19, 139–41, 152–57. *See also* evangelist; soldier(s).
Titus, 2–5, 11, 22, 34, 61, 108, 112–13, 130, 140
tradition(s), 3, 8, 108n, 112n
transgression (*parabasis*), 72–74, 105
translation(s), 1, 80–84
trial(s). *See* temptation(s).
truth, 3, 25, 28, 43, 45, 49, 52, 61, 67, 70, 73, 93–95, 103, 118, 131–32, 138, 143–48, 152, 157n, 164–65
type. *See* prototype.
violence (*hybristēs*), 36
vow, 114, 124, 128, 130–33, 140–41
widow(s), 7, 9, 25, 28, 47, 68n, 75, 80–81, 85, 87, 93, 105, 122–35, 143, 147, 157, 162, 164n
wine, 75, 91, 100, 114–15, 139–41. *See also* drinking.
Winter, Bruce W., 123n, 126n, 127

Witherington, Ben, 66n, 141
women: 77, 92, 109, 147, 162;
    elder(s), 9, 61, 80–84, 87–88,
    90, 93; prayer(s), 53, 55–57,
    69–70; quiet/silent, 48, 60–
    62, 67; teacher(s) (teaching),
    28–30, 61, 65, 72–73, 86.
    See also clothing; education;
    prayer(s); quiet; widow(s).
word, trustworthy, 37–38, 78, 108,
    110–11, 159

word-battle(s) (argument[s]),
    145–47. *See also* teacher
    (teaching), false.
yoke (*zygos*), 143
youth, 22, 112–14, 121, 154. *See also*
    child(ren).
Xenophon, 16n, 57, 79, 81–82
Zacchaeus, 150
Zeus, 15n, 23, 50, 148n
Zinserling, Verena, 57

www.ingramcontent.com/pod-product-compliance
Lightning Source LLC
Chambersburg PA
CBHW020848160426
43192CB00007B/831